MAKING CHAIRS
& TABLES

MAKING CHAIRS & TABLES

GUILD OF MASTER CRAFTSMAN PUBLICATION LTD

This collection first published in 1997 by
GUILD OF MASTER CRAFTSMAN PUBLICATIONS LTD,
Castle Place, 166 High Street, Lewes,
East Sussex BN7 1XU

© GMC Publications 1997

ISBN 1 86108 053 0

Printed and bound in Hong Kong by Dai Nippon Printing Company

**Front and back covers: boardroom furniture by Anthony Jackson and Neil Edgar
Photographs by Tony Ruocco, of Hamilton Photographic Studio**

CONTENTS

NOTES

PLEASE NOTE that names, addresses, prices etc were correct at the time the articles were originally published, but may since have changed.

MEASUREMENTS

THROUGHOUT the book instances will be found where a metric measurement has fractionally varying imperial equivalents, usually within 1/16in either way. This is because in each particular case the closest imperial equivalent has been given. A mixture of metric and imperial measurements should NEVER be used – always use either one or the other.

INTRODUCTION

CHAIRS AND TABLES are essential items of furniture in any home or workplace. At a pinch we can live without cupboards, bookcases, wardrobes and so on, but the need for a chair asserts itself as soon as we stop walking, and at least three times a day a table is needed if only for meals.

It's not surprising, then, that these two basics have been developed into a huge variety of specialised forms. We now have different chairs for dining, relaxing, and working, even different chairs for use in the house and garden – and yet a third for that in-between room, the conservatory.

Tables follow suit; but without the chair's restrictions – all chairs have to accommodate the human form – they have evolved into even more diverse types, from a low coffee table just large enough to support a tray to the vast and impressive boardroom table that bears the weight of corporate decision-making.

So chairs and tables are fertile ground for the furniture-maker, approachable by the very beginner who might start with a simple stool, a good exercise for the more confident woodworker using more complex joints and adding a decorative element, and a lifetime's challenge for the expert developing new ways of interpreting the form and structure of these most fundamental articles.

In these pages, compiled from the magazines *Woodworking International, Woodworking, Woodworking Today, Furniture,* and *Furniture & Cabinetmaking,* are examples to suit all woodworkers, together with approaches to such associated techniques as seat-caning and upholstery.

Whether planning a traditional kitchen chair or a contemporary office suite, this book will provide the practical advice and the inspiration needed to create something both beautiful and useful.

Paul Richardson, Editor,
Furniture & Cabinetmaking *magazine*

A meshing of struct
and aesthetics

CUTTING LIST
finished sizes in mm, (inches in brackets)

Back legs x 2	830 x 35 x 35	(32⅝ x 1⅜ x 1⅜)
Front legs x 2	610 x 35 x 50	(24 x 1⅜ x 2)
Side rails x 2	530 x 68 x 25	(20¾ x 2¾ x 1)
Front and		
back rail	520 x 68 x 25	(20⅜ x 2¾ x 1)
Top rail	575 x 35 x 35	(22⅝ x 1⅜ x 1⅜)
Arms x 2	530 x 35 x 27	(20¾ x 1⅜ x 1³⁄₃₂)
Stiles x 2	485 x 25 x 23	(19 x 1 x ⅞)
10mm ply		
seat	475 x 475	(18⅝ x 18⅝)
6mm veneered MDF		
back	392 x 387	(15½ x 15¼)

Leading designer-maker, Rod Wales, discusses the problems posed, and how he resolved them, when fulfilling a commission for a chair to be used as part of an office suite.

There are few certainties in life saving death and taxes, but one is how easy it is to get chairs wrong. Now, getting them right is not a matter of adhering, limpet like, to a set of rules or preconceptions (although ergonomics can only be ignored at your peril). Initially, at least, a great deal depends on defining the exact purpose of the object. In the case of a chair, I hear you say, s'obvious, innit, it's for sitting on.

Well, that may be so in the majority of cases – although there are exceptions – but who will be sitting on it, in what kind of room and for how long?

Is it just about the relative position of the posterior or the social elevation of the sitter? These and many more questions should be asked when designing any piece of furniture, but chairs are especially dependent upon the successful meshing and balance of aesthetic, structural and ergonomic factors. These three compete for attention and nowhere in furniture design do small adjustments have such a significant effect.

The chair featured here is by no means a general purpose, all things to all men kind of object. It was commissioned to go with an office desk and meeting table which are featured in my book *Rod Wales: Furniture Projects*. The customer required a fairly commodius and formal solution and particularly specified one that did not present itself as a self consciously designed – that is, 'designer' – object. The chair is for working from, not sprawling over, and will rarely be used by one person for more than one hour.

Upholstery was not part of the specification, but seemed appropriate as a means of visual as well as literal softening of the upright severity of the framework.

By using the cushions as discreet elements, rather than mere padding, we were able to introduce the curvature necessary to proper and comfortable lumbar support within a simple rectilinear framework.

The potential boxiness of the framework is further offset by subtle tapers, curves and rounding of the legs and arms. Much of the labour in this piece has to do with this shaping but this, if anything, affords satisfaction in the making process and is the chief means of achieving any delicacy of outline.

The construction itself is on the whole relatively simple, using straightforward joinery techniques without any of the compound angles so common in chair making.

PRECISION

As ever, a reasonable level of precision is necessary. And, again as ever, remember the design is there as a starting point. The conclusions we came to are not the only possibilities.

After the preparation of the parts, start with the back frame and panel. The panel is veneered 6mm (¼IN) MDF grooved into the frame. The stiles are tenoned into the top and bottom rails, the tenon being offset to allow this grove to run through.

The mitres on the back and arm frame are not essential structurally, but do afford a kind of linear flow in these elements. On the back legs they are sawn and, if necessary, shot with a plane, then mortised to take a double loose tenon using 6mm (¼IN) ply.

Be careful to position the mortises to allow for the eventual radiusing of the front edge (FIG 2). Notice, too, that the stiles are set back from the front edge of the top rail but remain flush at the front of the bottom (seat) rail.

All shaping, except the radiusing of the front edge, should be done before assembly. To mark out the shaping accurately and consistently make a template from sheet material. The curve itself is sprung between two points using a long rule or strip of wood. The bulk of the waste is sawn away and cleaned up by routing (following the template) or by hand.

I don't think it's necessary to describe the

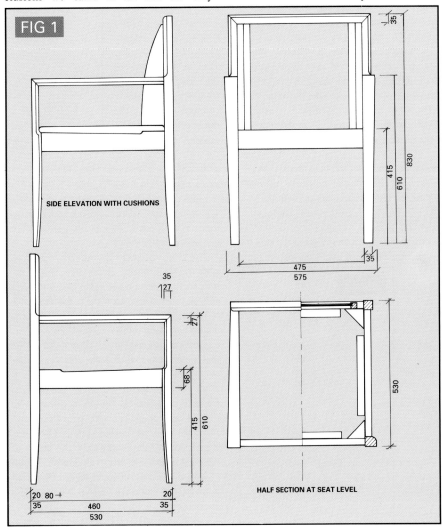

FIG 1

SIDE ELEVATION WITH CUSHIONS

HALF SECTION AT SEAT LEVEL

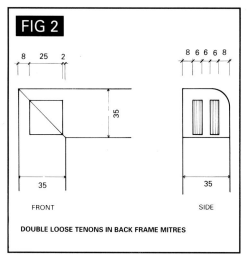

FIG 2

8 25 2

8 6 6 6 8

35

35   35

FRONT   SIDE

DOUBLE LOOSE TENONS IN BACK FRAME MITRES

seat rail mortise and tenoning in detail – they are, after all, absolutely conventional and their position and sizes are indicated on the drawings.

Assemble the stiles with the panel to the top and seat rail then, having mortised the back leg for the arm and side rail joint, complete the back frame with the mitred legs. Once this has been cleaned up the 13mm (½IN) radius on the front edge is routed, in stages, and is run out at the arm.

This radius serves a dual purpose. Practically, it serves to soften the top rail, which will be leaned on. Aesthetically, it breaks the line between the upper and lower parts of the frame and in doing so articulates and enriches the form by simple means.

The next stage is the front frame, which uses similar techniques. The legs are prepared to 50 x 35mm (2 x 1⅜IN) section throughout and mitred to take the arm.

The arm, however, is thinner (27mm – 1³/₃₂IN), so don't go merrily cutting mortises in the mitre until the shaping has been done. The front seat rail is tenoned into the legs as shown, the front face set back 2mm (³/₃₂IN).

To work the internal radius on the back face of the leg (at the junction with the side rail) it is easiest to cramp two legs together and, with a sharp 16mm (⅝IN) forstner or saw tooth bit, drill using the interface as the centre line. This will avoid the burning and

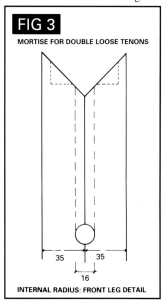

FIG 3

MORTISE FOR DOUBLE LOOSE TENONS

35   35

16

INTERNAL RADIUS: FRONT LEG DETAIL

chipping which is almost inevitable if the radius is routed.

After drilling, the remainder of the waste and the curves on the lower part of the leg (in both elevations) are sawn and cleaned up as before. The radius on the outside back edge of the leg is routed using a 13mm (½IN) cutter with its guide bearing run in contact with the back face – ie the cutter follows the side elevation profile of the leg.

After cleaning up – and sanding of shaped parts is always easier while still in component form – the front frame can be glued up, watching out, as always, for twist and squareness. Twisting would be catastrophic for the mitre joint at the arm.

The arm itself tapers from the front and is tenoned to the back frame. The twin loose tenons in the mitre at the front are made from 10mm (⅜IN) ply. The taper is sawn and planed. After fitting both back and front joints, ensuring all is flush, the radius is routed on the underside.

The bottom edge of the seat rail is horizontal, while the top edge tapers down 9.5mm (⅜IN) before flipping up 80mm (3⅛IN) from the back. This detail relates to the shaping of the front leg and visually connects the rail to the thickness of the back cushion. The radius is cut as described before, only this time using a 19mm (¾IN) diameter bit. The taper is sawn and cleaned up by routing against a template or judiciously placed straight edge. The frames are assembled using sash cramps (one vertical, one horizontal) to put pressure on the arm mitre.

The seat rail tenons are offset where possible to maximise the gluing area. But as the rails themselves are not offset the joints are still a little short. However, the frame is reinforced by the simple and traditional method of using screwed corner blocks.

The seat is made from 10mm (⅜IN) ply, the dimensions being 5mm (³/₁₆IN) smaller overall than the seat space in the chair, to allow for thickness of the calico and top fabric of the upholstery. The ply is drilled with nine, 25mm diameter, well spaced holes, to avoid the whoopee cushion effect. The ply is supported on fillets screwed to the inside of the seat frame. It is covered with 38mm (1½IN) of CMHR40 foam, held in position with contact adhesive. Leave 10mm (⅜IN) overhang all round.

Lay 12mm (½IN) of Dacron over the foam,

then add a calico cover. Take the calico round the edges, under the ply and staple it in position. The cover material is applied over this and stapled in the same way.

Mark the centres of the sides of the ply and the covering materials and match them to make sure that the warp and weft of the fabric lie evenly and do not deviate.

The edges of this drop-in seat need to remain fairly square so they produce a tight fit with the chair frame.

The underside of the seat is neatened up with a panel of black holland, similarly stapled down.

The back cushion profile is cut to a template from 100mm (4IN) HR40 foam. You will need the services of a specialist foam cutter (see *Yellow Pages*). The foam fits into the recess made by the stiles and the top rail, and sits on top of the seat cushion.

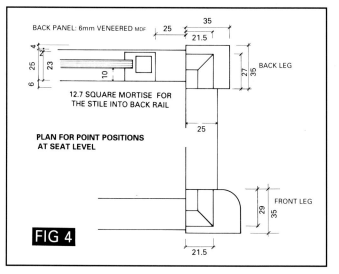

BACK PANEL: 6mm VENEERED MDF   25   35   21.5

4   2   25   23   10   6

BACK LEG   27   35

12.7 SQUARE MORTISE FOR THE STILE INTO BACK RAIL

25

PLAN FOR POINT POSITIONS AT SEAT LEVEL

FRONT LEG   29   35

FIG 4   21.5

A calico cover is made to cover the cushion. It is best to make a paper pattern to ensure that all the cushion covers are identical. Anyone who can follow a dress pattern and confidently use a sewing machine will be able to do this. The cover has panelled sides and is made a tight fit so the foam is slightly compressed.

The top cover is again cut to the pattern, the raw edges overlocked before the seams are stitched and a zip inserted along the bottom back edge. A strip of Velcro is stitched close to the top edge of the back of the cushion cover to match a strip stuck on to the inside face of the back panel on the chair frame so when the cushion is pressed into position it will stay there.

Finishing will depend on the timber used and the likely wear. But take into consideration that chairs receive a great deal of handling and oiled wood quickly achieves a remarkable patina as a result of this. In this case, I gave the cherrywood I used three coats of teak oil applied over two weeks, cutting back lightly with 0000 wire wool between coats □

LOUNGING AROUND IN STYLE

MARK WESTWOOD

This award-winning garden lounger made from Western red cedar makes an attractive and distinctive addition to any garden. Here's how to make it.

B efore attempting to design this lounger I laid down some of my own specifications about the function of the piece as well as undertaking a few experiments involving the properties of the timber. I wanted to know how strong and durable it is. I also wanted to know if it can be steam bent and laminated, and how it works with hand and power tools.

The timber is very light and soft, so its surface durability is limited. It dents and bruises easily and is strong only when used in fairly thick sections. However, it is excellent to work with machines. Even when feeding a plank the 'wrong way' through a thicknesser there is almost no break-out of the grain. Machine sanding brings the surface to a clean finish.

Because of the constraints of working the timber I decided before starting any design sketches that I had to make as much of the lounger as possible from machine cut parts.

I had already been told by COFI of the timber's good weather resistance. This I confirmed by repeatedly boiling and oven drying a piece. It did not appear to make any difference to the timber, apart from a slight discolouration. It hardly warped or cupped at all and did not split even under the harshest of conditions.

With the groundwork done, I set about designing the piece. My own requirements were that it had to be comfortably large, stable and adjustable to three positions.

The lounger may be divided into four basic sections – the side arches, the seat, the back, and the arm rests. I shall deal with each section in turn.

Side arches

These two, semi-circular, laminated parts form the frame into which the seat is set and work with the arm rests to provide the adjustment mechanism. To form the shape of these arcs I first designed a solid blockboard male and female mould.

The circumference was drawn and the centre marked and drilled on the male mould. The circumference was then bandsawn out roughly to within 2mm or so of the line. A dowel peg was put through the centre

hole and into an MDF base so that the mould could be swivelled around an overhead router cutter to clean up to the line. Two sheets of blockboard were glued together to give the thickness required for the 80mm wide laminated arcs.

The female mould is made using an MDF template, pinned to the blockboard and run around a ring fence on a spindle moulder. The radius is 36mm longer than that of the male mould's 510mm to allow for the laminates to fit in between. A strip of constructional beech veneer was glued to the surface of each mould to give a smooth, uniform finish.

The arcs are laminated from 12 pieces of cedar 1740mm long – allowing for cleaning up. The pieces are cut on the bandsaw 5mm thick and sanded down to 3mm ready for gluing together in the moulds. I used Cascamite for gluing – plenty of it. The wood soaks up glue like a sponge.

When it was dry it was cleaned up on one side with a surface planer and then passed through a drum sander to clean up the other side.

The floor rail is cut to length (finished length is 1092mm) and dovetailed to the arcs. The exact centre is marked and drilled with a 25mm hole side to side. This will be the pivot point for the lounger.

The arc for the other side is constructed in the same way and the two joined together with three cross members of the wood. The piece joining the floor rails should be 760mm × 80mm × 35mm and be positioned just in front of the pivot hole. The two pieces joining the arcs need to be thinner to take into account the curve of the arcs. The cross member at the front will be the front support of the seat and should be 340mm vertically from the ground at its top. The back cross member is at the same vertical height as the front member. Mortice and tenon joints are used to join the arcs and cross members.

Seat unit

A 2.5m length of string, a pencil and a nail were used to draw the circumference required on to an MDF template (the radius is 2220mm) to form the seat planks. The template was carefully sawn and cleaned up, then pinned to each of four blockboard formers needed and passed around a spindle cutter to give a neat edge. It was necessary to sandwich four pieces of blockboard together to get the required thickness (150mm).

The steam bending was relatively simple. A 2ft high tin drum fitted with a kettle element made an ideal steam chamber. A plywood box was put over the tin so that it filled with steam. The planks of cedar were put inside that.

Each plank was steamed in turn for an hour and then pulled over the former and clamped at the centre and at each end for three days until it was dry. No steel bands or supports were needed because the curve was fairly shallow. There was very little spring-back from the wood when it was removed from the former and there was little subsequent movement.

The planks of the seat are joined in five places and need to be drilled through to the size of rod you are using plus Nylon bushes to separate the metal and the wood and provide practically frictionless movement at the pivot points. I used 15mm Nylon bushes with 9mm steel rods

through them. The outside planks need a larger, 25mm hole to a sufficient depth to accommodate the bolt on the end of the rod.

I used steel rods powder coated red (for decoration) to join the planks of the seat. I put a joining rod through every 320mm with the first hole 40mm in from the foot end of the lounger. The rods are passed through the planks and bolted at each end. I used 15mm wide, 30mm DIA turned beech separators between the planks. I painted these red as a decorative feature. They are drilled with 9mm holes to accommodate the rod.

The seat is joined to the back by four open mortice and tenon hinges held in position by a steel rod and incorporating the Nylon bushes. This allows the seat to move in unison with the back when the position is adjusted.

The front of the seat rests on the front cross member between the two semi-circular arcs. Use has shown that this simple system could well be improved. Friction between the crossbar causes a wretched squeak when the seating position is changed. The use of rollers or some other frictionless component would improve this.

Each year the Council for Forest Industries of British Columbia (COFI) gives Buckinghamshire College of Higher Education some timber and sets up a competition for students to design and make furniture from that wood.

A couple of years ago the wood provided was Western red cedar and the students were required to design three pieces of garden furniture and to make one of those pieces.

According to COFI, Western red cedar contains natural oils which give it excellent durability, good working and finishing qualities, and outstanding intrinsic beauty, all of which makes it a natural choice for outdoor furniture. So it was outdoor furniture they wanted the students to make from it.

The winner of the contest was Mark Westwood. He agrees Western red cedar is a good timber to look at but says: "It does not work very well with hand tools. It chips rather than cuts – it doesn't matter how sharp your chisel is. It's soft. You sit on it and you leave 'Levi' printed on it. It does take a nice, clean finish, though."

This is Mark Westwood's winning entry in the COFI competition for you to follow if you want some distinctive garden furniture.

The back

The back is constructed in much the same way as the seat.

Like the seat it is made from four planks. Each one is 1200mm × 150mm × 35mm. The planks are held together with four metal rods and have red-painted beech separators between them like the seat. The lower rod needs to be right at the end and joins the back to the floor rail. Red beech separators should come between the back and the floor rail where they are joined. The back pivots at this point to allow the lounger to be moved into its three positions. The next hole is 320mm up the back. It goes through the loose mortices of the back and the tenons of the seat. Make sure the mortices are cut large enough to allow for the movement of the seat when the lounger is moved through its three different positions.

The next hole accommodates the arm rest and the one above it joins the planks of the back.

Arm rests

The arm rests are made in a similar fashion to the arcs, using lamination. Make the inside radius 546mm and the outside radius 36mm greater to accommodate the 36mm of lamination. The arms hold the key to the adjustment of the chair.

A 25mm wide groove is routed through each arch where the arm rest will be. Drill three sets of 15mm holes through each side arch (see FIG 3 and Detail 3). These pegs need to be strong because much of the leaning weight of the person using the seat will be placed on them.

A single beech hook under each arm rest screwed into position runs neatly within the groove and locates on to turned pegs to hold the back in the required position.

Two metal rods hold the arm rest in position. The back one secures them together and acts as a lever so that when one arm rest is lifted the other follows. The centre rod, which is cranked to give clearance to the mechanism (see Detail 1) passes through the planks of the back rest and beech spacers to the arm rest the other side. Because both ends of the rod are cranked and you cannot easily bend the rod once it has been ▷

pushed through the back planks it is easier to bend two pieces of rod and join them with a grub screw and thread where the straight rod emerges from one side of the back.

Finishing

The lounger is finished, after a lot of sanding, with Cuprinol Clear Wood Preserve which, when dry, turns the timber only slightly darker and highlights the grain, giving a subtle golden finish to the wood.

Western red cedar is one of the few woods which is virtually rot and worm proof so it does not actually need a finish to protect it. However, it does turn silver grey with age if it is left outdoors without a finish on it.

Indoors this lounger seems a little on the heavy side, but once it is in the garden it needs its bold sections and chunky feel to assert itself – as well as to stay grounded in the wind. □

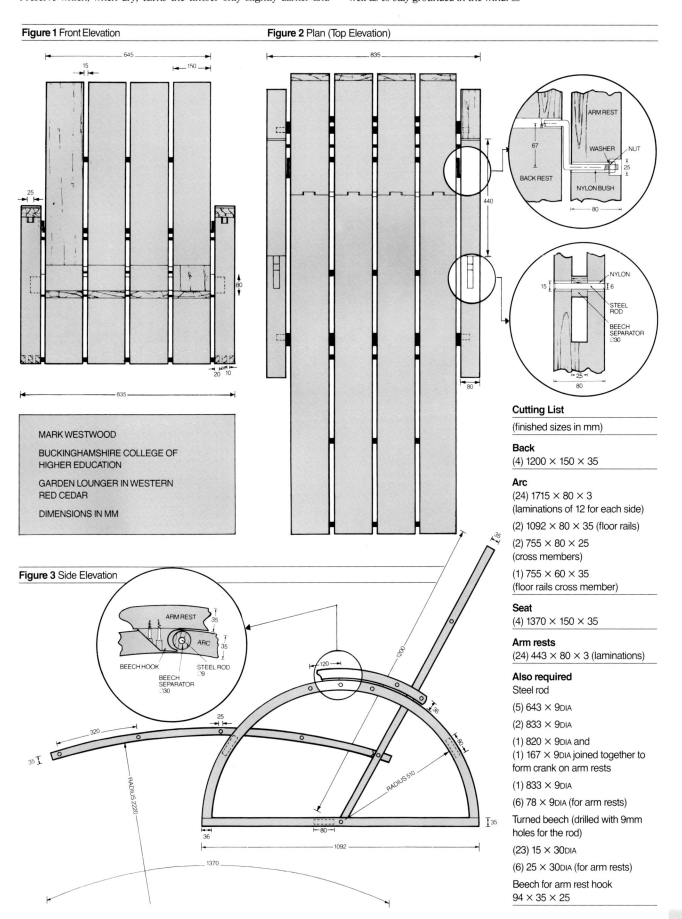

Figure 1 Front Elevation

Figure 2 Plan (Top Elevation)

MARK WESTWOOD

BUCKINGHAMSHIRE COLLEGE OF HIGHER EDUCATION

GARDEN LOUNGER IN WESTERN RED CEDAR

DIMENSIONS IN MM

Figure 3 Side Elevation

Cutting List

(finished sizes in mm)

Back
(4) 1200 × 150 × 35

Arc
(24) 1715 × 80 × 3
(laminations of 12 for each side)

(2) 1092 × 80 × 35 (floor rails)

(2) 755 × 80 × 25
(cross members)

(1) 755 × 60 × 35
(floor rails cross member)

Seat
(4) 1370 × 150 × 35

Arm rests
(24) 443 × 80 × 3 (laminations)

Also required
Steel rod

(5) 643 × 9DIA

(2) 833 × 9DIA

(1) 820 × 9DIA and
(1) 167 × 9DIA joined together to form crank on arm rests

(1) 833 × 9DIA

(6) 78 × 9DIA (for arm rests)

Turned beech (drilled with 9mm holes for the rod)

(23) 15 × 30DIA

(6) 25 × 30DIA (for arm rests)

Beech for arm rest hook
94 × 35 × 25

ABOVE: Dining table in sycamore.

Chamfered edge

Andrew Lawton on an interesting table which could be tackled by a relative newcomer to fine furniture-making

SEVERAL YEARS AGO I was commissioned to make a simple dining table of oak (*Quercus robur*) measuring 2300 by 915mm, 7ft 6 by 3ft. It was considered to be a success, and an almost identical table, this time in ripple sycamore (*Acer pseudoplatanus*), was recently made for another client.

This table would make an ideal project for the 'improver' in fine furniture-making wishing to develop skills and to turn out a large piece.

The techniques and joints used are straightforward, yet demand care and accuracy if the finished table is to be structurally sound and visually satisfying. The design need not be copied exactly; the dimensions can be varied and the methods used can be applied to other projects.

The table is intended to seat 10 comfortably, with minimum interference from legs and rails. The simple design is raised from the commonplace by bold, light-catching chamfers which alter the apparent shape of its outlines when viewed from different angles. The chamfers also reduce weight without sacrificing strength.

While the table might not turn

many heads at an exhibition, its unassuming lines blend with a variety of interiors and should stand the test of time.

Timber

The choice of timber can alter the overall mood of any piece of furniture, quite apart from obvious differences of colour and grain. The original oak table has a quieter, more traditional feel than the more striking and vibrant sycamore version.

Whatever species is chosen, however, the timber should all come from the same tree – difficult with imported wood.

Buy more than required because, particularly with home-grown timber, wastage from waney edges, shakes, knots and other defects must be taken into account. Having extra boards to hand provides greater scope for creating, say, a balanced, well-matched top.

Sycamore was bought in at 75mm, ▶

● **ANDREW LAWTON**, a member of the Society of Designer Craftsmen, has been making furniture full-time since 1980. He rescued Goatscliffe Workshops – run by pioneer craftsman Ben Coopland from the 1920s to 1960s in Grindleford, Derbyshire – from near dereliction. Lawton's 1991 Spiral Table in English walnut (*Juglans regia*) inlaid with sycamore received a Guild Mark from the Worshipful Company of Furniture Makers.

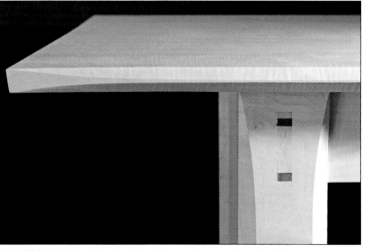

ABOVE: Detail showing the chamfers and exposed wedged tenon.

ABOVE: After the drawknife, a spokeshave is used to tidy the chamfers.

"I had to learn to chop mortises entirely by hand before being allowed to use a machine"

ABOVE RIGHT: Planing the chamfers with a Norris smoother.

3in thickness for the legs, 38mm, 1½in for the rails and top. Over a length of 2000mm, 6ft 6in, stock must be sawn initially at 40mm, 1⁹/₁₆in to be sure of achieving a finished thickness of 25.4mm, 1in or 32mm, 1⅛in.

The timber must be thoroughly seasoned, either naturally or kiln dried – and even then it cannot be assumed that it is dry enough for the construction of fine furniture. Timber air-dried in the UK rarely has a moisture content of less than 18 per cent (see Charles Hayward's *A Woodworker's Pocket Book*, now published by Harper Collins, ISBN 0583 314392), even in a hot summer like last year's, while kiln-dried timber is invariably stored in unheated, often open-sided sheds which allow it to draw in moisture from the atmosphere.

It is therefore important to rough out all the components well oversize, machine plane them and stack them so air can circulate around them in a warm, dry environment for at least six weeks before building begins. Ideally, the wood should be stored in the room the piece will live in.

Underframe

In my workshop the underframe of a table is usually made first so as to allow the boards selected for the top as long as possible in which to settle down. Others may argue that it is

better to make the top first, set it to one side while the frame is made, and give it a final truing-up should any movement have taken place; this avoids the snag of ending up with a base that is too big for the top!

All the parts for the sycamore table were machined almost to final dimensions, but allowance was made for a final planing by hand, even on normally unseen surfaces. Even with newly ground planer knives ripple sycamore can tear out, so it pays to take great care at this stage.

Arrange the legs to present the most symmetrical grain orientation, then square off the bottom ends on the dimension saw, leaving 'horns' of 50mm, 2in projecting from the top ends. The job of the horns is to absorb the pressures set up by the cramps when gluing up the joints; they are sawn off later.

Marking out

Mark out shoulder lines and gauge all mortises. For accuracy and to save time, cramp legs and other identical parts together or hold them in a vice when marking out; the various lines can then be carried across them all; the components can be separated and the lines taken round individually.

The rails, which at this stage are longer than necessary, are marked out next, together with the mortises for the central stiffening rail and

framework anchor buttons. Initial dimensions can be indicated with a sharp 3H or 4H pencil but all shoulder lines should be lightly cut in with a marking knife.

The lengths of the uncut tenons are determined, ensuring that those on the long rails are 3mm, ⅛in shorter than the depth of the blind mortises, and the tenons on the short rails are a little longer than the through mortises.

Blind or stopped tenons must always be slightly shorter than their mortises to allow for surplus glue; through tenons which project a few millimetres are easy to flush off later.

Cutting tenons

The tenons are cut with a hollow chisel mortiser, the stopped mortises being tackled first, then temporarily filled with scrap softwood to prevent spelching as the through mortises are chopped, working from each side to meet in the middle.

Chop the shallow mortises for the stiffening rail and buttons next. When I was training in the 1970s I had to learn to chop mortises entirely by hand before being allowed to use a machine and, although there is a certain satisfaction in doing so, I wouldn't recommend cutting them by hand if there are other means available.

If you have a dimension saw it may be used to cut the shorter end-

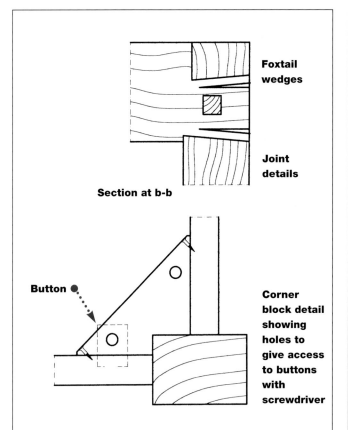

Foxtail wedges

Joint details

Section at b-b

Button ●

Corner block detail showing holes to give access to buttons with screwdriver

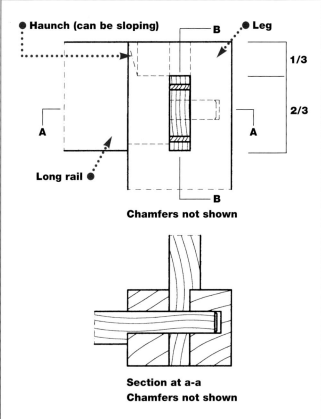

● Haunch (can be sloping)   B   ● Leg

1/3

2/3

A   A

Long rail ●

B

Chamfers not shown

Section at a-a
Chamfers not shown

rail tenons, with the blade lowered; strictly speaking this is illegal since it involves removing the guard, but I don't consider it inherently any more dangerous than any other machining method – providing care is taken.

The tenons on the long rails are cut on a bandsaw.

The strength of a mortise and tenon depends largely on the length or depth of the joint, but a potential source of weakness of this design is that the position of the through tenons restricts the length of the joints of the long side rails. My solution is to cut a 19mm, $^3/_4$in mortise through the wedged tenons and into the leg beyond it, *see photo/drawing*. A corresponding tenon is cut to fit it, adding strength and rigidity to the rail and leg joint.

Each joint is offered up to its mate and fitted dry; the kerfs for the foxtail wedges are sawn and the shoulders checked for accuracy, with adjustment as needed.

The walnut (*Juglans regia*) chosen for the wedges gives a pleasing colour contrast and is carefully sawn from straight grained material – not from scrap wood because this is prone to snapping off when being driven home.

Leg chamfers

With the joints cut out and fitted up, including screw slots bored into the central cross rail to hold down the

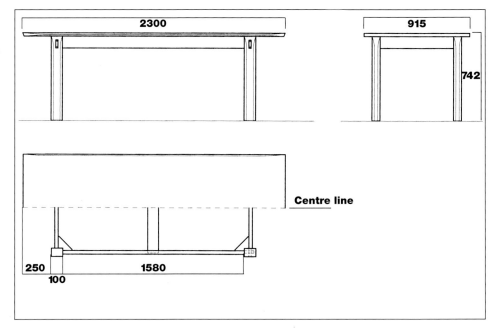

2300

915

742

Centre line

250   1580

100

top, it is time for the legs to be chamfered.

The purpose of chamfers is to lighten the structure physically and visually and to create light-catching planes and curves. George Sturt relates in *The Wheelwright's Shop* (published by Cambridge University Press, ISBN 0521 0919 50) how his craftsmen used to "refresh themselves" by cutting chamfers on wheel spokes and wagon frames, but sometimes overdid it.

As with most applied decoration it is best to keep chamfering restrained and simple. Each chamfer should be crisp, flat and parallel, and should run out to nothing in a smooth curve.

A drawknife is used to remove the bulk of the waste, followed by a spokeshave, then a block plane on the parallel sections. On an easier timber, such as straight grained oak, the chamfers could be made solely with a drawknife.   ➤

"Fitting corner blocks anticipates abuse and minimises joint strain"

ABOVE: Flattening the table top across the grain.

BELOW: The table was commissioned to accompany this sideboard with chamfered detail.

Gluing up

A finely set smoothing plane is stroked over all accessible surfaces before glue is spread carefully into the through mortises and saw kerfs; each end is pulled up with sash cramps.

Check that all is square and true before driving in the wedges, giving each a tap until a change in pitch and feel indicates they are fully home. Saw off each projecting wedge, applying the plane to level off the tenon until it is flush, and reveal a tight-fitting joint with evenly sized rectangles of end grain.

With the two ends safely assembled, the tenons of the long rails are offered up again, care being taken to ensure the middle square part of the mortise will accept its partner.

After gluing up the long rails and stiffener to form an 'H' structure, the final assembly takes place. Check that no stray shavings or chips have infiltrated the mortises and that the whole is pulled up tightly with extended T-bar cramps – hideously expensive but invaluable on this sort of work.

The tenons should be a good hand fit, with cramps drawing the shoulders tight but allowing the joints to be pulled apart. Glue is applied to both mortise and tenon, the adhesive acting as a lubricant.

The table is checked for squareness in all directions before being left overnight to fully set. Test for squareness by placing accurate pencil marks on strips of timber to match up the diagrams – steel tapes tend to flex, giving false readings. A long straightedge and a plain background are also useful for aligning by eye.

Corner blocks

Remove the cramps the next morning, saw off the horns and level off the top edges. The underframe is fairly rigid at this stage, but to stiffen it further fit corner blocks. This refinement is well worth the effort since this table will probably be dragged roughly across a carpet; fitting corner blocks anticipates this abuse and minimises undue joint strain.

Depending on the position of the buttons, holes may have to be bored into the blocks to give access for a screwdriver, *see drawing*.

Making the top

With the underframe complete, attention can be turned to the table top. The boards are re-machined and arranged to achieve a pleasing match. Adjacent edges are accurately shot using the surface planer against its fence, followed by a final shooting by hand with a try plane.

With an easier timber it is usually possible to achieve a perfect match joint straight from the planer but these boards needed a little hand work as well.

To ensure a close fitting joint it is good practice to run a stopped groove into each edge with a router or biscuit jointer for a ply tongue rather than relying solely on glue. This not only gives a mechanically strong joint irrespective of the adhesive, but makes gluing up easier, especially for the lone worker.

The top is assembled with six sash cramps, applied alternately top and bottom to prevent bowing, and set to one side until the following day. Surplus glue is removed with a damp rag before it goes off.

PVA adhesive is used in my workshop, except for laminating, veneering and outdoor work, for which I use Cascamite or similar urea-formaldehyde resins.

Cleaning up

Razor-sharp tools, the correct technique and a systematic approach make cleaning up easier. The underside of the table top is tackled first. A try plane is worked across the grain several times, from one end to the other, until all humps and hollows are removed to reveal a surface that is flat across its width but not necessarily along its length.

Flatness in length is then obtained, and a finely set smoothing plane followed by a cabinet scraper gives an acceptable surface to the underside.

The top surface is trued up in the same way, with more effort put into ensuring that it is as blemish-free as possible; this entails working through the grades of garnet paper down to 400 grit.

The ends of the top are bevelled inwards and the long edges chamfered as described.

After a final check in flaw-revealing slanting, late afternoon sunlight, the whole table is sprayed with pre-catalysed lacquer.

Had the table been made of elm or some other richly coloured, open grain wood, an oil finish would probably have been applied; but it is important to preserve the paleness of the sycamore while ensuring it has a resistant surface.

The metal connection

Glyn Bridgewater decided he needed a change from making complex pieces of furniture

WHEN I DESIGNED this chair and table I was interested in triangulated structures and constructions which involved combining wood and metal components.

After making some complicated furniture, I was also keen to design something which was easy to make. After endless models and full-size mock-ups I arrived at a design that used simply machined wood components and forged steel rods.

Design

The chair design uses two planks for the seat and back and four vertical sticks for the legs. Triangulating steel rods and brackets are screw-fixed to the wood, this combination making a very strong chair.

The design for the table, which serves as a writing desk, uses a similar construction to the chair and the two work well together.

The table and chair are made from American white ash (*Fraxinus sp*). As well as being a tough wood, ash contrasts well with the black steel.

Ash is readily available and reasonably priced. However, as is the case with many imported timbers, ash is normally only available as narrow boards.

The table top and the seat and back of the chair are made by gluing boards together. The metal components are 'forged' – heated up with a welding torch and then bent and/or hammered flat – from round-section steel rod.

Chair preparation

The seat and back are made from one board, 200 by 254 by 25mm, 8 by 10 by 1in. The board is first cut crosscut in half, then both pieces are surface planed one side and thickness planed to 18mm, ^{3}/4in.

With the grain pattern exposed, the best arrangement of the boards can be decided. Square up the two edges that are to be butted together and join; biscuits will locate the joint and strengthen it, but a good rubbed joint with PVA or a sash-cramped butt joint with Cascamite will do as well.

Cut the board into two pieces for the back and the seat, leaving an equal amount of waste on each. The taper shapes of the seat and back are marked out using the glue line as the centre line.

The waste is removed with the bandsaw, keeping to the waste side of the line, then the sawn edges are taken to the line with a bench plane.

Making the legs

The legs are cut from a board 470 by 200 by 38mm, 18^1/2 by 8 by 1^1/2in. Cut four 40mm, 1^9/16in

strips from this then face and edge each one, leaving the other faces sawn at this stage.

On each piece mark out the shape of the tapered leg on to one of the rough sawn sides. Cut to the waste side of the line with a bandsaw, ➤

● GLYN BRIDGEWATER, who is based in Lewes, East Sussex, studied furniture at Loughborough College of Art and Design and the Royal College of Art, and has worked with Trannon Furniture in Salisbury and Richard La-Trobe Bateman.

ABOVE: The completed table and chair

ABOVE RIGHT: The metal rods and brackets are both simple and functional.

allowing extra for working back to the line on the surface planer.

This done, mark out the same taper on the sides that have just been planed and remove the waste as before. Square off each leg at the thick end. The angle brackets that fix the legs to the seat are screwed to the inside corner of each leg.

A 45° bevel is planed off the legs at this point. This detail can be achieved by passing the leg over a surface planer while the leg is supported in a 45° jig — practise on a scrap piece of wood in order to judge how many passes are needed and at what point to clamp a 'stop'.

Drilling the holes

All the metal rods and brackets are fixed to the seat, back and legs with black, round head slotted screws. Every hole is drilled at 90° to the surface.

The holes used for fixing the brackets to the legs are drilled at 90° to the bevel and for this it is best to use the same jig that was used for creating the bevel.

Where angle brackets are fixed to the seat and back 19mm, $^3/_4$in by No.8 screws are used, and for every other fixing 25mm, 1in screws are used.

Pilot holes are drilled at all the points indicated on the component drawing. Practise drilling a pilot hole in an ash offcut to arrive at the best combination of hole size – two drill sizes will be needed – and depth. Remember to take into account the thickness of the flattened rod. The screws should be tight fitting, but not so tight that the screw shears.

Metal components

Bright mild steel round-section rod is normally bought in 3m,10ft lengths from specialist metal suppliers. To produce all the components, start by cutting the rod with a hacksaw to the exact lengths given in the cutting list. Use a file to clean up the ends.

The metal rod is then forged to produce the parts shown in the component drawings. If you are not familiar with heating, hammering and bending metal, it is advisable to practise.

A large hammer will be needed, also an anvil or metal block, two pairs of pliers, a heating area – a metal sheet lined with fire bricks – and a heat source. I used an oxy-acetylene torch – welding goggles protecting the eyes from the white flame – but a plumber's blow torch would be sufficient. When hammering the hot metal goggles must be worn to stop the hot oxide flakes getting in the eyes.

Cooling hot metal by drenching it in water will harden its surface, so' making it difficult to drill. It is best to let the metal cool naturally.

Safety check

Support the rod over two bricks to heat one end. Before starting, make sure that the rod can be picked up at its mid-point with a pair of pliers, leaving one hand free for hammering the rod over the anvil.

Heat more of the rod than needed to flatten until the metal becomes cherry red – but before it goes shiny and melts – and then as quickly as possible hammer the rod flat.

After practise the rod will be flattened with one heating, but there is no harm in reheating the metal for further flattening.

Metal rod is also flattened in this way, so that holes can be drilled through it, as an industrial process. The rod is hammered once only and without heat being used.

Angle brackets

To produce the angle brackets, flatten the ends first and then bend the rod. Heat a 25mm,1in portion of the rod at the point of the bend, until it is cherry red. Grip the rod at both ends with pliers and bend it to the angle shown in the component drawing.

Drill holes through the metal rods at the points indicated on the drawing. Mark the centre of each hole with a centre punch and drill a hole to take the shaft of the screw.

File off any sharp edges and remove all traces of grease with white spirit.

To imitate gun metal, I applied a clear liquid called 'gun metal blue', bought from gun shops. It is quickly brushed on and, no matter how it is applied, gives a uniform finish. A chemical reaction turns the metal surface black; this can then be neutralised with water.

Assembling/finishing

Assemble the chair, stand it on a level surface and prop up the legs with small scraps of wood until the seat is straight and at the correct angle to the floor. Then measure from the floor to the top of the seat at the front.

When cutting the legs to length the front of the seat should be 450mm, $17^3/_4$in off the ground. Subtract this amount from the actual measurement to establish how much to cut off the legs.

Cut a square block of wood to this height and use this to mark around the bottoms of legs. Double check the marks by measuring directly from the seat to the marks on the legs and, if everything works out, take the chair apart. Cut the legs to length using a tenon saw.

Remove all sharp corners with a block plane and scrape and sand every surface. Give everything a ➤

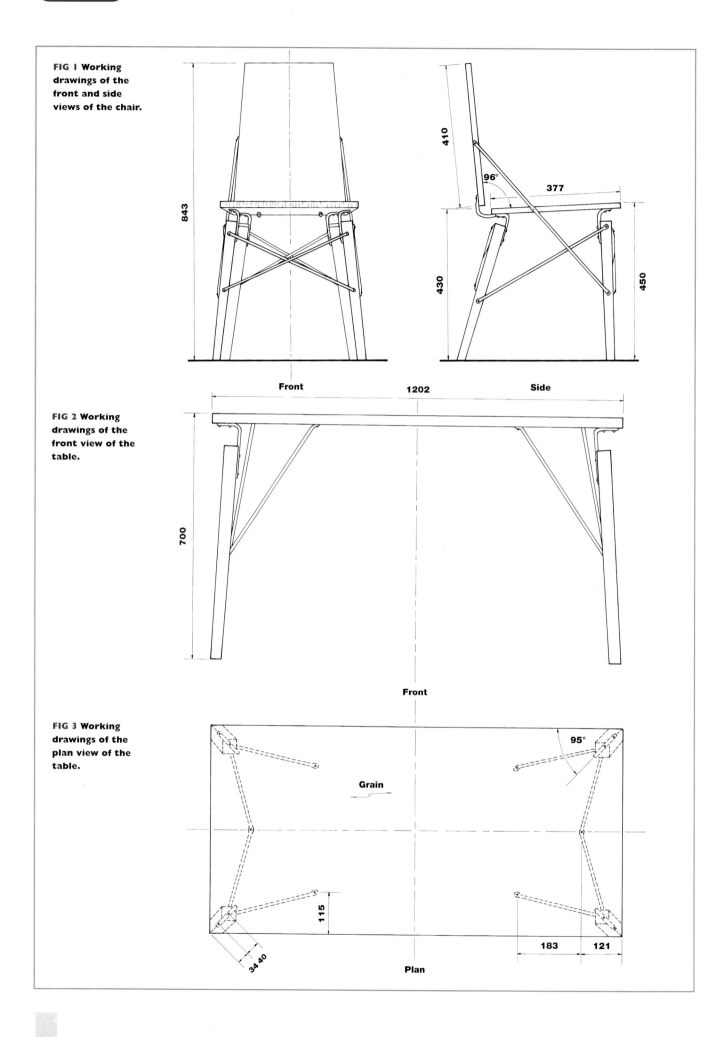

FIG 1 Working drawings of the front and side views of the chair.

843

410

96°

377

430

450

Front   1202   Side

FIG 2 Working drawings of the front view of the table.

700

Front

FIG 3 Working drawings of the plan view of the table.

95°

Grain

115

34 40

183   121

Plan

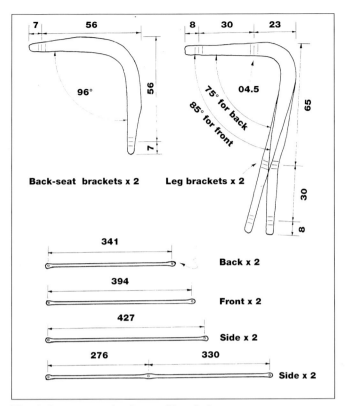

The chair components – legs and brackets.

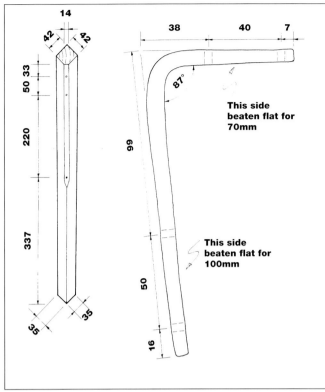

The table components – legs and brackets.

final sanding before applying a finish – matt cellulose lacquer, brushed on matt polyurethane varnish or tung oil are appropriate finishes.

Lastly, assemble the chair.

Making the table

The table top is made from four boards joined together. The finished surface measures 1202 by 591 by 30mm, $47^5/_{16}$ by $23^1/_4$ by $^{13}/_{16}$in.

If the boards go together well it takes only a little sanding to achieve a flat surface. The boards are first surface planed one side and then thickness planed down to 30mm, $1^3/_{16}$in.

As with the chair, the boards should be arranged to best effect, alternating heart-side up and down for stability. The same technique for gluing up the chair seat and back is used for the table.

Cutting the legs

The table's legs are produced in the same way as the chair legs. The four tapered sections can be cut from a 700 by 228 by 5mm, $27^1/_2$ by 9 by 2in plank. Cut the top of the legs square, but leave extra length on each leg as these will be cut to size on assembly.

The 45° jig is used for producing the beveled corner and for drilling the screw's pilot holes. No.8 x 25mm, 1in black round head slotted screws are used for every fixing.

Fitting the legs

At either end of the table just one continuous length of bent steel is used to brace the legs against the top. This can be produced quite successfully by eye and any irregularities can be compensated for by adjusting the position of the screw hole partway down each leg.

An alternative would be to set up a jig using the working drawings for reference; this would help when bending the steel rod to the correct angles.

The rod can be flattened on each bend by hammering a length of square section rod over the hot metal. Label each component and its position in the table when assembling it before finishing.

The same method for cutting the legs to length in the chair is also used for the table. ■

MATERIALS LIST

CHAIR ....
American white ash:

Back – 410 x 328, x 18mm, $16^1/_8$ x 13 x 1in x one off
Seat – 403 x 377 x 18mm, $15^7/_8$ x $14^7/_8$ x 1in x one off
Legs – 430 x 35 x 35mm, 17 x $1^3/_8$ x $1^3/_8$in x four off

Bright mild steel rod, 8mm, 5/16in diameter:

Long side – 620mm, $24^{13}/_{32}$in x two off
Short side – 445mm, $17^1/_2$in x two off
Front – 421mm, $16^1/_4$in x two off
Back – 357mm, $14^1/_{16}$in x two off
Long brackets – 140mm, $5^1/_2$ x four off
Short brackets – 100mm, 4in x two off

TABLE ....
American white ash:

Top – 1202 x 591 x 30mm, $47^1/_4$ x $23^1/_4$ x $1^1/_4$in x one off
Legs – 640 x 42 x 42mm, $25^3/_{16}$ x $1^2/_3$in x $1^2/_3$in x four off

Bright mild steel rod 10mm, 3/8in diameter:

Triangulating components – 2000mm, 78 in – includes excess length – x two off
Brackets – 230mm, $9^1/_{16}$in x four off

A stool for Emily

Dr Stanley Purser has made a stool for each of his grandchildren. The latest was Emily's. This is how he made it.

Consider the constructional problems. The feet of this stool have to be splayed out to give stability. But how far? Ideally they should extend to the perimeter of the design, but this is asking a lot from the joints, so in this stool I have settled for 25mm (1IN) inwards from the outline. At this spread the stool is not easy to tip over and the appearance is satisfactory.

Next, strength. Putting the legs outwards at an angle demands the strongest tenon it is practical to make and the largest surface area of the shoulders that can be achieved – hence the initial bulk of the legs at 90 x 90mm (3½ x 3½IN).

THE SEAT

The seat will be made in two stages. First, plane the wood to an even thickness. The shape is drawn from a template and cut out. Mark out and cut the mortises.

The second stage involves routing and carving. From FIG 1 it is apparent that the shape of the seat is based on an equilateral triangle within a circle of 190mm (7½IN) radius. Having drawn this on card so as to make the template, strike off three arcs from the three corner points. The radius from one point to another is 330mm (13IN). There must be a special name for this particular shape, but I am unable to find it and until I am corrected I shall call it an "emigon".

Using the cardboard template, mark the outline and prick through the card to position the centre point. Inscribe the circles for the birth date numerals and mark out for the mortises. The mortises will be 19mm (¾IN) by 38mm (1½IN) and are best made by drilling two holes 25mm (1IN) deep with a Forstner bit. Complete the job with paring chisels.

It is better to leave the carving and lettering until later as there will be a certain amount of handling of the seat during the fitting of the legs and there would be a risk of damage to the finer tool work.

The wood available to me for the legs was 51mm (2IN) thick. In order to get the massive joint and shoulders necessary to give

strength to the splayed legs I glued up two pieces to give the required size. It would have been better, and quicker, to work from a single solid piece. However, in due course and with careful matching of the grain, the joint is unobtrusive.

It is important that the surfaces to be glued are true and their sides square, for only then will you be able to mark and cut tenons and shoulders accurately.

Marking out on the legs can now start. Set the sliding bevel to 74DEG. Mark the top of the leg on one side with the bevel, strike across the two surfaces with the try square and then check on the fourth side with the bevel that the marking has been accurate.

Mark out the tenon, using the try square and sliding bevel (FIG 2). The same care and time as has been spent in marking out must now be given to cutting the tenon. In both procedures you will be at times working off the square and this adds to the difficulty of getting all four shoulders in precisely the same plane. Judicious finishing with a sharp paring chisel may be necessary.

You can now start shaping the legs, starting by drawing rough outlines (FIG 3) using cardboard templates. Waste wood is cut off with the bandsaw. A useful tip after cutting off the waste, tape it back on before flipping over to cut the other side. In this way the cutting can be kept relatively square.

Do not forget to leave the step on the inner side of the leg. This is essential for clamping in the final gluing and also useful in the next

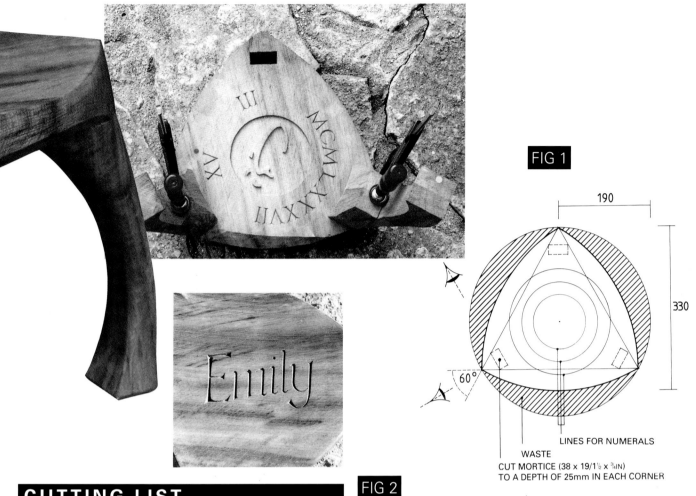

FIG 1

190

330

60°

LINES FOR NUMERALS

WASTE

CUT MORTICE (38 x 19/1½ x ¾IN)
TO A DEPTH OF 25mm IN EACH CORNER

FIG 2

FIG 3

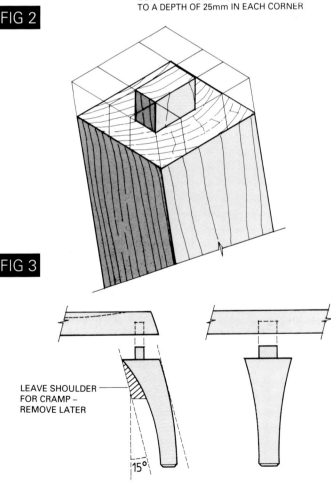

LEAVE SHOULDER
FOR CRAMP –
REMOVE LATER

15°

CUTTING LIST

Finished sizes in mm (inches in brackets)
Seat   355 x 355 x 51 (14 x 14 x 2)
legs x 3   255 x 90 x 90 (10 x 3½ x 3½)
I have used brown oak, but other strong hardwoods could have been used.

stage of shaping, which you start once you are satisfied it all fits perfectly.

The leg is held firmly in position with the clamp applied to the step and seat top. Shaping is done by rasp, file and gouge, the aim being for the lines of the seat and leg to flow into each other when viewed from all angles. Proceed as far as you are able, but do not use abrasive paper yet. Put the legs on one side and start on stage two of the seat.

SEAT (PART II)

Carving the name and birthdates can now begin, but first some guide-lines on drawing.

The birthdate numerals will be circular in the final carving, but draw them out between horizontal parallel lines, leaving excessive space between each numeral. Cut out each numeral in vertical strips, each strip a fraction wider than the number. Each strip is then laid on the underside of the seat, the base line of the numeral forming a cord with the inner letter circle.

Spacing will have to be by eye so time spent on this important detail will be well repaid. In this case, I have tried to get equal spacing between the year, month and date of birth and this is viewed from the centre of the circle.

The numerals are transferred to the wood using blue carbon paper under the strips but do not indent the wood with excessive pressure.

The Arabic lettering in the inner area is raised, which means routing out the grounding or removing the wood with a grounding tool.

For some ideas about lettering see the previous article in this magazine (starting page 16). Suffice for me to suggest you take your time over this most enjoyable part of woodwork and do not hesitate to bring your own 'signature', or style into the letters.

With the underside completed, cut a piece of hardboard, tape it over the carving for protection and start on the upper side of the seat.

As you will see, I have scooped out the top of the seat. I went to a depth of 12mm (½IN) so you will have to make a simple jig on which the router will rest. FIG 4 shows this easily made accessory. The two blocks (B) are a fraction less than the thickness of the seat so that when the jig is in position the blocks can be clamped to the bench, holding the seat steady when routing.

CARVING THE NAME

Rout out the top of the seat, but do leave flat areas at the three points where the cramps will rest when the legs are fitted. By moving the position of the jig, most of the wood can be removed by the router. A shallow gouge will be required for the areas around the points.

Smooth the surface thoroughly using the different grades of garnet, ending with 320.

The name can now be marked (gently) on to the wood. I prefer lower case lettering for this name as opposed to Roman numerals for the dates.

With lower case, of which there are many variants, the craftsman can allow his own particular flair to show itself. It is worth spending much time on the drawing, viewing from all angles, and in the mirror, too, to make sure mistakes do not happen in the wood and the spacing is correct.

Before the final gluing up, make sure the legs fit nicely and you are confident with the appropriation and positioning of the cramps. I have used Resin 'W' adhesive, which gives satisfactory results.

The author
Stanley Purser

Each of Dr Stanley Purser's grandchildren has a stool made specially for them by their grandfather, inscribed with the child's name on top of the seat and the date of birth underneath.

Emily's stool, featured here, was number five. Like most of the others it is made of oak. It has some interesting design features, too, as Dr Purser explains.

"Emily was born in Dubai, therefore some Arabic is appropriate as well as a suggestion of Eastern arches in the legs. By coincidence, the feet resemble those of a camel.

"Emily's father, Ian, was consulted about the stool. He wanted it in brown oak, which is a lovely wood, not easily obtained and sometimes a little temperamental for fine work (no connection, we hope, with Emily)."

It was Dr Purser's idea to make a three legged stool, which presented some problems of stability. The legs had to be splayed, which meant they had to be joined to the seat with strong, robust joints.

Leave cramped overnight. Cut another hardboard protective cover for the lettering, tape it on and start the final shaping of the legs.

This shaping will include removing the 'step' that had assisted in cramping. Although the legs and seat are now strongly united, go with gentle care at this procedure, removing a little wood at a time with sharp gouges followed by wood files.

Cut the legs to the correct length: being a three legged stool, the precise length is of secondary importance to the squareness of the base of the feet. Put a 3mm (⅛IN) chamfer around the base edges of the feet.

Remove the hardboard and finish the corners which had been left flat for cramping with a sharp shallow gouge leaving a decorative diamond, or whatever device you prefer.

FINISHING

The garnet can now be used on the legs and edges of the seat. Start with grade 80 or 100 and go through to 320. When you are satisfied with the surfaces (remembering that all imperfections will be magnified in the final polishing) wet the stool all over using a damp cloth, but be careful not to allow wetness into the lettering.

Let the work dry and go over again with 320 garnet. Repeat a further wetting and garnet. The wood can now be sealed with a cellulose based sealer. Two applications are required, each being allowed to dry. Finish again with fine old paper. Brush and vacuum once more and give a final attention to the lettering with delicate tools such as the fishtail.

Finally, I applied Danish oil, several coats, at daily intervals. This oil gives a beautiful but tough finish and Emily will enjoy the feel of the surface and the aroma of the oil. When little dents and abrasions occur, as they will, a bit more oil and rubbing will put the matter right.

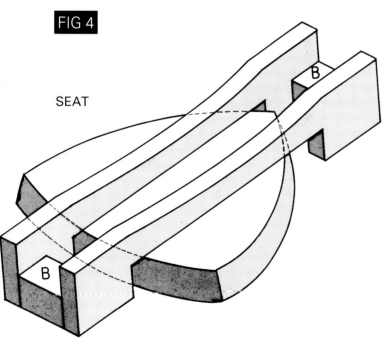

FIG 4

SEET

B

B

Jig for routing out the top of the seat.

Taking the backache out of the kitchen

It's not only the food which rises in this kitchen – the table does, too. You can prepare the food without getting backache and sit down to eat it without needing a high chair. Ron Doel explains how he made this adjustable height kitchen table.

PROJECT TABLE

Most of the furniture I am commissioned to design and make is fairly run of the mill – dressers, tables, television cabinets and the like. Usually people want the pieces made to fit into a particular space, or because they cannot find any furniture to match existing pieces they have. But every now and then I get asked to solve a particular problem, which I like because it keeps the grey matter working and is interesting.

This kitchen table was one of those problems. The commission came from a lady who is an excellent pastry cook. But, while she loves cooking, she suffers from a bad back and preparing food on an ordinary height kitchen table is painful for her.

What she needed was a table 150mm (6IN) higher than an ordinary kitchen table. Now, that would have

been easy enough, but she only had room in her kitchen for one table and most of its life it would have to serve as an ordinary kitchen table, 735mm (29IN) high.

The problem was to make a table 735mm high for normal use which could be raised by 150mm when my client wanted to make pastry. In the raised position it had to be firm

CUTTING LIST FOR ADJUSTABLE-HEIGHT KITCHEN TABLE		
Finished sizes in mm (inches in brackets)		
PINE		
Legs	x 4	64 x 64 x 737	(2½ x 2½ x 29)
Top	x 3	200 x 32 x 1220	(7¾ x 1¼ x 48)
	x 1	172 x 32 x 1220	(6¾ x 1¼ x 48)
Rails	x 2	96 x 32 x 990	(3¾ x 1¼ x 39)
	x 2	96 x 32 x 813	(3¾ x 1¼ x 32)
Supports	x 2	45 x 20 x 1067	(1¾ x ¾ x 42)
IROKO		
Flaps	x 2	178 x 20 x 534	(7 x ¾ x 21)
Under bars	x 4	32 x 20 x 534	(1 ¼ x ¾ x 21)

You will also need four pieces of 19mm x 3mm x 355mm (¾ x ⅛ x 14IN) steel bars in order to make brackets.

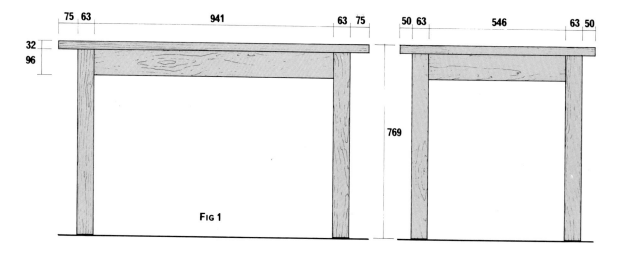

75 | 63 | 941 | 63 | 75

32
96

769

50 | 63 | 546 | 63 | 50

FIG 1

enough to endure the rigours of making and rolling out puff pastry. The firmness and stability of the table was the most important problem to be solved. I thought about this for a very long time – probably longer than it took me to make the table.

It had to be simple in design and easy to operate. The table I eventually designed and made is shown here.

You will see from the cutting list that the legs were 64 x 64mm (2½ x 2½IN), the rails 96 x 32mm (3¾ x 1¼IN) and the top 32mm (1¼IN) thick. This all helped make the table extremely rigid. The overall size of the top was 1,220 x 762mm (48 x 30IN).

The table was made of best quality pine with the top of side boards.

It is advisable to see how the top boards join together and if there is any bowing. If there is, put two end pieces across the grain to keep the table top flat. You can use an electric router for this, cutting grooves and inserting a strip of 6mm (¼IN) ply. Make sure it is well glued and cramped. Do not cut the grooves right to the end because if you do they will show on the side edges.

I did not put these extra two pieces at each end but, on reflection, I would advise it because you may not be as lucky as I was in obtaining such flat boards.

But back to the beginning. First order the timber. I am old fashioned and I work in feet and inches. I order finished sizes with lengths in the sizes I wish to finish up with and the timber merchants send a little extra to allow for cutting. When the timber arrives, I use a belt sander (a Bosch PB5 75) and finish with an orbital sander before putting the pieces together. I sand down to 120 grit.

I cut the legs first. I used a radial arm saw using a stop on the saw bench on the left of the blade to guarantee four legs of the same length.

Then I cut the rails the same way, but allowing 20mm (¾IN) on each end for the mortise joint. When you have prepared these parts mark out the

mortises on the top of the legs and drill to the correct depth (ie 20mm). This makes chopping the mortises easier work – even if you are using an electric mortiser as I was. I use a Wolf chisel mortiser making a trial run on an offcut before making the mortises in the legs of the table.

Take the corners off the legs with a plane. This makes a better finish. You could, of course, have turned legs, or any other type of leg, but in this instance I used a straight, square leg with just the corners off. I cut off the inside top corner of each leg to a width of 25mm (1IN) and length of 254mm (10IN).

I make the tenons on the rails with the help of my radial arm saw using a stop 20mm (¾IN) to the right of the blade. If you choose this method, take

off 3mm (⅛IN) at a time on each side until you reach the correct depth. Cut the shoulder the same way and clean off the tenon with a sharp chisel.

You are now ready to put the base together. I glue it up with Resin W glue, keeping a damp cloth handy to wipe away any surplus. This is important because stain will not take on the glue. Cramp up the frame and leave it to set for at least 24 hours.

Now to the top. The boards have to be joined together and for this I use an Elu router to make finger joints ▶

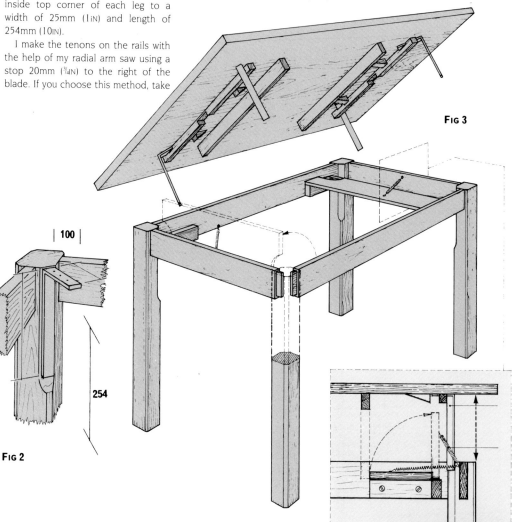

FIG 3

| 100 |

254

FIG 2

between each board. Again, don't make the joint go quite the whole length of each board or it will show. Cramp the top from above and below and leave it for well over 24 hours.

When the top is ready I sand both sides with a belt sander and finish off with the orbital sander, starting with 80 grit, then 100 grit and finishing off with 120 grit.

Now comes the difficult part – making it possible to adjust the height of the top. It would have been easy to use metal brackets and wing nuts, but this would be too complicated and tedious to use. Instead I screwed 20mm x 3mm (³/₄IN x ¹/₈IN) right angled steel brackets (FIG 2) on to the underneath of the table top. These are positioned so they will act as runners against the flattened surfaces on the inside of the legs.

I couldn't find any brackets of the right size so I had them made up by a local engineering firm. I painted them with white Hammerite before fixing them.

To get them positioned properly place the table top upside down on the bench (making sure the bench is clear of any debris because softwoods mark easily) and put the base in place with the legs upright. Position the angle irons in each corner allowing 1.5mm (¹/₁₆IN) for easy movement and screw the irons into the underside of the top.

Now you have a table with a top which can be raised 150mm (6IN). All you need now is a device to keep it in place.

To make such a device I used some 50 x 25mm (2 x 1IN) pine running parallel to the end rails (leaving enough room for the metal brackets to slide) and continuing on the return by 230mm (9IN). This is screwed on to the

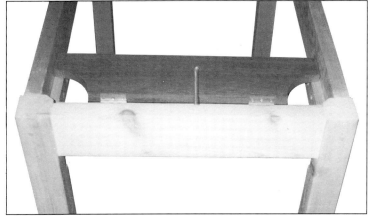

front and back rail so it is 32mm (1¹/₄IN) lower than the top of the rails. Hinge two pieces of 179 x 20mm (7 x ³/₄IN) iroko the width of the table (but allowing for movement and cutting out two corners [FIG 3]) to the 50 x 25mm pieces so that when the iroko flaps are laid flat they rest on the returns.

Now stops have to be fixed to the underneath of the table top at each end so that when the iroko flaps are raised at right angles to the base they are locked into position. The flaps slide over two wedge-shaped pieces of iroko and slip down between them and an iroko bar of 25 x 38mm (1 x 1¹/₂IN). Cut out a 50 x 13mm (2 x ¹/₂IN) recess in the middle of the bar before fitting to allow for a spring. The spring, which can be bought from a garage, is fixed between each iroko flap and end rail so it is under tension when the flap is down. This way, when the table top is lifted the springs pull the flaps into the upright position and the table top is lowered on to them.

I thought it advisable to use two additional supports across the grain to make sure that the table top remained absolutely flat.

Now came the moment of truth when I made this table. With it all assembled I lifted the top, one end at a time – and the theory worked in practice. As the flaps fit into the space between the iroko wedges and batten on the underneath of the table top, the top is rigid. Raised or lowered it is as firm as any table.

To revert it to normal kitchen table height all you have to do is lift the top

a little and push the flaps forward, one end at a time.

It is advisable to have the angle irons reasonably tight to the legs because, with wear, they may become too loose. In the first instance, a little candle grease smooths the movement.

Before I deal with the finishing, there is a point I would like to make about the type of timber which could be used. I had no option but to use pine because the table had to match the other kitchen furniture.

If, however, a hardwood was used (such as elm, oak, iroko or ash) the top does not need to be as thick. It could come down to 25mm, or even 19mm (1IN or ³/₄IN) for the top, 50mm (2IN) for the legs, and 25mm (1IN) for the rails. This, of course, cuts down the cost of the timber you will need for the project.

To finish, I gave the whole piece a final sanding and then a coat of Jenkins shellac sealer No S053. It is a natural colour when finished. Of course, you could use a light brown shade, bearing in mind pine gets darker as each month goes by.

Whichever you care to use, leave it for at least 12 hours before continuing with the finishing. When it is dry, rub it down with fine paper, say PSF P360. Clean it off and coat up with a hard varnish, rubbing down after each coat. When this is dry, use 0000 steel wool dipped in a finishing wax polish (such as Colron finishing wax) and rub it well into the whole table. This gives a smooth finish which is also serviceable ●

This commission was to make a refectory table, four chairs and two carvers. The design had not been finalized by the client, although he did have something in mind. I explained to him I could not possibly start this work for about six months. He was not put off and the time gave us ample time to confer and finalize the shape, at least for the table.

What he was quite concerned about was that the wood should be English oak. Not American, or Japanese, but English. Well, that was all right by me because I only work in home grown woods such as elm, cherry, yew and oak. And I always keep a good stock of oak.

I buy the wood from logging firms of long standing. I select the butt and get them to saw it through and through, which is less expensive than having it quarter sawn.

Still, I'm not too unhappy. Cut through and through I still get nearly 20% quarter sawn and I use this in prominent positions to show off the grain, particularly in oak.

I air dry the planks for at least a year or more according to thickness and finish them off in my small kiln.

The client for this dining table and chairs was the head of a woodwork and metalwork department at a public school in the north west of England. Being an artist and designer, it should have warned me of what was to come. For it ended up not being the straight-forward design I imagined. It developed from the idea of a Gothic arch, inverted to make the table frame.

PROJECT

TABLE

Going
Gothic

Gothic arches and English oak were the inspiration for a dining suite which cabinet-maker Oswald Tat was commissioned to make. Here he explains how the table was made, and in the following article he talks about the chairs.

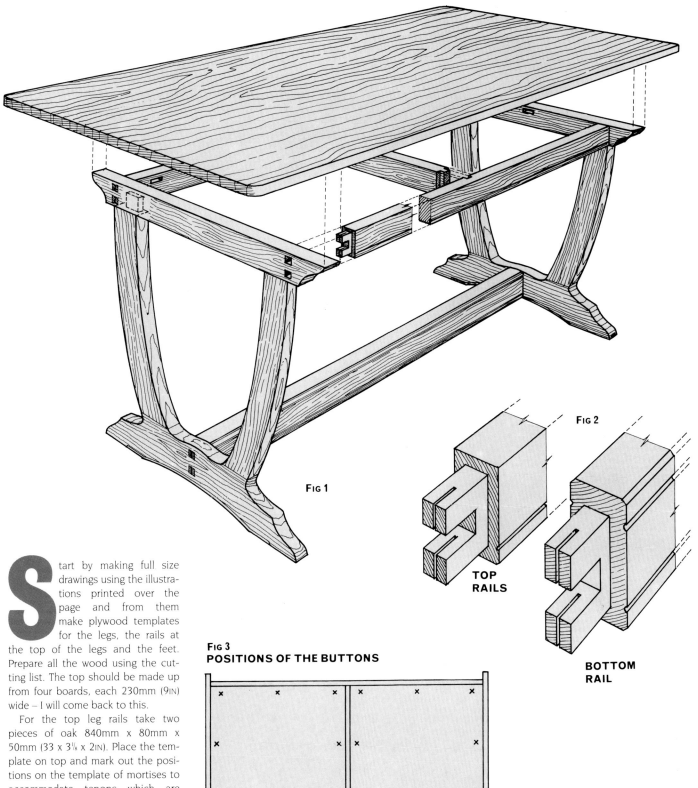

Fig 1

Fig 2

TOP RAILS

BOTTOM RAIL

Fig 3
POSITIONS OF THE BUTTONS

S tart by making full size drawings using the illustrations printed over the page and from them make plywood templates for the legs, the rails at the top of the legs and the feet. Prepare all the wood using the cutting list. The top should be made up from four boards, each 230mm (9IN) wide – I will come back to this.

For the top leg rails take two pieces of oak 840mm x 80mm x 50mm (33 x 3⅛ x 2IN). Place the template on top and mark out the positions on the template of mortises to accommodate tenons which are 20mm (¾IN) thick. With two clamps to hold the template rigid, cut the through mortises in the rail in the positions indicated by the template. Remember to put a piece of scrap wood on the underside so the work is protected when the chisel breaks through. Draw round the template and saw out the shape.

Use two pieces of oak 660mm x 130mm x 50mm (26 x 5⅛ x 2IN) for the feet. Place the template on the material and secure it with two clamps for rigidity. Outline the shape in pencil and mark the positions of

the mortises for the leg tenons. Cut the through mortises at the centre for the bottom rail, cutting through the template. Remove the template. Chop out the blind mortise between the two through mortises to take the tenons shown in FIG 2.

Set the table leg template against the outside of the foot, aligning the tenon with the mortise marks on the foot. Draw round the tenon. This will give you the angle of the mortise.

Again, I cut these on a mortiser. To do that the foot has to be tilted to the required angle. I do this by placing a piece of wood towards the end of the foot, the middle of which rests at the end of the moving table of the mortiser. This is shown in FIG 5.

By moving the block of wood left or right you can set the angle using the vertical mortise chisel as a guide on the outside of the foot. I used the clamp on the moving table to ▶

hold the foot firmly. Align the chisel to the cutting position and cut the mortise.

Cut the shape of the foot, leaving plenty of waste (about 30mm – 1⅛IN) either side of the leg for forming the legs to the foot.

Use the leg template on four pieces of oak 660 x 125 x 50mm (26 x 5 x 2IN) and, in pencil, mark out the legs. The tenon shoulders are marked with a marking knife for greater accuracy. Align an adjustable square to the shoulder marks, secure the angle and scribe with a knife. Use a try square to mark the edges. On the opposite side scribe the angle using the adjustable square.

Using the adjustable and the try square respectively, deepen the scribed lines with a chisel. This acts as a guide for the saw. Mark out the tenon using a two pin gauge and saw the shoulders with a tenon saw.

Match up the two pairs of legs and, with each pair clamped in a vice, finish them using a spokeshave.

When all the tenons and mortises are complete fit them dry.

Invariably some adjustments have to be made (in my case it is usually that the tenons are too tight, but these can be pared). When everything fits well the legs can be glued and clamped. Peg the mortises and tenons with 12mm (½IN) dowels and put the assembled legs aside for the glue to cure.

When the glue is dry, shape the legs where they meet the feet using a rasp and a file so they blend in. I finish them off with a drum sander of a suitable diameter fitted to my drill. I make my own drum sanders to suit the job and over the years have collected quite a range.

Finally clean up the leg, finishing with 150 grit paper, and bevel the edges with a router.

Cut to length the two upper and one lower rails which run the length of the table, not forgetting to allow for the tenons. Make the tenons as shown in FIG 2 and saw the ends to receive mahogany wedges.

Dry fit the legs and the rails and mark the position of the cross bar between the centre lines of the top cross rails. Make and dry fit the cross bar into position.

When all the parts fit well, glue, clamp and drive home the mahogany wedges.

Plane the four pieces of wood for the top making sure the edges are square. I do this on a surface planer. Having cleaned each edge, mark them to show at a glance which belongs to which.

On the edges that are to be glued,

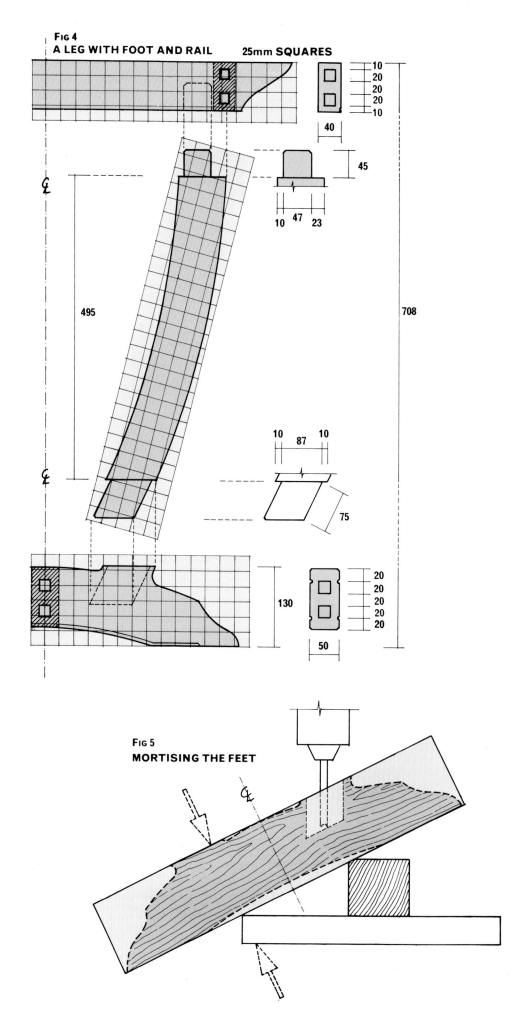

FIG 4
A LEG WITH FOOT AND RAIL   25mm SQUARES

FIG 5
MORTISING THE FEET

cut grooves, stopping them about 75mm (3IN) from the ends. For this I use a router. The grooves are 10mm (³⁄₈IN) wide by 15mm (⁵⁄₈IN) deep. Make the tongues for the grooves so they slip in and out by hand with a width of 2mm (³⁄₃₂IN) less than the total depth of the two grooves.

Apply glue to the grooves with an old paint brush, making sure there are no pockets of thick glue in the

I used a melamine, pre-catalysed lacquer satin finish. It is particularly appropriate today when people are not fond of polishing. Also, a table has to take all sorts of abuse. No doubt at some time wine or spirits will be spilt on it and hot items put on it. Melamine will not mark.

I am fortunate to have a small portable spray machine. I coat the surface with one coat of sanding

sealer. It dries in half an hour so I am able to sand it lightly and proceed with two coats of satin finish.

If you apply a similar finish, leave it for 24 hours then add a good wax using steel wool grade 0000. Apply a liberal spread and leave it for 36 hours – then go over it with virgin steel wool grade 0000 to remove the odd thickness of wax that is invariably left. Polish it up to finish ●

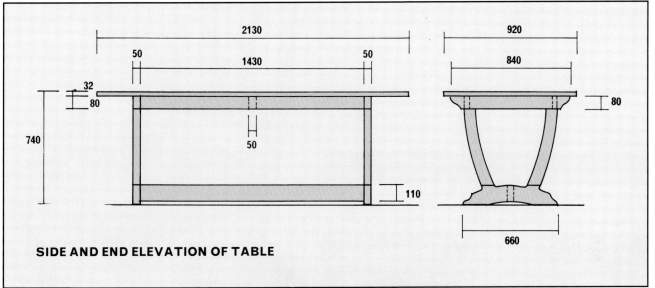

SIDE AND END ELEVATION OF TABLE

grooves. Put the tongues in position and clamp the pieces together using two clamps about 460mm (18IN) from the ends and another clamp on the opposite side in the middle. I always protect the workpiece where the clamp touches it with a thin piece of plastic – a carrier bag is ideal. This stops the metal clamp from staining the wood.

Clean off all the surplus glue, first with an old piece of wood and then a damp cloth. Leave to set overnight.

When the glue is cured the top needs finishing. I have a 100mm (4IN) belt sander. I start off using 80 grit, then 100 and finally 150.

Bevel the edges of the top with a router – and make sure you use a sharp cutter.

Use buttons to fit the top to the legs. I always use this method because no matter how well the wood has been seasoned, it will move. I season my timber down to a 10% moisture content, which is reasonably safe to put in centrally heated rooms. When I do church work I'm happy with a moisture content of between 14% and 16%.

Cut 16 grooves with a router on the inside of the upper rails, spaced as shown in FIG 3. The buttons are 60 x 40 x 30mm (2³⁄₈ x 1⁵⁄₈ x 1¹⁄₈IN) with a hole to take a No 12 or 14 screw.

The table I made was not going to be stained, which I was pleased about. I much prefer natural wood.

GOTHIC TABLE-CUTTING LIST
finished sizes in mm (inches in brackets)

OAK

Table top	x1	2300 x 920 x 32	(90³⁄₈ x 9¹¹⁄₁₆ x 1¹⁄₈)
Legs	x4	650 x 125 x 50	(25⁵⁄₈ x 5 x 2)
Top rail of legs	x2	840 x 80 x 50	(33 x 3¹⁄₈ x 2)
Leg foot	x2	660 x 130 x 50	(26 x 5¹⁄₈ x 2)
Top rails	x2	1530 x 80 x 40	(60³⁄₁₆ x 3¹⁄₈ x 1⁵⁄₈)
Bottom rail	x1	1530 x 110 x 50	(60³⁄₁₆ x 4³⁄₈ x 2)
Member across top rails	x1	590 x 80 x 50	(23³⁄₁₆ x 3¹⁄₈ x 2)

You also need a board 800 x 40 x 30 (31⁵⁄₈ x 1⁵⁄₈ x 1¹⁄₈) to make 13 buttons, each 60 x 40 x 30 (2³⁄₈ x 1⁵⁄₈ x 1¹⁄₈) for securing the top.

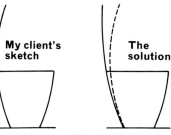

My client's sketch

The solution

A month after I delivered the dining table (featured in the previous article) to my client, he approached me about making the chairs to complete the suite.

When he visited me I was still thinking of chairs being straight, upright and square. My client had other ideas. He drew four lines on the back of an envelope and asked me if anything like that could be done. His simple sketch showed me why he is heading a design department at a prominent public school. It was simple and direct.

He was following the basic design of the table legs with an extended upright for the back of the chairs. It looked unusual and had possibilities. More importantly, it excited me.

I told him it could be done, submitted a sketch and told him I would make a sample chair in pine before attempting the final pieces.

The pine model demonstrated how uncomfortable the chair would be in its initial design. The continual curve of the back kept the body leaning forward all the time and made you feel hunched up.

The solution was discovered by putting a piece of wood under the feet at the front of the chair, which tilted it backwards. It became comfortable. The design was amended, effectively tilting the back legs backwards as shown in the drawing above. The dotted line represents the original position of the back.

This was agreed and I started making the four side chairs and the two carvers.

Going Gothic 2

PROJECT CHAIR

In the previous article Oswald Tat explained how he made a dining table based on Gothic arches and English oak. Here he details the making of the chairs and carvers which concluded the commission.

Before getting to work on the wood, make full scale working drawings of the side chairs and the carvers. You can scale these up from Fig 1.

From the drawings make templates – for which plywood is useful – of the sides, rails and uprights showing the positions of mortises and tenons. Cut the 12mm (½in) through mortises in the templates in the appropriate positions. Prepare the wood according to the cutting list.

Four back legs can be cut from one piece of planed oak 1200 x 260 x 25mm (47³⁄₁₆ x 10¼ x 1in) as shown in Fig 2. Four front legs can be cut from a piece 600 x 200 x 25mm (23⅜ x 8 x 1in). I extended the top part of the legs by 50mm (2in), which is cut off when the sides have been assembled and the top is shaped.

Pencil round the templates, cut accurately following the pencil line on the waste side and allow 50mm for the tenons.

Cut out the wood for the feet but do not shape them at this stage. It is easier to chop out the mortises with the wood still square. I used a mortiser, sup-▶

CARVERS

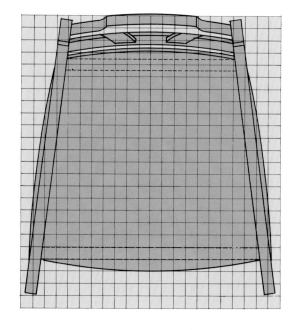

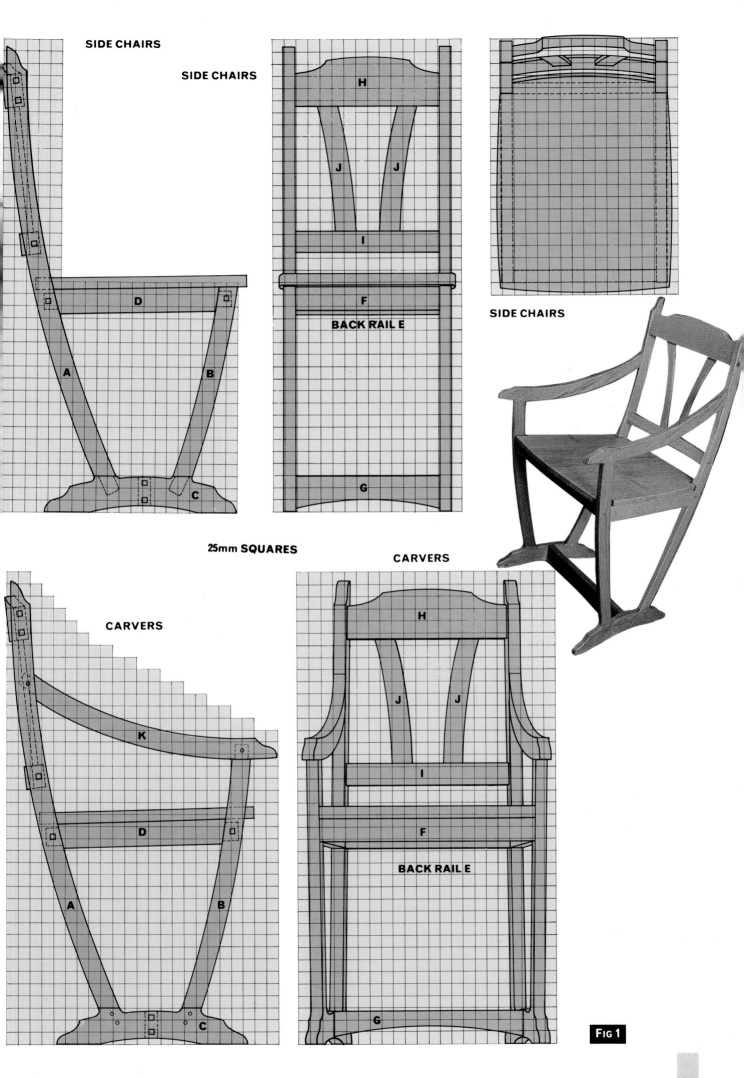

SIDE CHAIRS

SIDE CHAIRS

D

A

B

C

H

J   J

I

F

BACK RAIL E

G

SIDE CHAIRS

25mm SQUARES

CARVERS

CARVERS

K

D

A

B

C

H

J   J

I

F

BACK RAIL E

G

FIG 1

porting the wood on an offcut to achieve the required angle (see previous article, page 24). With the mortises cut you can shape the feet, but leave enough waste either side of the joints to be able to blend the feet and the legs together later.

Match the legs in pairs (ie put the back legs together in pairs and the front legs together in pairs). Clamp a pair of back legs together and clean up the saw marks using a spokeshave on the curves. Do the same for all the pairs of back legs then all the pairs of front legs.

Mate pairs of back legs with pairs of front legs and use the appropriate template to mark the position of the mortises for rail D on FIG 1. The same template will give you the angle of the tenon shoulders on the legs.

Chop the mortises and cut the tenons. The tenons at the feet (C) are pegged with 6mm (¼IN) dowels after the legs and feet have been glued up and the glue is dry.

Tenon the rails D (FIG 1), dry fit and if all is well glue up and clamp together the front and back legs with the feet and rails D.

FIG 3

JIG FOR GETTING CHAIRS UPRIGHT

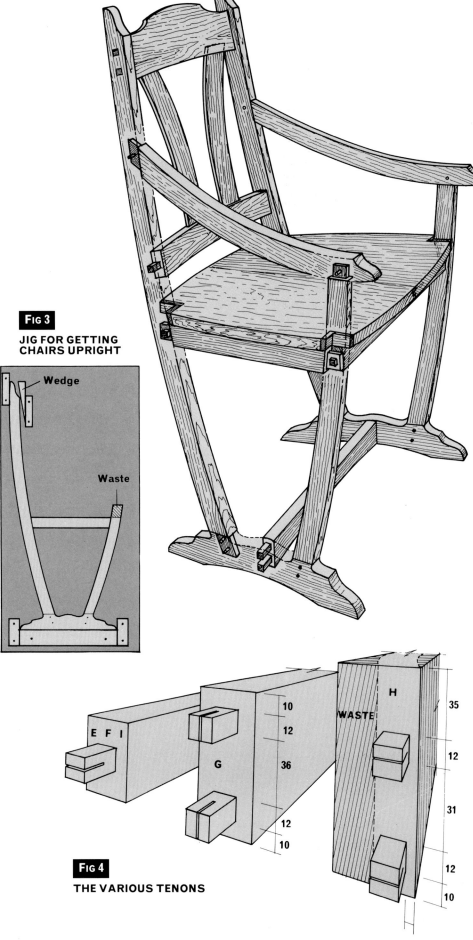

FIG 2

THE BACK LEGS

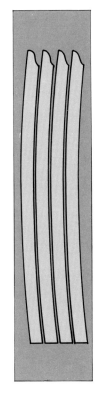

THE FRONT LEGS

FIG 4

THE VARIOUS TENONS

CUTTING LIST FOR CHAIRS AND CARVERS
sizes in mm (inches in brackets)

CHAIRS x4

OAK	PART		
Back legs x8 cut from 2 pieces	A	1200 x 280 x 25	(47³⁄₁₆ x 11 x 1)
Front legs x8 cut from 2 pieces	B	600 x 200 x 25	(23⅝ x 8 x 1)
Foot x8	C	450 x 80 x 25	(17¾ x 3⅛ x 1)
Seat rails x16	DEF	450 x 50 x 25	(17¾ x 2 x 1)
Top back rail x4	H	400 x 100 x 40	(15¾ x 4 x 1⅝)
Top middle rail x4	I	400 x 45 x 40	(15¾ x 1¾ x 1⅝)
Foot rail x4	G	400 x 80 x 25	(15¾ x 3⅛ x 1)
Splats x8	J	200 x 50 x 10	(8 x 2 x ⅜)
Seat x4 cut from 2 pieces		1900 x 180 x 25	(75 x 7 x 1)

CARVERS x2

	PART		
Back leg x4 cut from a piece	A	1200 x 280 x 25	(47³⁄₁₆ x 11 x 1)
Front leg x4 cut from a piece	B	750 x 280 x 25	(29⅝ x 11 x 1)
Arm rest x4	K	850 x 50 x 25	(33⅜ x 2 x 1)
Seat rails x6	DE	500 x 50 x 25	(19⅝ x 2 x 1)
Seat front rail x2	F	600 x 50 x 25	(23⅝ x 2 x 1)
Top back rail x2	H	500 x 100 x 40	(19⅝ x 4 x 1⅝)
Middle rail x2	I	500 x 45 x 40	(19⅝ x 1¾ x 1⅝)
Foot rail x2	G	500 x 80 x 25	(19⅝ x 3⅛ x 1)
Splats x4 cut from 2 pieces	J	200 x 150 x 10	(8 x 6 x ⅜)
Foot x4	C	500 x 80 x 25	(19⅝ x 3⅛ x 1)
Seat x2 cut from 2 pieces		1000 x 240 x 25	(39⅜ x 18¾ x 1)
Buttons x30		50 x 25 x 20	(2 x 1 x ¾)

Because of the curves and angles on these chairs the cutting list does not give finished sizes, but rather the amount of timber you will need. Refer to drawings for dimensions.

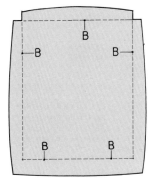

FIG 5

RAILS H AND I   R = 960mm.

FIG 6

POSITION OF BUTTONS HOLDING SEAT IN POSITION

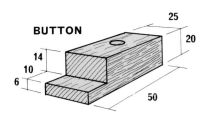

BUTTON

To make sure all the chairs ended up with the same upright angles I made myself a jig (FIG 3).

When the glue has set, shape the legs to the feet using a rasp and file and dowel the tenons. Bevel the edges and sand smooth.

Through mortises next. Place the template on one of the legs. Tape it at each end with masking tape and also use two clamps for security. As the chair is a square design the cut of the chisel is at right angles to the surface.

Mortise through on the positions you marked on the template. (Remember to put a scrap piece of wood under the leg so the chisel cuts through cleanly.)

Now the sides need joining together, so cut the tenons on all the cross rails – parts G, E, F, I and H on FIG 1. Parts E, F and I have single tenons. On parts G and H the tenons are doubled (FIG 4). Cut slots into the tenons as shown to receive mahogany wedges.

Note that the tenons on the top rail, H, and middle rail, I, are offset because of their concave shape (FIG 5). When the tenons have been cut, the concave shape can be sawn out and the mortises cut to receive the decorative pieces, J, between them. Cut out the pieces J and fit them between the rails H and I. Dry fit and, if satisfactory, the chair can now be glued and

clamped and mahogany wedges inserted into the ends of the through tenons and hit home.

So to the seat. This is made up from two pieces of oak board. The grain goes from back to front. The two pieces are grooved to accept a mahogany tongue which I allowed to show through front and back because I liked the look of it. If you do this it has to be a good fit.

The sides of the seat and the front are slightly curved, the front being 20mm (¾IN) each side wider than it is at the back. This gives it an attractive appearance.

The seat is held in position by five buttons, made and positioned as shown in FIG 6. They are ▶

screwed into the bottom of the chair seat and located into grooves cut into the rails. This allows the wood to move.

The carvers

So far we have talked about the ordinary chairs. The carvers are slightly different. The sides are constructed in the same way as with the other chairs – ie glued and clamped – but with the arm rests fitted. Only the cutting of the through mortises is different because the carver is wider at the front than at the back. The mortises will have to be cut at an angle. The precise angle is gauged from the working drawing in the way shown in FIG 7.

To chop the mortises using a mortiser a piece of wood at the correct angle is made long enough to go beyond the moving table of the mortiser. This means the side frame of the carver and the template can be clamped to the angled wood on the mortiser, which itself is held firmly on the moving table by its clamp (FIG 8).

The back rails, I, E and H on FIG 1, are all the same length. The front rail, F, is longer as the carver is wider at the front.

The length of the rails is taken from the working drawing, adding

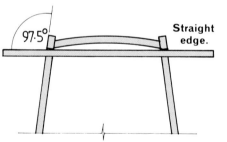

FIG 7

Gauging the angle of the carvers. With a straight edge across the legs the angle can be gauged by using an adjustable level.

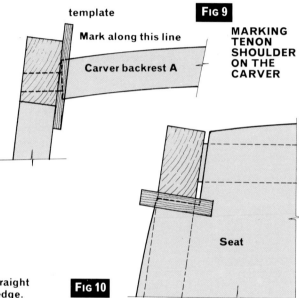

FIG 8

MORTISE CUT FROM OUTSIDE OF SIDE FRAME OF CHAIR TO INSIDE

FIG 9

MARKING TENON SHOULDER ON THE CARVER

template

Mark along this line

Carver backrest A

Seat

FIG 10

Mark with a marking knife along these edges on all four legs. Remove the waste. Insert the 10mm (⅜IN) mahogany pieces the same thickness as the seat. Glue and pin. Trim the edges. Sand the top and bottoms flush with the seat. It is a nice touch.

5mm (³⁄₁₆IN) at each end for the square tenons to protrude.

The tenons at this stage are all cut with square shoulders. The top and middle rails are the same as for the side chairs. Dry fit them to the sides of the carver and lightly clamp. Measure the length of the piece that goes across the feet (G). Cut this to size and tenon.

The carver is again reassembled and lightly clamped. Because the shoulders of the tenons are square all round, they will not close up. So now take a piece of 6mm (¼IN) thick oak and place it on the inside of the carver sides and on the rail. Mark the edge that is on the rail with a knife. This gives the exact angle needed. Pare off the excess with a chisel (FIG 9).

Re-fit the carver dry again to measure the two splats (J) that fit between the top and middle rails. When done, refit the whole again and check all fits well. The carver can now be glued and clamped.

The seat is made in the same way as for the chairs. I had a slight difficulty in getting the corners to fit snugly, so I decided to fit inserts of mahogany. I replaced the seat, aligned it, and clamped it to the rails. I prepared a 10mm (⅜IN) thick piece of mahogany. I used this as a template placed against the inside edges of the chair and marked the seat with a marking knife (FIG 10).

The chairs are finished to match the table (see page 25). In my case, I sprayed them with a sealer and added two coats of spray-applied satin finish. After 24 hours I waxed them, applying the wax using 0000 grade wire wool. I left that for 36 hours, went over it again with wire wool of the same grade and polished it up to finish. ●

The finished table and chairs inspired by English oak and Gothic arches.

The six-way standard

Cane woven seats and panels can produce attractive furniture. Whether it is for a new piece or to restore an antique, Ricky Holdstock explains how to weave in cane.

Ricky Holdstock weaving a medallion into a 'spiders web' panel.

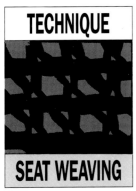

TECHNIQUE

SEAT WEAVING

The variety of seat and panel shapes is almost endless, although the choice of woven pattern is relatively limited. For our purposes the pattern known as the six-way standard of open weave is described. This is the strongest and most aesthetically satisfying way of caning a piece of furniture.

The method for weaving seats and panels is the same, though chair seat weavers have their own individual variations.

The procedures I shall describe are those which I have refined over the years – different, maybe, in detail from others, but the result comes out the same.

Seating cane and pre-woven cane can be purchased from most good craft shops or specialist mail order houses. A quarter kilo hank (or bundle) of seating cane is enough for several chair seats, though you can get it in smaller quantities. If there is some of the original canework left, take a section of the pattern to your supplier, who should be able to identify how much and of which size of cane you will require.

You will have to remove every piece of the old work from the holes in any case, so don't worry about taking some out.

Any repair to the chair frame is easier to do before, rather than after, the weaving.

The relationship between the diameter of the holes and their distance from each other determines the size of cane to be used, but as a rough guide you can establish the sizes yourself in the following way:

Measure a distance of 150mm (6IN) from the centre of any hole in a straight or nearly-straight frame rail and count the number of holes in that distance. If there are 16 holes, size No 1 cane will be used; 15 holes, sizes 1 and 2; 14 holes, size 2; 13 holes, sizes 2 and 3; 12 holes, size 3; 11 holes, sizes 3 and 4; 10 holes, size 4.

There should be the same number of holes in each of the side rails, but in most dining chairs the front rail is longer than the back rail, which usually means there are more holes in the front than there are in the back. This is as it should be, provided that both rails have an odd (or even) number of holes in each.

The tools required for caning are minimal and simple: a pin hammer, a handyman's knife, a pair of sharp pointed scissors, a bradawl, blunt penknife, bowl of cold water, sponge, short pegs to hold the cane firmly in the holes (golf tees make good temporary pegs during weaving) and supplies of seating cane.

Right. The simplest shape for caning – a rectangle.

Below. From a Victorian nursery.

Left. Caning a tub-shaped elbow chair is time-consuming, but no different from a balloon back.

Far Left. A medallion inset.

Left. Rectangle and shield shapes on the same chair.

Although the cane can be worked dry, it is better for it to be kept damp throughout the weaving process – not only the strand being woven but also those which are already in place.

It is not necessary to *soak* the cane before using it, just dip it in water for a few seconds.

It dries quickly from the warmth of your hands (even quicker if the work is being done in a centrally-heated home) so keep drawing it through a damp sponge. The cane has a shiny top surface which repels moisture. Only the underside is absorbent.

The six-way standard pattern is so called because there are, in effect, six directions in which the strands are woven: two from the back rail to the front, two from side to side, and two diagonally.

You begin with what is called **first setting**. Mark the central holes in the back and front rails. If there is an even number of holes, mark those which are immediately to the left of the centre of the rail.

Feed a strand down through the marked hole at the back until about half its length is above and half below the hole. Place a peg firmly in that hole, but not so ▶

Top. Ricky Holdstock demonstrating the six-way standard.

Above. Another example of the standard being used, this time by William Coddon.

There is no substitute for chair seating cane. True, my grandfather told me that his grandfather used the tendrils of ivy and honeysuckle to replace the odd broken strand in the family's chair seats, but that was because he was a poor shepherd and couldn't afford the proper material.

Rattan cane (the generic name given to around 300 species, not related in any way to bamboo) is a creeper growing in the jungles of the Far East – Malaysia, the Phillippines, Indonesia are the chief exporters of this multi-billion dollar trade in rattan furniture. For centuries the people of those countries have used it for making huts, baskets, suspension bridges, fish traps, mats, and all sorts of everyday items as well as furniture. Indeed, in recent years the development of the rattan furniture trade came near to denuding the jungles of this vital resource.

Caners use only a small proportion of the plant. The stems grow to hundreds of metres long and vary in thickness from a few millimetres to the size of your arm. Sharp-thorned runners support the main stem, making the harvesting a perilous affair. The native people who cut the cane have to wear thick hide gloves to protect themselves.

Having released the tangled creeper from the jungle canopy and cut it at the base, it is left out in the sun. The outer bark shrivels before it is stripped from the main stem to reveal the shiny surface of the inner bark.

It is then cut into lengths of 8-9 metres, and taken to a local processing yard to be cured.

After examination for size and quality, the individual lengths are mechanically processed to separate the inner core (which is then prepared as centre cane for basket making and similar crafts) from the bark. The inner bark is then split into flat strands of varying widths. This is our chair seating cane.

firmly that it is difficult to remove. Its job is merely to hold the strand in position temporarily.

This temporary pegging is necessary in every hole throughout the weaving, each peg being removed whenever another strand has to be fed through. Always keep the glossy surface of the cane uppermost, both on the surface of the rail and beneath.

Feed the half of the strand coming up out of the hole through the marked hole at the front and peg it. It must not lie too taut across the frame. Just how tight the cane should be is a matter of preference, but bear in mind the weaving will tighten as the work proceeds.

Take the end of the strand going through the front rail hole and feed it up through the next hole to it, either to the left or the right (it doesn't matter which). Make sure the strand is not twisted and that the glossy side is visible.

Pull the strand up tight and hold it in place with another peg. Take it to the opposite hole in the back rail, feed it down and through, and peg. Then come up through the next hole and peg. Continue feeding through and pegging in the appropriate holes at the front and back. When there is not enough of the cane left to continue, take it up through the next hole and peg it.

Take the other end of the strand and repeat the procedure in the same way but going in the opposite direction.

It is unlikely that any strand will be long enough to complete the first setting, so new strands must be joined in.

This is done by putting a new end down through the last hole from which the old end is emerging (having first removed the peg).

Thread the new end through the loop on the underside of the rail, between the cane and the rail, then through itself to make a single knot. Pull both old and new ends firmly to tighten it (making sure it is not pulled up into the hole), and peg both strands. The old end will be trimmed off later.

The knot will be tapped flat against the underside of the rail but it must be damp when you do this. If it isn't it will probably split when you hit it.

Continue weaving like this until every hole in the back rail, apart

from the corners, has a strand in it.

Unless you are working on a square or rectangular frame, when there will be the same number of holes in the front rail as there are in the back, there will be some spare holes at the front.

These are threaded through in the usual way, but after coming up through a hole at the front, the strand must be threaded down through a suitable hole in the side. But do not use any of the four corner holes yet.

The next step is called the **first weaving** and goes from side to side across the frame.

Peg the end of a new strand in the hole in a side rail which is immediately below the corner hole. Leave 25mm (1in) or so hanging.

Despite its designation, the first weaving is not actually woven through the strands of the first setting, but laid over them. The procedure is the same as for the first setting, pegging as you go.

The **second setting** repeats the first setting, the cane being laid over the previous two steps.

There are two points to watch out for.

1. On the underside of the rails, the loops lie between alternate pairs of holes. With this setting, the strand must be woven and fed through the holes in the opposite direction so that loops are made between all other pairs of holes.

2. As the strand comes up out of each hole it has to be persuaded to lie at the side of the cane already there, not on it. Whether the new strand lies to the right or left of the old one is immaterial, but they must all lie to the same side or you won't be able to complete the weaving.

So far, no actual weaving has been required. It starts with the **second weaving**. As with the second setting, the direction is reversed to create matching loops on the underside. Likewise, the strand on the second weaving must come out of each hole to lie at the side of the strand laid in the first weaving.

Start by pegging a new strand into the hole next to the back corner, in the opposite rail to that in which you began the first weaving.

From now on, get used to working with one hand below the work and the other above it. This is so the end of the strand being

woven can be passed easily from one hand to the other as it is threaded between the strands of the first and second settings.

As you come to each pair of strands, weave contrarywise to the first weaving – that is, under one and over the other, and between the horizontal strands of the first weaving and the back rail.

Continue down from side to side across the frame, pegging and joining as necessary. You will notice the tension of the weaving increasing.

Before you start the next stage, carefully persuade all the horizontal and vertical pairs of strands to lie straight and parallel, each as close to its partner as possible. Finger and thumb are the best tools for this, but two pegs can be used to press them into position.

The **first crossing** requires careful attention. It is the first diagonal, starting from one of the back corner holes and woven in the general direction of the opposite front corner.

The cane used for the diagonals can be one size larger than that

Concave and convex back panels create no difficulties in the weaving.

The craft of seat weaving in Ricky Holdstock's family dates back at least as far as his great great grandfather, who was born in 1795. And it continues. Holdstock has taught the skills to his son and is now passing them on to his son's 10-year-old son. Once, seat weaving was just a hobby for Holdstock, a relaxation away from his job in international banking in the City and 100 miles a day commuting into London and back to his home in the Kent village of Hernhill.
In 1978 he left the world of high finance to become a full time seat weaver in rush, cane and cord (if you need his services you can contact him at the address below). His only regret, he says, is that he did not do it 25 years earlier.
In this article he has explained just one technique of seat weaving in one material. He explains a great deal more in his book, *Seat Weaving, Practical Crafts Series*, published by GMC Publications Ltd, ISBN 0 946819 46 7. Ricky Holdstock, Hillside Cottage, The Forstal, Hernhill, Faversham, Kent ME13 9JQ. (Tel: 01227 751204)

used for the settings and weavings to make an even more durable seat.

The weaving goes under *or* over both settings, and over *or* under both weavings, depending on which sides of the first settings and weavings the second settings and weavings have been laid.

What is important is that both diagonals should nestle snugly in

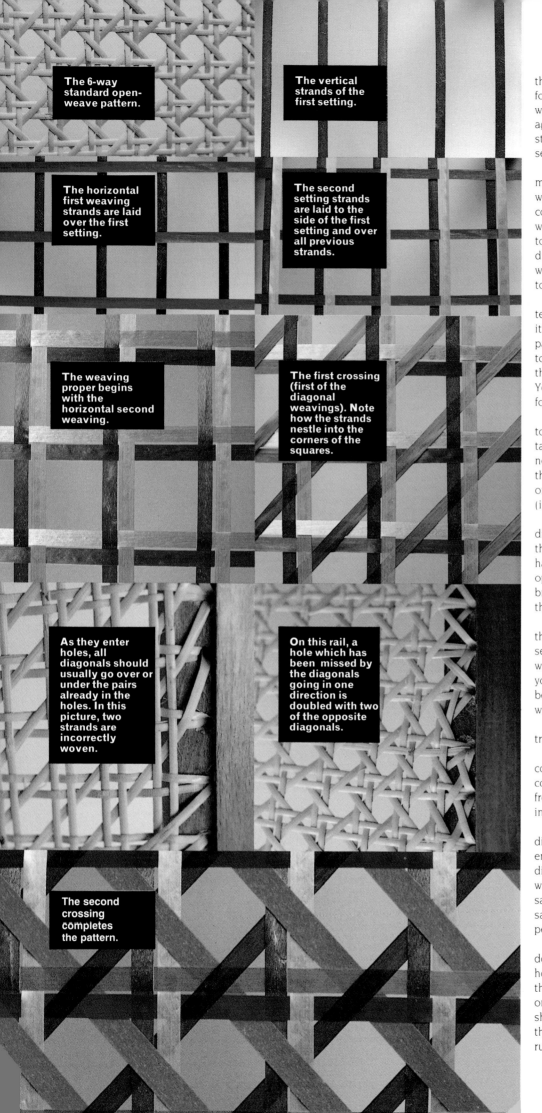

The 6-way standard open-weave pattern.

The vertical strands of the first setting.

The horizontal first weaving strands are laid over the first setting.

The second setting strands are laid to the side of the first setting and over all previous strands.

The weaving proper begins with the horizontal second weaving.

The first crossing (first of the diagonal weavings). Note how the strands nestle into the corners of the squares.

As they enter holes, all diagonals should usually go over or under the pairs already in the holes. In this picture, two strands are incorrectly woven.

On this rail, a hole which has been missed by the diagonals going in one direction is doubled with two of the opposite diagonals.

The second crossing completes the pattern.

the small squares of the pattern formed by the settings and weavings. If the diagonals snag against them, they will not lie straight in the pattern, and the seat will wear at these points.

Unless the frame is square it is most unlikely the diagonal strand will go directly into the front corner hole. So thread it through whichever hole is nearest in order to form a relatively straight diagonal. It does not matter whether the hole you use happens to be in the front or the side rail.

Because of the increasing tension of the seat as you proceed, it may be necessary to raise the pairs of strands entering the holes to insert the diagonals between them and the surface of the rail. You can use a blunt penknife blade for this.

Having woven diagonally towards the opposite corner and taken the strand down through the nearest hole, bring it up through the next hole to the left or right (if on the front rail) or the next below (if on a side rail).

You might now begin to find it difficult to get the new strands through the holes, which already have two strands in them. An opening can be made with a bradawl, but take care not to split the strands already in the holes.

Weave back towards the rear of the chair, still going under/over the settings and over/under the weavings, as the case may be, until you reach the hole in the side rail below the back corner hole from which the first crossing began.

Continue weaving until that triangle of the seat is completed.

If the pattern has been worked correctly, the last diagonal at each corner will be very short and go from the holes next to the corners in adjacent rails.

In irregularly shaped frames, diagonals will tend to bend as they enter some holes. To maintain the diagonals' alignment, some holes will need to be doubled, that is to say, two diagonals going in the same direction will have to be pegged in the same hole.

Corner holes are always doubled. On the rails, doubled holes should be the second or third from a corner, and the second or third hole from the end of a short strand, whichever is easier, though there is no hard-and-fast rule on this. ▶

Note that holes which have been doubled on a side rail are missed on the opposite rail so they can be doubled in the weaving of the other diagonal of the pattern.

With the triangle of the first crossing done, weave the other one starting from the same back corner hole.

The final stage of weaving (the second crossing) is a repeat of the first crossing but in the opposite direction. It starts from the opposite back corner hole to the first crossing. This diagonal is woven under those pairs of strands which the first crossing went over, and over those which it went under. When finished, the pattern should form crosses as the diagonals enter most holes.

Many caners do not weave the second crossing with long strands but cut each one to length. However, they only do this to save time and it does not make for as durable a seat.

Tie off the loose ends underneath by making a single knot as for a join. Tap them firm with a hammer and cut off the excess length. Loose ends sticking upwards from holes are not cut off until after the final pegging.

There are several ways of finishing off. The simplest method is by pegging every hole using a piece of round cane from the centre of the plant. It should be of appropriate diameter and cut to length. Pegs are tapped down to just below the surface of the wood so they hold all the strands firmly. They should not protrude beneath the seat.

However, the most popular finish is 'sewing', or 'couching', a length of beading cane to cover the holes. The beading cane should be wide enough to conceal the holes.

For a symmetrical finish, start at the back rail and tap pegs into the holes next to the corner holes. Keep pegging alternate holes, working towards the centre of the rail. Do the same with the front rail. For the side rails, having pegged the holes next to the back corners, peg alternate holes towards the front.

For circular and oval frames, and those with sharp curves, the beading is couched in every hole, because only using alternate hole couching prevents the beading from bending sideways to produce a smooth curve.

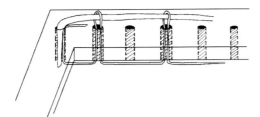

The initial stages of couching the beading.

This three-seater bergère settee had seen better days ...

Cane ends protruding above the frame from holes which have not been pegged should now be cut off in their holes.

To couch the beading, insert one end of a strand of No 2 size cane down the first couching hole nearest a corner of the back rail. Bring the end under the rail and up through the corner hole to leave 25-50mm (1-2IN) protruding. Push one end of the beading cane down into the same corner hole. Hold both couching and beading canes in the corner hole with a temporary peg. Take the long end of the couching cane over the beading (glossy surface towards the centre

of the frame) then back down the hole, keeping both canes taut.

With the couching cane held firmly against the underside, bring it up through the next unpegged hole, over the beading (towards the outer edge of the rail), and down the same hole. Continue to the end of the rail. At the end the couching cane is brought up through the corner hole and the beading brought down it. Cut off the ends of both canes to leave about 50mm (2IN) protruding.

To start the beading of the adjoining side rail, insert couching and beading canes into the corner hole as before. Tap a peg of suitable diameter into the hole against the underside of the beading cane so the beading can be bent over to conceal the peg.

Add the beading to each rail in the same way.

When the last length of beading has been couched, the corner hole from which couching began is

... which returned after renovation (though the caner's work is largely concealed).

pegged. This is the only corner hole in which the peg is not concealed as it is not possible to bend the beading over it●

Mail order suppliers of cane and caning products: Jacobs, Young & Westbury, JYW House, Bridge Road, Haywards Heath, E. Sussex RH16 1TZ (Tel: 01444 412411).
Fred Aldous, 37 Lever Street, Manchester M60 1UX (Tel: 0161 236 2477).
The Cane Store, 207 Blackstock Road, Highbury Vale, London N5 2LL (Tel: 0171 354 4210).

ABOVE: The finished table.

Coffee table wit

The work of Danish designer Hans Wegner inspired
Andrew Skelton when a client asked him to make a coffee table

● **ANDREW SKELTON has been making high quality hard — wood furniture for the past 15 years. He trained as an architect and says furniture making is a natural progres- sion from that discipline. He lives and works in the Derbyshire Peak District.**

SINCE I HAVE been running my own workshop I have made so few coffee tables that I was beginning to think either they didn't like me or I was going to have to come up with a reason why I didn't like them.

Until, that is, a client put such thoughts out of my mind with a commission which specified only that the table should be of an interesting grained timber and have some 'red' in it.

I remembered the sketch I had made of a table when I saw an exhibition of work by Danish designer Hans Wegner.

With his beautifully simple and direct chairs Wegner stretches the use of machines and I was particularly struck by the often intricately shaped, rosewood (*Dalbergia sp*) tongues he uses both structurally and decoratively in otherwise plain ash (*Fraxinus sp*).

It occurred to me that I could have 'red' and tongues. These tongues are more than a whim, providing both a practical and a visual way of joining the components.

This method of construction allows most of the work to be done before gluing the pieces together. This simplifies the making but demands a high degree of accuracy.

Whether, if I were to repeat this design, the tongues would be red again I don't know. Up to the moment of putting them in I was wavering on the brink of using something sensible – like American walnut (*Juglans nigra*) – but then the results would have been fairly pre- dictable. I was interested to know what the red would look like!

Suitable woods

Some designs look right in only one timber, but I feel a number of differ- ent woods could be used successfully to make this table. Cherry (*Prunus avium*), ash, a wild grained oak (*Quercus sp*) or knot free pine (*Pinus sp*) would all be suitable.

Here I have used elm (*Ulmus sp*) with a linseed oil finish worked up over numerous applications. This does not take long to do but does require several weeks to achieve a good result.

One of the advantages of a small piece is that the full-size working drawing will fit on the drawing board. Not only is this easier, cheap- er and more accurate than drawing on a sheet of MDF, but paper is considerably more convenient to store.

At times I wonder whether the workshop is for making furniture or for storing rods and templates which will not be needed again until the week after they have been destroyed!

The drawing for this table should show details of the tongues and joints. While as much information as possible should be included, this does not mean that some decisions cannot be left until later.

Perfect fit

With all the pieces planed up and thicknessed, the grooves for the tongues are run using a 6mm, $^1/_4$in winged cutter in a table-mounted router.

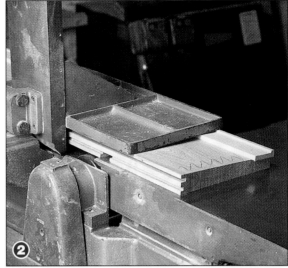

> "At times I wonder whether the workshop is for making furniture or storing rods and templates"

h colour

My tongues were made from $^1/_4$in birch ply which needed planing down to fit and, although one could use 6mm ply, the $^1/_4$in does enable a perfect fit to be achieved.

After all, the whole piece depends on these tongues – too loose and the joints are useless – too tight and it will be a struggle to get them up.

The centre leg pieces are housed into the centre rail while it is still square. When it is rounded the shoulders are scribed to fit.

Not having a spindle moulder, I removed the waste on the saw bench and finished the round with one of my great grandfather's wooden planes. The gouge to scribe the shoulders came from the same source.

This joint can be simplified by cutting the housings the full thickness of the leg. But take care to avoid a loose fit when the legs are finally cleaned up.

Mortises and tenons

The pairs of 12.5mm, $^1/_2$in mortises in the two halves of the top were cut on a mortiser, setting it up for the near mortise with a spacer block against the fence. Simply remove the block, without altering the setting, to cut the second mortise of the pair.

The tenons are marked on the legs and cut with a fine saw to the haunch line – but don't remove the waste at this point.

Now, the two halves of the top are temporarily joined with tongues cramped together and the 12.5mm, $^1/_2$in deep housing is routed against a fence, see picture one.

Separated again, the tops can have their undersides bevelled. There are many ways of doing this, from thrashing off the waste with a hand plane to making sophisticated jigs.

I simply pinned a batten into the waste at both ends of the top board and, with a little double-sided tape to hold it in the middle, put the whole thing through the thicknesser several times, see picture two.

At this point you find out how well the timber has been conditioned. Removing a large proportion of a piece of wood can release built-in stresses to wreak their cupping and twisting havoc.

Finishing

Finish the legs by first cutting the long shoulders across their width and then removing the waste from between the paired tenons. These joints are now pared to a fit ensuring that the inside edges are flush and square, see picture three.

As each of the legs is fitted, use a block to knife a line that will serve as an alignment mark when joining the three components together, see picture four.

Prepare all the tongues and the internal spacer strips, which are cut 10mm, $^3/_8$in short of the ends of the top to allow the red tongues to be knocked in later. With all the parts cleaned up, the top and leg assemblies can be glued together.

The glue must be applied careful-ly, ensuring that there is enough to make a good joint but keeping the grooves that will take the red as far as possible glue free.

My choice is to use Cascamite here as it has a relatively long open time and allows the components to slide. The curve on the bottom of the legs and the moulding on the edge of the top are cut when the glue has set.

Final check

Make a final check to see that every-thing still fits before gluing the legs to the top. Use a softwood caul shaped to fit the curve on the bottom of the leg and another cut around the ➤

PICTURE 1:
Routing the housing.

PICTURE 2:
Thicknessing the bevel.

PICTURE 3:
The joints are ready to assemble.

PICTURE **4:** Scribing the alignment mark.

PICTURE **5:** Gluing up.

PICTURE **6:** Fitting the red tongues and lines.

> "Removing a large proportion of a piece of wood can release built-in stresses to wreak their cupping and twisting havoc"

BELOW: Perspective drawing of the table.

through tenons for the top.

Pull up each assembly with sash cramps, removing the cramps to drive in the wedges and then replacing them until the glue has set, see picture five.

All that remains is to make and fit the 'red' – which is laminated from dyed veneer – being careful to keep the grain in the same direction.

Machine it to size – I recessed it about 1mm, $^1/_{16}$in, below the elm, further emphasising the meeting of two materials.

Remember that these tongues have a structural purpose and must be properly fitted and glued in. If the glue is applied carefully then little further cleaning up will be required, *see picture six.*

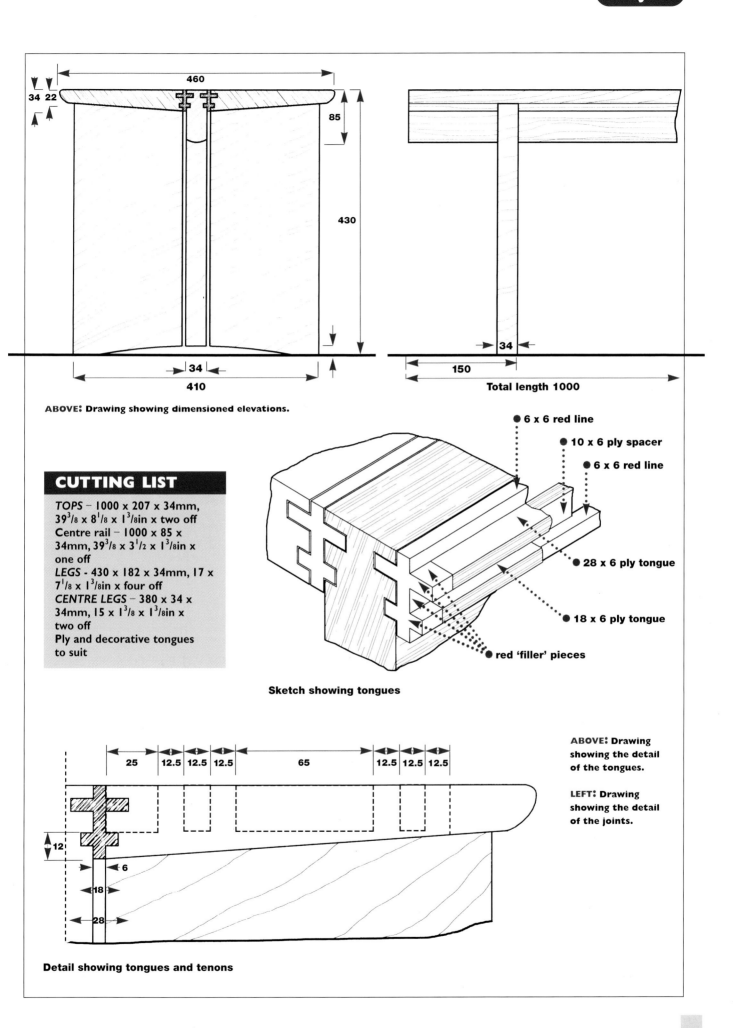

ABOVE: Drawing showing dimensioned elevations.

- 6 x 6 red line
- 10 x 6 ply spacer
- 6 x 6 red line
- 28 x 6 ply tongue
- 18 x 6 ply tongue
- red 'filler' pieces

Sketch showing tongues

CUTTING LIST

TOPS – 1000 x 207 x 34mm,
39³/₈ x 8¹/₈ x 1³/₈in x two off
Centre rail – 1000 x 85 x
34mm, 39³/₈ x 3¹/₂ x 1³/₈in x
one off
LEGS - 430 x 182 x 34mm, 17 x
7¹/₈ x 1³/₈in x four off
CENTRE LEGS – 380 x 34 x
34mm, 15 x 1³/₈ x 1³/₈in x
two off
Ply and decorative tongues
to suit

ABOVE: Drawing showing the detail of the tongues.

LEFT: Drawing showing the detail of the joints.

Detail showing tongues and tenons

A seat that folds

This dining chair really looks like a dining chair. But it folds up. It was designed by Beaversdam, the Lincolnshire company set up by Nigel Halliday and Dennis Smith.

Folding chairs can all too often look like garden or school room furniture. This folding dining chair, made in beech, would not look out of place in any dining or living room. Prepare the timber from the cutting list and the drawings of the finished chair, FIG 1. Make a template for the back legs and mark on it the positions of the mortises so they can be transferred on to the wood later.

The tenons on all the rails are 20mm (³⁄₄IN) long. The edge shoulders on the back seat rail are 20mm (³⁄₄IN) and the tenon is barefaced and positioned at the back of the rail.

The edge shoulders on the bottom back stretcher rail are 5mm (³⁄₁₆IN) and shoulders on all other rails are 10mm (³⁄₈IN). Use a 10mm (³⁄₈IN) chisel to cut these mortises.

The three banisters have 10mm (³⁄₈IN) long tenons, with 5mm (³⁄₁₆IN) shoulders. Use a 6mm (¹⁄₄IN) chisel for their mortises.

Use the template to mark out the back legs, but before cutting them out mark and chop out the mortise for the side seat rail on the left hand leg (as viewed from behind). After cutting out the legs, plane them to shape and mark on the mortise positions from the template.

Mark out the front legs, including the mortise positions, and cut out and shape.

Mark out and cut out all the back rails, including the mortises and shapes of the two scalloped rails, and the three banisters. After cleaning up, glue and cramp the rails and banisters together.

Also glue and cramp together the pieces prepared for the seat, butt joining the planks with the heartwood sides alternatively up and down to control movement.

Mark and cut out the side seat rails and cut the left hand rail into two sections. Cut all the tenons and chop all the mortises.

When the glue has cured on the back rails and banisters, finish shaping and cleaning up the back legs and the two other back rails and glue and cramp the whole of the back together.

Plane and sand the seat. Clean up the side seat rails and fit the hinge to the left hand rail. Pre-drill the holes and use steel screws – these will be removed and brass screws inserted later. Remove the hinge and glue the short section into the back.

Fit the hinge to the right hand rail and, using the left hand rail as a guide for the level, mark the position for the hinge on to the back. Chop out the recess, fit the hinge with steel screws, then remove.

Clean up the two front legs and glue and cramp the side rails into them. When dry, finish the legs to the correct length and refit the hinges.

With the framework of the chair complete and standing the seat can be fixed. Mark the positions for the cylinder hinges, drill and fix.

Tap a panel pin into the centre of the tops of the front legs and press the seat down to mark the positions for the centres of the dowel pegs. Drill holes in the legs and the underside of the seat and glue the short dowel pegs into the legs. The seat should now locate on the dowel pegs.

Measure the exact size of the false front rail. Mark the position of the front legs on the underside of the seat. Cut and shape the front rail to size and fix to the underside of the seat. Screw through from the top of the seat with two screws and then plug.

The seat can be left its natural shade, stained or varnished as required.

Cleaning up the glued scalloped rails and banisters before fitting the back legs.

Fitting the hinge to the right hand side seat rail.

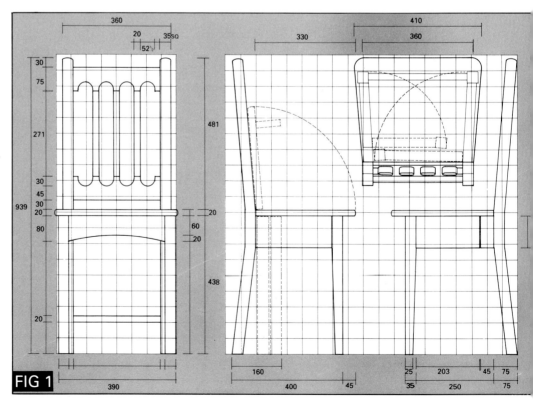

FIG 1

FLAT

The finished chair.

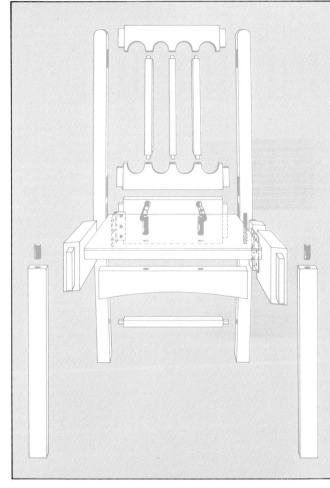

The finished chair
folded flat.

CUTTING LIST
finished sizes in mm, (inches in brackets)

Back legs x 2	939 x 75 x 35	(37 x 3 x 1⅜)
Front legs x 2	438 x 35 x 35	(17¼ x 1⅜ x 1⅜)
Back rails x 2	330 x 75 x 20	(13 x 3 x ¾)
Back seat rail	330 x 120 x 30	(13 x 4¾ x 1⅛)
Bottom back rail	330 x 20 x 20	(13 x ¾ x ¾)
Banisters x 3	271 x 20 x 20	(10¾ x ¾ x ¾)
Side seat rail	290 x 100 x 30	(11⅜ x 4 x 1⅛)
Side seat rail	270 x 100 x 30	(10⅝ x 4 x 1⅛)
Front seat rail	320 x 80 x 20	(12⅝ x 3⅛ x ¾)
Seat	330 x 410 x 20	(13 x 16⅛ x ¾)
Dowels x 2	30 x 9 DIA	(1⅛ x ⅜ DIA)

2 x 75mm (3IN) steel washered brass hinges
2 x 14mm (⅝IN) cylinder hinges

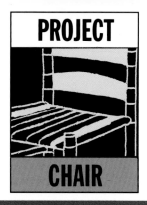

PROJECT CHAIR

Making a continuous arm Windsor

This continuous arm chair might be considered America's interest on the debt it owes Britain for the basic Windsor. Harriet Hodges describes how she made this one in the style of Curtis Buchanan.

Master chairmaker Curtis Buchanan of Jonesborough, Tennessee, designed this chair – or rather developed it from chairs made by David Sawyer, of Vermont.

As with all Windsor chairs, the principle behind it is wet-dry joinery. That is, what is dry on assembly (tenons and wedges) takes up moisture from what is wet (mortises). The dry wood swells, so tenons and wedges become larger, and the wet wood shrinks, making mortises tighter. This way the joints lock together, with the direction of the wedges opposing the direction of the pulls. Because of this the assembly of such a chair has a certain urgency to it.

To make the chair you will need a 610mm (24IN) bolt of green maple or beech for the legs and stretchers, and an oak log 1625mm (64IN) or so for the back and arms. Both should be of the finest quality. Use lime, or some similarly carvable wood, for the seat. I use American hickory for the spindles, but you will find oak or beech come closest to this for strength and elasticity.

Some jigs and other aids are needed, so it is best to read through the project and make sure you have these ready before you start. Trace the shape of the seat and paw (handhold) on to heavy cardboard. Make a drying box of foil-coated insulation board and a light bulb, a bending form and a back support jig.

Make a steamer for bending the back, test tapers to match your reamer, and a gauge to measure the diameter and depth of the fit of spindles. You could also make a square-notched gauge to measure your stock as you dimension it.

Back and arms. Start by cutting the oak for the back and arms to its final 1486mm (58½IN) length. The ends of the arms, or paws, where your hands will rest when sitting in the chair, should be 48mm (1⅞IN) wide. It is better to use stock of this thickness than it is to glue an extra piece on. If you have a choice let the thickness be in the quarter-sawn orientation – that is, with the grain running vertically down the ends (FIG 1).

Drawknife one surface at right angles to the growth rings and square an adjacent side following a growth ring. Mark a line 21mm (¹³⁄₁₆IN) down from the top and thickness the wood to that. Make sure it is square.

Using a cardboard or ply template mark on the best surface the shapes of the paws on each end (FIG 2). Carve out the shapes of the paws, taking extra care when cutting into the grain on the curves.

You might also like to mark an arrow pointing to the bark side of the timber. Bending timber with the bark side up is more predictable than putting the bark side down.

Mark a line round the piece 367mm (14½IN) from each end. This is the point at which the piece narrows towards the ends. Placing the wood top-side down, use a drawknife to taper the wood from the marked lines quickly down to 11mm (⁷⁄₁₆IN) and continue this thickness to the tips of the paws (FIG 3).

The undersides of the paws are rounded. With the wood still face down on the bench, first drawknife the two corners making the shape of half an octagon. Using first a drawknife and then a spokeshave remove the corners between the flats until a rounded shape is achieved (FIG 4). Soften all sharp edges.

The back and arms piece is now ready to be steam bent. Mark a line round the centre of the piece and lay it flat on the bench with the flat, inside edges of the paws towards you.

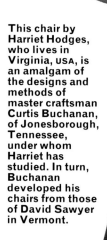

This chair by Harriet Hodges, who lives in Virginia, USA, is an amalgam of the designs and methods of master craftsman Curtis Buchanan, of Jonesborough, Tennessee, under whom Harriet has studied. In turn, Buchanan developed his chairs from those of David Sawyer in Vermont.

FIG 1

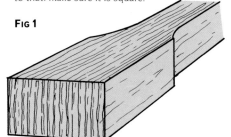

Draw arrows on the top near the centre line to show that this flat side goes towards the bending jig, and so will be on the inside (Fig 5).

I made a steamer from a length of 100mm (4IN) PVC drainpipe with a cap over one end and a piece of sponge in the other. Steam is provided by a metal kettle on a hotplate, connected to the pipe with a length of rubber hose. You will also need to make a jig using ply, dowel pegs and wedges for bending the steamed wood. Use the shapes in Fig 6.

Take care not to overdo the steaming – about 45 minutes should suffice. While you are waiting, get your bend-

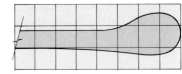

CONTINUOUS ARM WINDSOR CHAIR CUTTING LIST

Finished sizes in mm, (inches in brackets)

		mm	(inches)
Back		1486 x 48 x 48	(58½ x 1⅞ x 1⅞)
Seat		460 x 460 x 48	(18 x 18 x 1⅞)
Spindles	x 1	585 x 14 x 14	(23 x ⁹/₁₆ x ⁹/₁₆)
	x 2	580 x 14 14	(22¾ x ⁹/₁₆ x ⁹/₁₆)
	x 2	555 x 14 x 14	(21¾ x ⁹/₁₆ x ⁹/₁₆)
	x 2	510 x 14 x 14	(20 x ⁹/₁₆ x ⁹/₁₆)
	x 2	442 x 14 x 14	(17½ x ⁹/₁₆ x ⁹/₁₆)
	x 4	280 x 14 x 14	(11 x ⁹/₁₆ x ⁹/₁₆)
Legs	x 2	505 x 55 x 55	(19¾ x 2¼ x 2¼)
	x 2	485 x 55 x 55	(19 x 2¼ x 2¼)
Stretchers	x 3	460 x 45 x 45	(18 x 1¾ x 1¾)

You will also need oak wedges of various lengths cut with the growth rings running down their length.

FIG 2

FIG 3

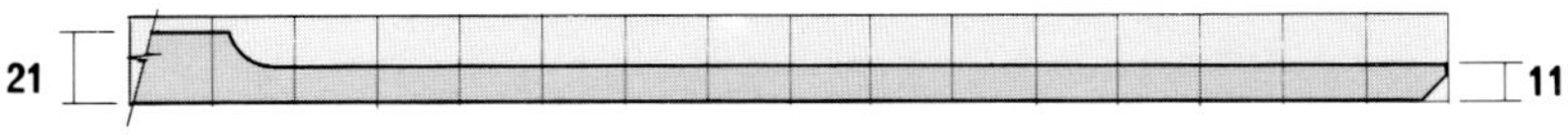

21   11

FIG 4

FIG 5

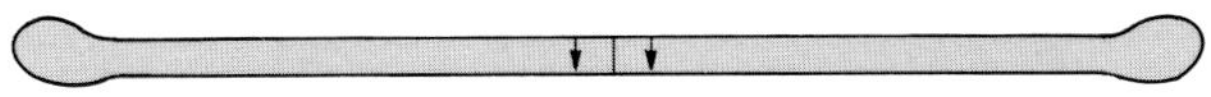

ing jig set up and secured to the bench and have a practice run through with the clamps and pegs. Make sure the clamps will not obstruct the bending of the the wood, which must be brought round flat and smoothly in one sweep.

When the wood is ready, take it out of the steamer pipe (wear gloves – it's hot) and place it on the jig. I secure the wood at the top of the jig first, lining up the centre line on the wood with the centre line on the jig.

Pull one end round steadily, wedging it quickly as you go. Press hard with one hand to hold the wood flat on the jig while you make the second, downward bend for the elbow.

Having secured one end, bend the other end in the same way. Tighten the wedges, making sure the curve is flat and even, and insert extra, small wedges where necessary. If the wood bows up from the jig, knock it down with a mallet. Leave the wood cramped up for a week to dry.

Back spindles. You will need to split out 13 spindles of 14mm (⁹/₁₆IN) square wood (plus a few extra for insurance): one 585mm (23IN) long, 2 x 580mm (22¾IN), 2 x 555mm (21¾IN), 2 x 510mm (20IN), 2 x 442mm (17½IN), and 4 x 280mm (11IN), Mark a line round each spindle 305mm (12IN) from one end and taper the wood down to 11mm (⁷/₁₆IN) square at the other end (Fig 7).

Cut the corners off to make an

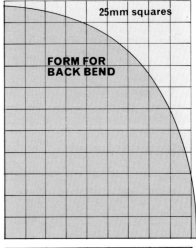

FIG 6

25mm squares

FORM FOR BACK BEND

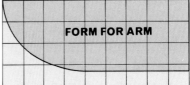

FORM FOR ARM

Fig 7

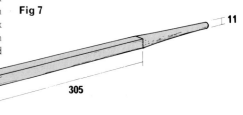

11

305

14

octagon, then finish rounding each spindle using a draw knife and spokeshave, but leave the bottom (thicker) tenons square as they will not be finished until the wood is dry. You will find two simple jigs (FIG 8) helpful

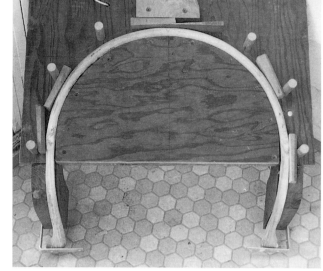

FIG 8

10   12

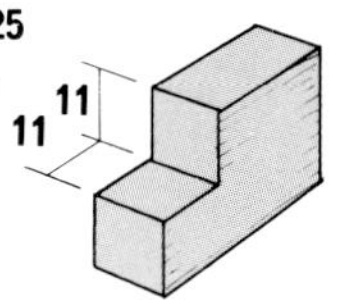

FOR MEASURING AS STOCK IS DIMENSIONED

25

20   11   11

FIG 9

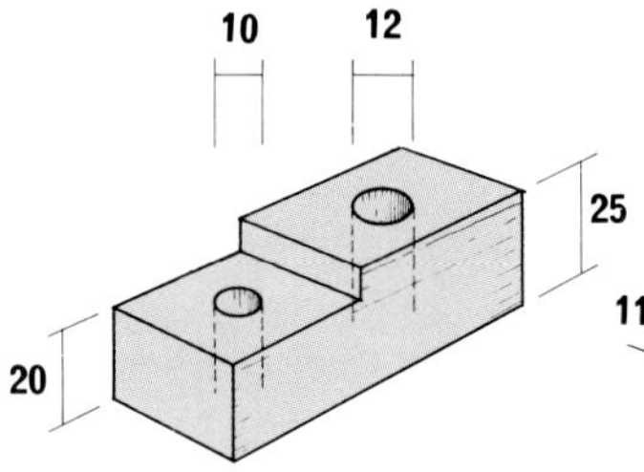

FOR MEASURING DIAMETER AND DEPTH OF FIT OF SPINDLES

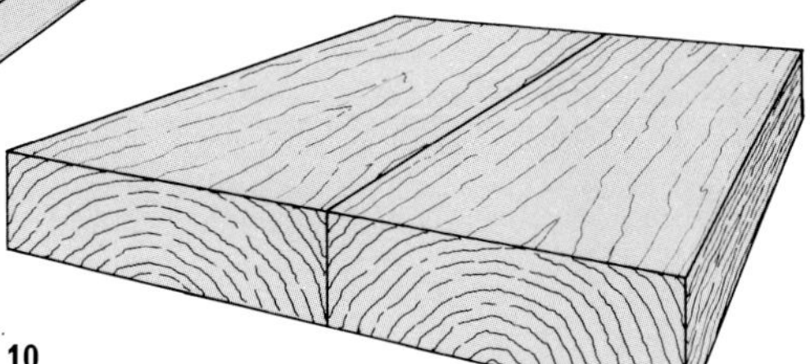

in preparing the spindles to size. The spindles will later be kiln dried for at least eight hours with the legs and stretchers.

Seat. Carving the seat from a single blank is ideal, but two pieces of wood glued together well is just as strong. Glue up as in FIG 9. The wood should be air-dried and be at outdoor humidity. Keep it outside until you are putting the chair together.

Make a card or ply template for the shape of the seat (FIG 10) and use it to mark the shape. The growth rings of the blank should be turned downwards.

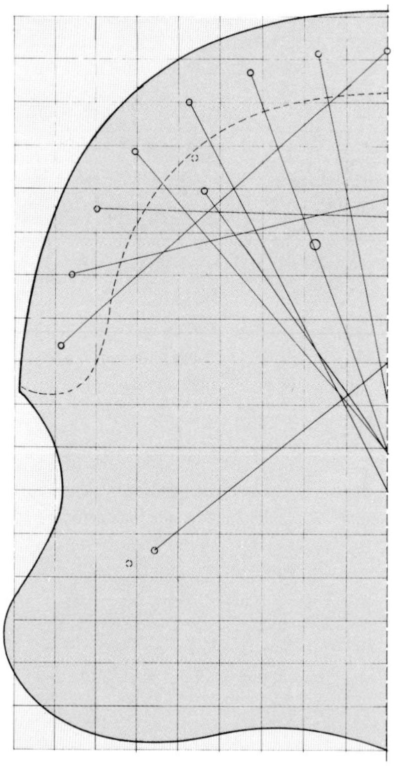

Mark the positions of the spindle and arm post holes with a bradawl and the sight lines (to make sure the spindles match) with a pencil. Cut out the front shape of the seat but leave the waste at the back for cramping the wood. Turn the seat over and mark the positions of the leg holes. You can drill the holes through from the top. but I find it easier to drill through from the bottom.

Drill 12mm (¹⁄₂IN) DIA spindle holes, starting with the centre hole. Rig up a depth gauge for 30mm (1¹⁄₈IN) deep and set your bevel gauge at 12DEG. Set your gauge on the sight line. A small mirror will help you check both angles while drilling.

Drill the rest of the spindle holes in pairs, changing the angle for each set. Then drill the 10mm (³⁄₈IN) holes for the armposts. Drill through until you can just feel the point of the bit, then drill through from the other side.

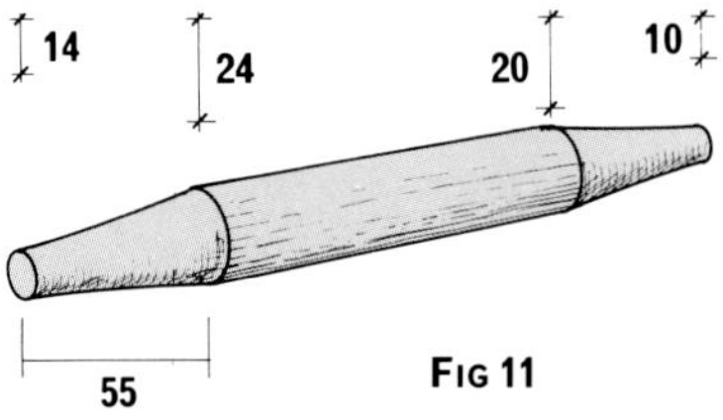

Use a test taper (FIG 11) and ream the armpost holes from the top until the taper just protrudes through the hole. Cut out the gutter, but before cutting out any more mark up the seat to set guidelines for carving out the contoured shape.

Mark a vertical centre line down the front of the seat and a horizontal cross mark 3mm (¹⁄₈IN) down. Mark a set of vertical lines 200mm (8IN) each side of

FIG 10

14   24   20   10

55   **FIG 11**

the centre, and cross marks 20mm (³⁄₄IN) down from the top. Draw guidelines from these cross marks to the bottoms of the gutter and to the centre pommel cross mark.

Bore depth holes 25mm (1IN) deep using a spoon bit, or 22mm (⁷⁄₈IN) using a forstner bit. Starting in the middle, cut a hollow with an adze or

chisel using the contour guide lines of FIG 12. Turn the seat as you carve, enlarging the bowl-shape gradually to get an even shaped hollow. The deepest point should be about 140mm (5¹⁄₂IN) from the back of the chair.

The wood should be thickest at the point in front of the leg holes, only a little below the planed surface. Here the seat breaks over and falls off gently. Use a drawknife and spokeshave for the edge.

Clean up the whole seat, looking at it from every angle in different lights to smooth out any bumps or hollows. Feel with your fingers for defects hidden to the eye. Finish by smoothing the top with scrapers, then cut off the waste at the back.

Mark lines round the back 20mm (³⁄₄IN) from the edge, one on the side and one on the top. Cut this larger chamfer with a drawknife and spokeshave and round it thoroughly.

The most difficult parts of the seat to shape are the S-curves of the front corners which start horizontal at the front and finish vertical at the sides. These are hardly attempted in any but the best hand-made chairs.

Showing contours of the seat.

FIG. 12

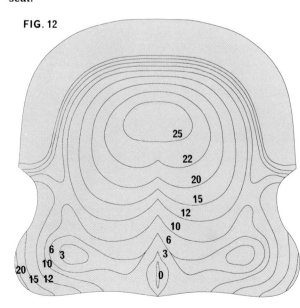

25
22
20
15
12
10
6   6
6 3   3
20 10   0
15 12

I start cutting the curves with a drawknife, then sometimes use rounded rasps and files and almost always, somewhere in the process, a strange little circular spokeshave that fits a very tight radius.

Although I've watched Curtis Buchanan cut this curve with his drawknife alone, if I do it I still wind up chewing into the end grain of the opposite side. I probably need a thinned knife with a rounded bearing surface on the underside.

With the seat fully shaped, bore the 14mm (⁹⁄₁₆IN) DIA leg holes using the bevel gauge on the sight lines and the mirror. I prefer to do this from the underneath. Stop when you just feel the tip of the bit breaking through and drill through from the other side in order to make clean holes.

Ream the holes, checking constantly with the bevel gauge, until the test taper just protrudes. Sight along a try square, its butt on the line, and make

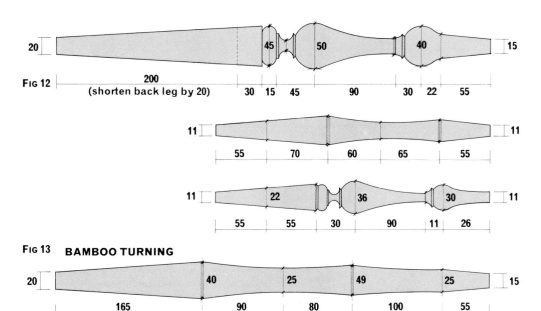

FIG 12 | 200 (shorten back leg by 20) | 30 | 15 | 45 | 90 | 30 | 22 | 55

20 | 45 | 50 | 40 | 15

11 | 55 | 70 | 60 | 65 | 55 | 11

11 | 55 | 22 | 55 | 30 | 36 | 90 | 30 | 11 | 26 | 11

FIG 13   BAMBOO TURNING

20 | 40 | 25 | 49 | 25 | 15

165 (shorten back leg by 20) | 90 | 80 | 100 | 55

FIG 14

FIG 16

sure the centre of the test taper, the blade of the square and the sight line all line up. If you overdo it and make a hole a fraction too big, make sure its mate is reamed to match. You will get a second chance to get them even when fitting the legs.

Legs (FIG 12). If you are not an experienced turner, give them to someone who is or go for bamboo turnings (FIG 13), which can be achieved with only a gouge and the tip of a skew. I turn the legs finished length to retain centre marks for rechucking for sanding (which shouldn't be needed but, alas, sometimes is) and for lapping the tenons. I do leave 3mm (⅛IN) extra on the tenon end so I can saw off most of the centre mark by tailstock leaves.

Buchanan turns his long and cuts them off. His tenons usually fit perfectly. I am less practiced and mark holes with a water colour pencil. If you put the tenon into the hole and twist it, the water colour marks high spots which can then be removed. When you

Final shaping of the seat.

have fitted a leg, mark it to the hole it matches and keep them as a pair.

Set the seat upside down on the bench. With the legs in their holes, twist them until the growth ring lines are at right angles to those in the seat. This enables the seat to tighten around them without splitting. Mark the depth of the tenons on the legs and on the tops of the legs mark the direction of the wedge cuts across the grain of the seat.

Stretchers. Measure the distance between a back and front leg and mark the centres of the legs with a bradawl (FIG 14). Repeat on the other pair of legs, but do not expect the measurements to be exactly the same. Add 50mm (2IN) to each measurement to allow for the 25mm (1IN) tenon on each end, and 5mm (³⁄₁₆IN) for the chamfers (FIG 15). These are the

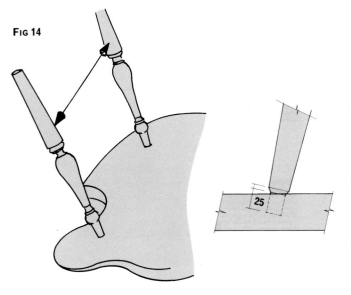

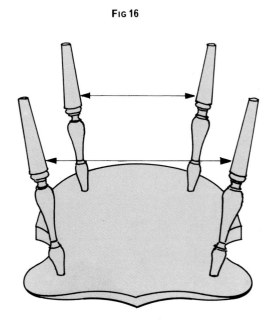

Measuring for the exact length of the stretchers.

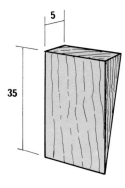

Make plenty of wedges

lengths of the side stretchers.

To calculate the length of the centre stretcher, measure the distance between the front pair of legs and the back pair between the bradawl marks. Add these two figures together and divide by two. Add a further 12-15mm (½-⅝IN) for the tenons and 3mm (⅛IN) for the chamfers (FIG 16).

I add a step here because I'm still cautious about my consistency. I put a straight edge along each pair (in turn) of front and back legs, measure the angle the leg makes with the seat using a bevel gauge against the straight edge, and write down the angle by each leg. Later I bore the hole in the leg to this angle.

Then I put another straight edge across the first, up against a set of back or front legs and record the angle at the intersection of the straight edges. That will be the angle at which the centre stretcher enters the side ones. I'm almost ready to quit this routine, but it's wonderfully helpful for boring the holes at the correct angles when you're beginning and your angles vary.

Turn the stretchers, being sure to make the tenons exactly 25mm (1IN) long x 17mm (¹¹⁄₁₆IN) DIA – they should shrink to 15mm (⅝IN) DIA. With dividers, mark the centre point on the side stretchers for where the centre stretcher will join them.

The legs, stretchers and spindles must now be dried. Wrap them tightly in aluminium foil, except for the tenons, and either put them in an oven at 82DEG C (180DEG F) for seven or eight hours, or in a home-made heat box of foil covered insulation board and an electric light bulb You could also use the traditional hot sand method.

Wedges, legs and stretchers. Make plenty of wedges now from strong, straight, dry hardwood. Make them of different sizes to match the different sized holes.

This is the stage where we begin to put things together and the process becomes more unforgiving. Start by making sure all leg and stretcher tenons are tight fits in their test holes – a good fit is so tight it has to be knocked in. If a tenon is oversize shave off minute amounts with a file.

When trying a tenon in a hole it should be tight but show little crescent moons of light on either side where shrinkage has taken place. Exaggerate these moons with a file – swelling will fill the gaps. Saw the leg tenons almost down to the depth marks ready for the wedges.

Line up the side stretchers and mark which ends fit in which legs – I use small, self-adhesive coloured labels for this. Mark the positions of the mortises on the side stretchers 3mm (⅛IN) off centre. If there are any flaws on the stretchers have them facing up now so they will be facing down when the chair is standing on its legs.

Use a three-peg holding system (FIG 18) to secure the legs and side stretchers while you drill the holes for the tenons. Starting with the stretcher assembly, mark an arrow in the direction of the acute angle and drill the hole using a bevel gauge and mirror. The hole should be 30mm (1¹¹⁄₁₆IN) deep at the shallow side, so check every few turns of the brace and bit. No, you don't need a jig. As Buchanan says: "We don't realize how accurate our hands and eyes can be."

Carve a chamfer on the acute angle side to clear the chamfer on the tenon. Glue the centre stretcher

tenons and knock them into the mortises in the side stretchers, checking as you go that they are in the same plane.

With the stretchers assembled, bore and glue a front leg mortise. Knock the stretcher assembly partially into the mortise and fit the leg to the seat. Correct the stretcher assembly by twisting while knocking if it is not parallel to the seat. Glue and fit the other front and rear legs, checking as you go that the pairs of front and back legs are parallel.

The undercarriage assembled, fit the leg tenons into their mortise holes in the seat with light blows of a mallet, having first applied glue to them and the wedge slots. Turn the seat right way up and hammer in the glued wedges. When the glue has dried, saw off the protruding tenons and wedges and make them flush with the seat using a gouge or chisel. Scrape and sand the seat smooth, going down to 180 grit paper.

Now to level the legs. Put the chair on something flat – I use a sheet of plate glass – and level the seat from side to side using slivers of wood. Adjust the shims until the back is 20mm (¾IN) lower than the front. I finish my chairs to 460mm (18IN) at the front pommel and 438mm (17¼IN) at the back, but make yours to suit.

Mark the legs using a pencil on a block of wood the thickness of which gives you your desired height. Saw off the legs carefully to the lines, following the line round the leg as if hand sawing a square tenon. Use a file to

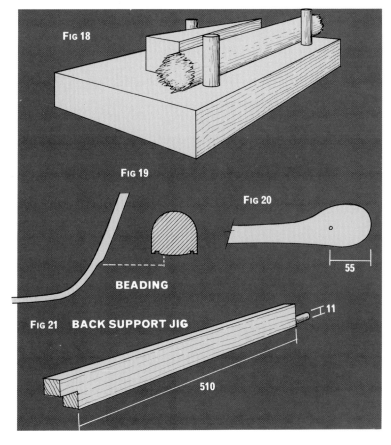

FIG 18

FIG 19

FIG 20

BEADING

FIG 21 **BACK SUPPORT JIG**

55

11

510

A scorp (top, centre) adze, spokeshaves, small plane and chisel used in shaping the seat.

know you have correctly seated them later.

All the spindles go right through the back except for the first each side after the four short spindles. Mark the angle for them on the back. Cut off all but the two blind spindles to within 6mm (¹⁄₄IN) above the back.

Mark the wedge lines to run across the growth lines of the back. Mark where the underside of the back intersects – wedge slots are sawn almost to this mark. Work the spindles until they fit into your test gauge. Saw the wedge slots.

Bore the 10mm (³⁄₈IN) holes, sighting through to the seat holes. A dowel fitted into each seat hole in turn helps sighting. A large mirror and a friend are a great help, too, as you struggle with two angles. Make sure the chair is held firmly against the bench as you carry out the drilling.

Put the back in a vice to finish drilling the holes through from the underneath. Stick a wooden dowel in the hole begun to help you get the angle right as you drill. Take extra care when boring the blind spindle holes – they are difficult. I start them with an auger bit and finish with a spoon bit. Try to keep a picture in mind of what the angle should be. Measure the depth of the blind holes and cut the spindles to length with one last dry run. Round the spindle tops.

Reassemble the back and spindles dry and check that all fits properly. You are now ready to glue up. Lay out all the spindles in their correct order and have a mallet and spare piece of wood (to use as a buffer handy). Again, an extra pair of hands helps.

Glue the spindle holes in the seat two at a time and knock the spindles in making sure they have the wedge slots in the right direction, their orientation marks line up, and they seat to the full marked depth. Put glue in all the back holes and in the spindle wedge slots. Fit the back on to the spindles and when every one is in its hole knock the back down firmly with the mallet and wood buffer. Hammer in the glued wedges.

When the glue has cured, cut off the protruding stubs and smooth them with a chisel, file or spokeshave. Fill any gaps with wedges or filler. Finish the chair to suit, but Buchanan uses milk, or casein, paint with penetrating oil over it. The chair is best painted because it does not come alive as a sculpture until the paint unifies its disparate parts. ●

smooth the bottom of the leg if necessary and chamfer the edges.

The back. The chair back may be beaded if you wish to use a scratch stock. Begin the beads just above the elbow taper (FIG 19). Round and smooth off any arrises. Check your dried spindles – they should fit tightly 25mm (1IN) deep into a 12mm (¹⁄₂IN) hole. Arm posts should fit in their holes in the seat so they protrude 3mm (¹⁄₈IN). Mark each one to match it to its hole.

Cramp the back to a waste board on your bench and mark lines 75mm (3IN) either side of the centre line. Set your bevel gauge to 26deg, put it on a line between the armpost hole mark and the further line on the back arch and mark 55mm (2¹⁄₄IN) from the tip (FIG 20). Drill the 10mm (³⁄₈IN) DIA holes for the arm posts. A mirror is useful.

Make a jig (FIG 21) to support the back while you work on the arm posts and spindles. Put this jig in the seat centre spindle hole. Insert the arm posts in the seat and ream the holes in the paws until you can fit the back on to them with the posts protruding a little.

With the jig straight and perpendicular, check that the centre line of the back is actually in the centre of the arc and that it matches the centre line on the jig. You can make slight adjustments by rotating the arm posts in their holes. When you are satisfied, cut the arm posts to within 6mm (¹⁄₄IN) of the arm, and mark depth lines round them underneath the arms and round the seat holes. Also mark the orientation so you can reinsert them in exactly the right way.

Mark lines for the wedge cuts on the tops and bottoms of the arm posts across the grain of the arms and seat. Saw the wedge cuts almost to the depth marks. I glue in the arm posts at

this stage as I like to have a fixed reference point when fitting the rest of the back, but they can be left until later to be fixed with the rest of the back spindles. Glue the seat holes, the bottom wedge cuts and wedges, knock the arm posts in and wedge from underneath.

When the glue has cured put the back on the arm posts and the back support jig. Bore holes in the arms for the four short spindles 75mm (3IN) and 150mm (6IN) from the centre of the armpost holes, offsetting them slightly from the centre line so the angled holes will be centred when done. Stop as soon as the bit point pokes through and finish boring from underneath.

Put the four short spindles into their holes in the seat and put the back on the arm posts and spindles and work them with a spokeshave until they fit tightly in the holes. Rotate each spindle until you are happy with its position.

Mark each spindle and hole so you can replace them later. Mark depth lines round each spindle under the arms. Cut the spindles off 6mm (¹⁄₄IN) above the arms and mark for the wedge cuts.

Mark on the back the positions for the rest of the spindles. Starting from the centre, the gaps are 68mm (2¹¹⁄₁₆IN), 73mm (2⁷⁄₈IN), 81mm (3³⁄₁₆IN) and 100mm (4IN). Make sure the holes in the seat are free of debris and insert all the spindles.

Set a marking gauge to 7mm (⁹⁄₃₂IN), put the fence against the front face of the back and mark the hole positions. Twist the spindles, taping them to the back if necessary, until you are satisfied with their positions. Mark the position and orientation on the spindles and circle each one with a pencil line through the hole junction so you will

The completed chair.

First commission

Two students from Bucks College went straight to the top when they teamed up to fulfil a commission for a marketing company. **Anthony Jackson** describes how they tackled the project

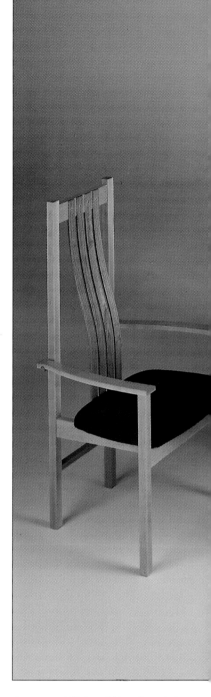

RIGHT: The boardroom table and chairs that Anthony Jackson and Neil Edgar designed.

BELOW: Anthony and Neil with two of the eight splat-backed chairs.

WHEN YOU ARE given the opportunity to work unpaid for eight solid weeks to a schedule so tightly packed that the words 'tea break' are removed from your vocabulary, you have to ask yourself why. On examination we found the motivating factor lay somewhere between drive, ambition – and being a student of Furniture Design and Craftsmanship at Buckinghamshire College.

Fellow second year student Neil Edgar and I had jumped at the chance to tackle a joint project, as part of our coursework, to design and make a boardroom table with eight accompanying chairs for DML Marketing in Uxbridge.

The company had recently taken over first floor office space and approached our course leader Phillip Hussey to see if any students would like to take on the project.

When Neil asked me to join him I did not hesitate. After all, designing and making a boardroom table and chairs is not a bad project at the best of times and to have it as our first commission would, we quickly realised, benefit not only our experience but our portfolios.

Research

Before the initial visit to the company Neil and I started to gather information about boardroom furniture, looking specifically at the work of designers in order to see what had already been done and how various design problem areas, like positioning table legs to allow for comfort, had been overcome.

From this background research we developed a greater awareness of what works well visually as well as practically. We noted high standards of excellence in workmanship and so set ourselves standards to strive for in our own work.

Presentation and image were of prime importance to the company and we deduced that our design should reflect that. The specification was left totally up to ourselves, with no preference given about either the type of timber to be used or the general appearance. Our only limitations were the size of the room (15ft by 12ft) and an eight week timescale.

After a short but busy Christmas break spent separately, sketching and model-making, Neil and I came together with our ideas, both of us having realised that to seat eight around the table comfortably, allowing ample clearance to pull chairs back and to walk behind a seated person, the room size dictated a rectangular shape of table.

Another possibility was to bow the sides, resulting in a boat shape, which seemed at first to be an attractive proposal in terms of aesthetic value and in terms of improving the sitters' visual contact with each other

due to the curved sides. However, introducing a curve in the table top would ultimately mean reflecting curves elsewhere in the design, and the shortage of time we had to complete the commission seemed to rule out this design approach.

Because we had both previously been involved in mechanical engineering it seemed inevitable we should apply this experience to our work and incorporate metal as well as wood in the design.

Presentation

The final design proposal was the result of many hours spent fine-tuning our ideas before making a

full-size mock-up of the chair design and, eventually, a 1:5 scale model of the table and chair, which we presented to our client.

We chose maple (*Acer saccharum*) for its striking blond appearance, hard, clean cutting characteristics and minimal waste. To complement this timber we included American cherry (*Prunus serotina*) for the chair back-splats and also for the inlaid stringing on the table top, so dividing the figured veneered surface from the solid edge lippings. In contrast, the pale grey of sandblasted stainless steel seemed to set the two off perfectly.

The scale model was made with

our intended materials, even to the extent of inlaying the tabletop, and obviously impressed DML as the company gave us the go-ahead that same day.

Our next task was to create a carefully structured time planner which would ensure completion, ➤

ABOVE: The table features clusters of legs.

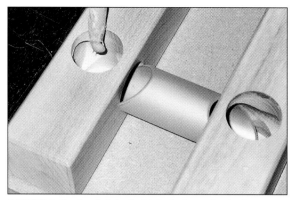

ABOVE: Adhesive is injected into holes prior to leg cluster assembly.

ABOVE AND BELOW: The veneer was pinned to the mould to prevent movement during pressing and then the back-splat laminate was cut, working from the centre line.

ABOVE AND RIGHT: The lippings were glued using sets of two sash cramps bolted together, then chamfers were hand planed on the lipping corners.

including delivery and photography, within seven weeks, even allowing for other college assignments, limited access to the machine shop and numerous journeys to suppliers for materials. There was only one way to accomplish such a challenge and that was by maximum efficiency, a phrase that was to become the project's motto.

However, being well organised is all very well in theory but practice can be different. As we found out, when you are working with wood it is all too easy to forget that you are manipulating a natural product which requires more understanding than merely how to work it. I am referring, of course, to the conditioning of timber and to its reluctance to adapt kindly to sudden changes in environment, a problem we experienced after having machined the table lippings.

Checking setback

Although we had allowed the rough cut boards to adapt to the workshop conditions, the combination of removing large amounts of material in a generously heated, dry machine shop proved too much too soon. The result was surface checking, luckily only in the two, smaller, end lippings.

After a bemused minute of silence gazing at the splits we agreed that the only option was to purchase more timber from our supplier some 60 miles away. There's nothing like learning the hard way!

Apart from this the project ran smoothly and we completed it earlier than anticipated, without making any compromises. On reflection I believe this was down to a combination of two very focused minds with similar attitudes, one goal and plenty of organisation. Seeing the finished

commission was more than rewarding, it gave us a buzz we will be striving to repeat in the future.

The big day

Delivery day involved hiring a removal service to deliver our pieces via Hamilton Photographic Studio, High Wycombe, to DML Marketing. Tony Ruocco ensured that our hiring of his studio was worth every penny and he was very helpful and patient about setting up the shots we wanted. After an enjoyable three hours it was time to load our baby onto the van once again and set off for Uxbridge.

The weight and size of the table, even with the leg clusters detached, caused an anxious moment and all hands to the rescue to prevent a catastrophe as it was carried up the stairs to DML, but with the table and chairs safely installed and admiring onlookers gathered around,

SUPPLIERS AND WORK LOG

FAR LEFT: Week One and the components are stacked and allowed to condition in the workshop environment.

LEFT: Week Four sees a 10° angle being cut on a lipping.

BOTTOM LEFT: Week Four and a 30mm medium density fibreboard sheet for the table top is being cut on the dimension saw.

BOTTOM RIGHT: Week Five and the chamfers on the lipping corners are being hand planed.

STUDENTS Anthony Jackson and Neil Edgar kept a log of the project, detailing the accomplishment of key stages and which suppliers they used for materials.

These included *Atkins & Cripps* of Bishops Stortford, Hertfordshire for maple; *J. Crispin & Sons* of Shoreditch, East London, for rippled maple and cherry veneers; *Righton* of High Wycombe, Bucks for stainless steel; *Isaac Lord*, also of High Wycombe, for saw tooth bit, epoxy resin, sandpaper, sash cramps, cordless drill and sander.

"Presentation and image were of prime importance to the company"

we were able to reassure the assembly that the chair back-splats were strong enough to lean back on and that the acid-catalysed lacquer would withstand the odd coffee spill. It was encouraging to know that our work was seen as precious and would be in safe hands, although I suspect there was some apprehension at first.

The company has since received a number of complimentary comments about the boardroom suite from their clients and has now enquired about a side unit to match. ■

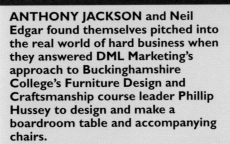

COSTINGS

ANTHONY JACKSON and Neil Edgar found themselves pitched into the real world of hard business when they answered **DML Marketing's** approach to Buckinghamshire College's Furniture Design and Craftsmanship course leader Phillip Hussey to design and make a boardroom table and accompanying chairs.

RATHER THAN being able to let their imagination dictate the final designs they were limited from the start by the twin disciplines of money and time. Not only did their designs have to satisfy DML's desire for an appropriate reflection of their corporate image, they had to ensure

their interpretation met the company's own budget and that they could complete the agreed commission within eight weeks. Something of a tall order for the pair.

THE PROJECT cost a total of £3,320, inclusive of VAT, the bulk of which went on timber, veneer, MDF, stainless steel and upholstery. To the total, the students reckoned, would normally have been added a direct labour charge of £5,474, reflecting 435.5 hours worked at £6.25 each.

Their costings also took into account jigs, adhesives, finishing, additional tools, petrol, photography and delivery.

A mahogany veneered dining table was the ideal Christmas present for Robin Anderson to make for his son. It was finished just in time to receive the turkey. Here's how to make it.

A table fit for Christmas dinner

t was at the request of my son that I made him a dining room table as a Christmas present. The top is 1370 x 915mm (4FT 6IN x 3FT), capable of extension to 1830mm (6FT), and it is based on a Sheraton design. The table top, support rails and plinth are made from 19mm ($^3/_4$IN) veneered medium density fibreboard (MDF). The advantages of MDF are that it is cheaper than solid wood, flat and stable, easy to machine, and allows an attractive matched grain pattern to be achieved by the use of veneer.

If you have not used veneer before do not be put off – it is not difficult and I will give a few hints on how to get a good result.

The central column (FIG 1) traditionally should be round, but as I do not have a wood turning lathe I made mine on my router set-up, giving it 16 sides decorated with flutes.

It is made from four pieces of mahogany glued together to form a section 118mm (4$^5/_8$IN) square. Of course, the top face must be at 90DEG to the central axis or the table top will not be level. The overall height of the table can be adjusted by changing the length of the column.

The legs (FIG 2) are marked out using a pattern to take the best advantage of the wood available, avoiding short grain. In my case the sawmill produced a piece of wood 460 x 460 x 50mm (18 x 18 x 2IN) which they sanded and, after marking out, cut out five legs for me as my band saw was not up to the task.

Being rough cut, these had to be cleaned up. This was done by attaching them to a pattern and using a guide pin on the worktable of my router machine. The taper was produced with the router.

The finished table, shown fully extended.
The table was finished just in time for Christmas dinner.

However, a plane will do the job equally well but with a bit more effort. The reeding decoration was done with a homemade scraper. The ends of the legs were shaped to fit the castors.

The joints between the legs and the column are unconventional. I wanted to ensure there were no gaps around the shoulder of the tenons and the column. The ends of the legs were machined flat and separate tenons, made to a good fit in the open-ended mortices in the column, were screwed and glued to the column using one 100mm (4IN) No 10CS screw per leg. The holes were counterbored and filled with plugs made from a scrap piece of wood from which the legs were made.

The legs and column should be stained before gluing as any surplus glue will prevent the stain from penetrating the wood and colouring it.

The two supporting rails and plinth are quite simple (FIGS 3 and 4). Solid wood can be used but it is more expensive than MDF. I made my rails with two pieces of 19mm MDF 1120mm (44IN) long glued together and veneered on all sides before the grooves are cut for the runners.

The groove for the runner (FIG 3) is cut with a 19mm (³⁄₄IN) DIA router cutter. When completed the rails must be screwed and glued to the plinth, which is made from two pieces of 19mm (³⁄₄IN) MDF glued together, measuring 510 x 355mm (20 x 14IN).

The plinth fits between the two runners. It is essential that the rails and plinth are flat, level, square and parallel or it will be difficult to slide the table tops in and out to insert or remove the centre section. To achieve this, place the plinth on a flat surface (I used an old mirror) lay the rails and plinth in position and drill the holes for six No 6 50mm (2IN) screws. Stain before gluing.

Fit the assembled plinth and rails to the top of the column, making sure the legs are at 45DEG to the rails when viewed from above (FIG 4). The plinth assembly is cen-

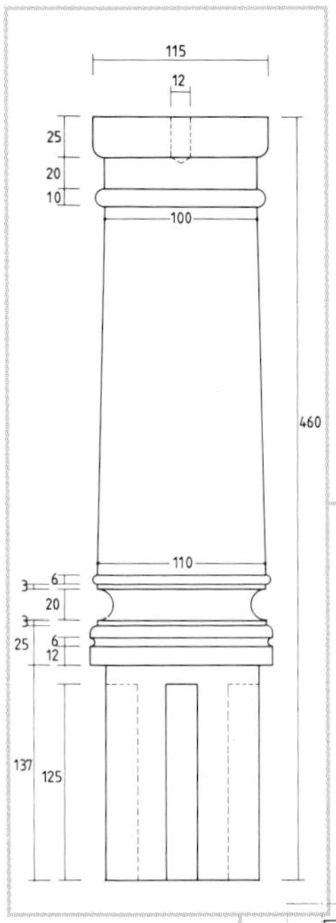

FIG 1

The central column.

FIG 2

The legs. Separate tenons are made 125 x 20 x 20mm (5 x ³⁄₄ x ³⁄₄IN) which are screwed and glued to the legs with 38mm (1½IN) No 8CS screws. Drill holes 5mm (³⁄₁₆IN) DIA, counterbored 10mm (³⁄₈IN) DIA to fix leg to column using 100mm (4IN) No 10CS screws. Holes are plugged after assembly.

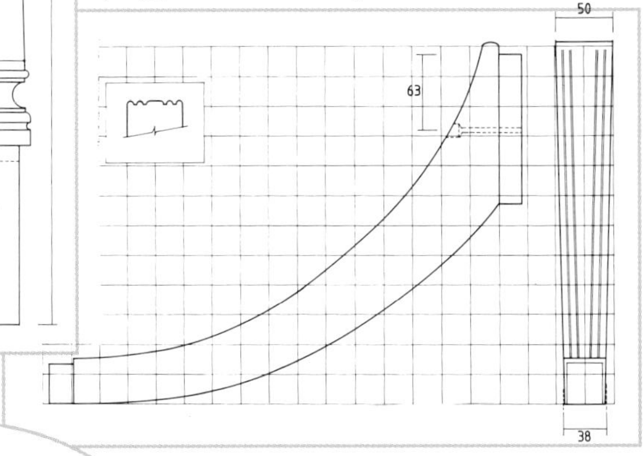

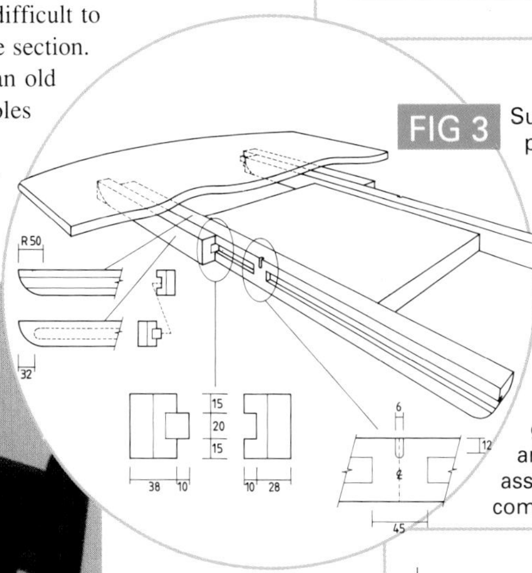

FIG 3

Supporting rails made from two pieces of 19mm (³⁄₄IN) MDF glued together. Veneer all surfaces before machining groove.

FIG 4

Supporting rails screwed and glued to the plinth. Plinth is made from two pieces of 19mm (³⁄₄IN) MDF glued together. The underside and ends are veneered before assembly, the top veneered on completion.

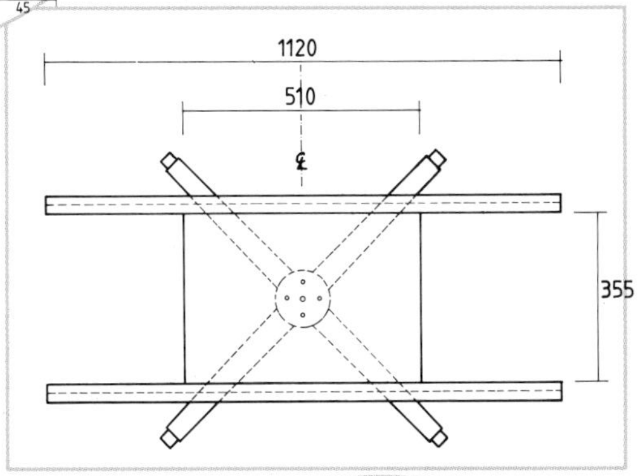

FIG 5

The table top with extension, showing the peg system viewed from the top.

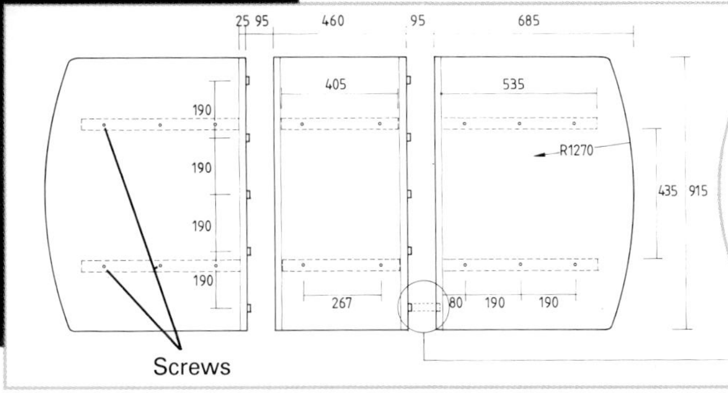

FIG 6

Details of the pegs used for locating the sections of the table top.

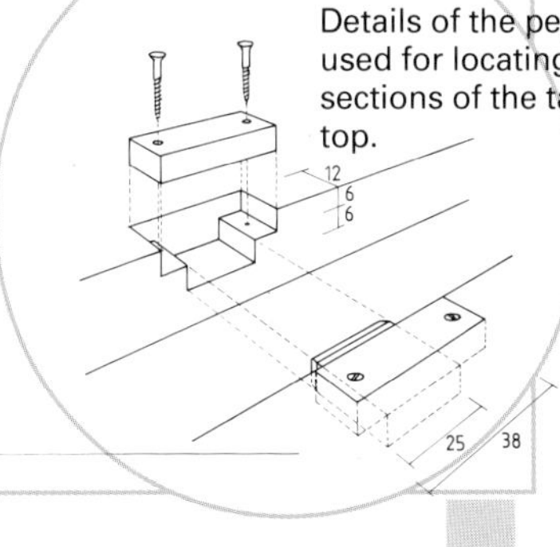

Screws

tralised on a 12mm (½IN) DIA dowel and fixed with four 100mm (4IN) screws to the top of the column.

The top of the plinth shows only when adding or removing the centre section but it looks better veneered. Before doing this any cavities should be filled and rubbed smooth to prevent air pockets under the veneer.

Cut the groove for the table top rails (FIG 3) in the same way as for the support rails. The table top rails are also made with two pieces of MDF 535mm (21IN) long glued together, and the runners are made with a piece of MDF 19mm (¾IN) square veneered on two sides and glued into the groove in the rail. The veneer on the top face of the table top rail is added after machining the groove to make sure that when the rails and runners are screwed to the table tops there is clearance to allow the tops to slide freely.

A 6mm (¼IN) steel pin in the rail of the top centre piece slots into the groove in the centre of the support rail (FIG 3) to ensure correct fitting.

The table top (FIG 5) consists of two ends and a centre extension piece. Five rectangular pegs, plus pockets for them to engage into, are used to ensure proper alignment. As MDF is prone to delamination, the edges must be lipped with 25mm (1IN) wide by 22mm (⅞IN) thick mahogany strips, which are glued on.

With the strips fitted, veneer the underside of the tops. Lay the three sections on a flat surface, underside up, and fit table forks, (catches) about 25mm (1IN) in from the edges to hold the sections together. After fitting the catches release them and turn the sections right way up. Remove the centre extension piece and fix the two end pieces together with the catches, making sure the sides line up.

The pockets for the pegs can be produced as mortises, but there are 20 and they must line up accurately. My method ensures perfect alignment and is much quicker.

First make two simple jigs as FIG 7. The sides are labelled A and B, and to avoid any inaccuracy with alignment they should be used the same way round each time – that is, replace side 'A' by side 'A'.

Fit a 12mm (½IN) DIA bush to the router base and use a 6mm (¼IN) DIA cutter. Screw jig No 1 to the top across join A-D in FIG 8 near one of the positions shown in FIG 5 and machine a pocket 12mm (½IN) deep. Replace the first jig with the second and machine to 6mm (¼IN) deep. Repeat for the other four positions. The depths must be accurate or the pegs will not fit properly.

Remove the screws from the jig in the end marked D and replace it with the extension. Refit jig No 1 to A and screw the B side to B on the extension. Repeat the machining operations. Repeat D to C.

JIG 1   JIG 2

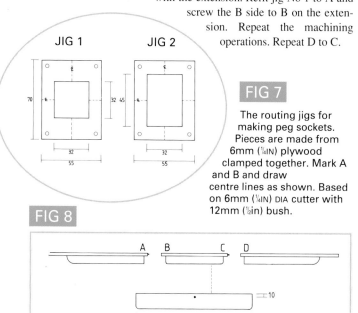

FIG 7

The routing jigs for making peg sockets. Pieces are made from 6mm (¼IN) plywood clamped together. Mark A and B and draw centre lines as shown. Based on 6mm (¼IN) DIA cutter with 12mm (½in) bush.

FIG 8

Item	Length	Width	Thickness	
Column, sections x 4	460	60	60	(18 x 2⅜ x 2⅜)
Legs x 4	560	140	50	(22 x 5½ x 2)
Lipping x 4	915	25	22	(36 x 1 x ⅞)
Tenons	125	20	20	(5 x ¾ x ¾)
Top sections and supports, cut from				
MDF sheet	2440	1220	19	(96 x 48 x ¾)
Plinth MDF	510	355	38	(20 x 14 x 1½)

Castors x 4 (No 1324) aperture 32 x 32mm (1¼ x 1¼IN) and Table Forks x 4 (No 1756) 75mm (3IN) can be obtained from Martin & Co. 119 Camden Street, Birmingham, B1 3DJ. (Tel: 0121 233 2111)

Veneer can be obtained from Art Veneers, Mildenhall, Suffolk IP28 7AY. (Tel: 01638 712550)

Next make 10 pegs from scrap mahogany and 20 packing pieces to dimensions shown in FIG 6. The packing pieces can be screwed into position over the peg recess and the fit of the pegs checked. When satisfactory, refit and glue the packing pieces. DO NOT glue the pegs at this stage, as they would impede the trimming of the veneer of the top surface.

The top sections must now be attached to their rails. The top rails (FIG 3) should be slid into the supports, and on one side a piece of veneer should be placed between them, above and resting on the runner to act as a spacer to provide clearance. Clamp them in position. Repeat this for the other end and the extension.

The top sections should be laid on the supports, and the pegs engaged. The assembled top should now be adjusted to be equi-spaced laterally and parallel to the supports. When this has been done, drill and fit the 16 No 6 38mm (1½IN) screws as indicated in FIG 5. Remove the clamps and, if all is well, remove, glue and refit the supports.

All the cavities must be filled and rubbed smooth prior to veneering. After veneering, glue the pegs into position.

For veneering I use Thixofix as an adhesive which has the advantage that, if you have a disaster, the veneer can be removed with a warm iron. Any subsequent local delamination can be rectified in the same way, even after polishing. A wallpaper roller is a good way of pressing the veneer on if you don't have a veneer hammer.

Joining and trimming the edges can present problems. Mahogany veneer can be very brittle and the grain changes direction. Using a sharp knife and a straight edge does not always produce a clean edge.

I made a simple jig from two pieces of MDF dowelled together and machined one edge straight. Two pieces of wood dowelled together and planed straight will do just as well. The sheet of veneer is placed between them so that the edge to be joined just protrudes – the less the better. With firm pressure on the top of the jig, use abrasive paper, (120 grit) until the edge is smooth.

Having laid them, hold the joins together with strips of masking tape at 90DEG to the join. This may stretch, so reinforce with a piece parallel to and along the whole length of the join.

Apply adhesive to both the groundwork and the veneer, leave it to dry for 10-20 minutes before laying the veneer and rolling down firmly. Once again, sandpaper (120 grit) makes an excellent job of trimming the edges. The paper should be held on a pad and angled slightly downwards. Surplus glue is removed with white spirit.

When you select your veneer make a careful choice and use adjacent sheets. The pattern should be repeated on all the top sections. How many sheets you need for the tops depends on the widths of the sheets, and hence the number of joins. In my case, two sheets were wide enough. To complete the suite, see page 62. ■

Stools with style

A spinning stool is a relatively simple piece of furniture to produce, yet the carving makes each one unique and an attractive piece to have in the home. Jeremy Williams explains how the stool is made and carved.

This project was a combined effort. The construction of the spinning stool was carried out by furniture-maker David White, while I provided the carved decoration.

The basic concept of the spinning stool, was taken from the design of one in Haddo House, Edinburgh. The wood used was English oak.

Firstly, the material has to be planed and thicknessed. With the seat block still rectangular, the mortise is marked out for the back using the thickness of the wood for the back as a guide. The mortise is marked in place and lines extended to the seat edge, taking them down the side using a sliding bevel set to provide a 5DEG slope for the splat.

The lines are then squared across the underside of the seat and the width of the mortise marked on both the top and bottom surfaces. But remember, it is wider on the top due to the angled shoulders.

Drill out the waste from the mortise

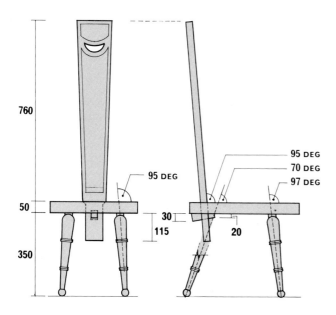

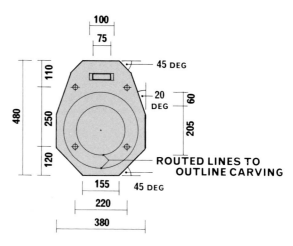

760

50

350

95 DEG

95 DEG
70 DEG
97 DEG

30
115

20

100
75
110
480
250
120
45 DEG
20 DEG
60
205
ROUTED LINES TO OUTLINE CARVING
155
220
380
45 DEG

Material used and one leg turned.

Turning one of the stool legs.

At this point David White had finished the first part of making the stool. Then it was over to me for carving.

and, using the bevel as a guide, trim with a mallet and chisel.

Mark and drill the holes for the legs 30mm DIA x 35mm (1⅛ x 1⅜IN) deep. Because the legs have compound angles – as shown on the drawings – David White used a home-made tilting table with a pillar drill to drill the holes.

Taper the back along its length and cut the tenon to width with angled shoulders.

Trial fit the back and mark it out under the seat to show the position for the wedge – we used a wedge with a 1:8 taper.

Mark out the mortise on the back splat allowing 2-3mm so the wedge will tighten up the back on to its shoulders.

The legs are turned – and note that the rear ones are longer than those at the front. Before turning the beads and spherical feet, make sure the lengths are correct. With this design there is little or no leeway for final adjustments later to get the chair level.

A simpler design of leg could be used and it may be worth noting that many early stools either had very plain turned legs of tapered, rectangular section legs.

As an aid to carving, 'V'-rout guides on both the seat and the back. These are shown in the drawings. Also cut out the finger crescent shaped hole in the back.

In its simplest form, chair carving can consist of incised lines cut with just a V-tool. But much more effect is achieved if the pattern is taken into low relief. It is, though, essential not to have too much undulation or the seat will be uncomfortable. Try sitting on a pebble beach and you will soon see what I mean.

So I planned to set the carving of

dog-roses and foliage in to a depth of only about 5mm (³⁄₁₆IN).

First you need to make drawings of what you intend to carve and this has to fit between the routed guidelines. So place some paper over the chair and crease along the routed guideline grooves. For the seat, divide the design into quadrants to allow the pattern to repeat four times.

The drawings are traced on to the wood in the usual way using carbon paper. With that done, it is always a good idea to take a good look at the imprints just to make sure the design is well balanced. It is not uncommon to find the look of the design changes once it is on the wood. When I put my design on to the seat it became obvious there was too much space between the quadrants, so I added extra leaves to fill in the gaps.

Once the tracing is complete, outline all of the pattern using a small V-tool just into the waste area.

It is a mistake to carry out the work in sections. So work progressively. Do all the outline, not just part of it, before going on to the next stage.

With so many small areas of background to remove I opted to take them out with a small cutter fitted to my Dremel Moto-Tool and router plate. With the depth at 3mm (¹⁄₈IN) maximum to allow a small margin for gouge work later on, I removed the background. Any parts of the background too small for the cutter were dealt with as the carving progressed using a veiner.

With most of the background removed, do as much as possible of the setting-in with just one gouge. This ensures the shapes of the leaves are similar. I used an elderly Henry Taylor No 4 gouge for the work. Being old it ▶

Design ready for carboning on to the wood.

was stubby, which meant it was easier to control the vertical stab cuts. Whatever you use, keep the bevel moderately short to compensate for the hardness of the oak.

Mirror images can present problems unless they are carved in sequence. In other words, carve the one on, say, the left and immediately transfer to the right-hand side and repeat the cuts. This way there is every chance the cuts will be similar, as if the brain automatically reverses the image.

If you carve all the detail in one part and then transfer to another area there will be much more variation. So, pick out where there is repetition and work the detail turn and turn about. All the leaves were formed in this fashion before the flowers were carved.

While I treated the chair back and the seat as separate entities, if you are a beginner at carving intent on uniformity, you might well carve all the leaves then all the flowers. I would certainly recommend this if you are doing the carving over a period of time.

Where the depth of relief is minimal, as it is with this stool, start with the lowest contour detail and work back to the next higher. This will help to make sure you do not run out of wood or have to dig deeper when creating the design.

At this stage, some thought needs to be given to the structure of the wood. Try and avoid having delicate leaftips, for example, rising up on cross-grain. Over years of dusting and polishing they are bound to get broken off. In fact, I made sure they all turned down to the background.

Old carvers used to describe a design as being 'nervous' if it contained plenty of variation of shape and contour. The petals, as well as the leaves, lend themselves to this treatment. How each curls, or overlaps its neighbour, needs to vary. It will provide a look of vigour and crispness.

When cutting the flowers, lower the centres first nearly to the background, then dome them. This allows the petals to dip steeply towards the centres. With a moderately quick-cut gouge, the petal contours are 'nervously' formed. I used a No7 gouge for this to create the

25mm SQUARES

right amount of undulation.

If your gouges have been kept razor sharp, as they should be, there should be no need for anything more than the gentlest sanding. Too much and the brightness of the cutting will be lost. More effective is to burnish the work using a polished pointed stick. I find bamboo works well for this. With it you can remove any persistent wood fibres and the natural oil in most wood will burnish to a pleasant sheen. You might at this stage seal the carving with sanding sealer, but I didn't as the stool was to be fumed.

After carving, David White carried on with the final construction. Mainly this was to provide a 6mm (¼IN) chamfer cut, top and bottom, all around the seat and a lighter chamfer around the back, stopping just above the seat bevel.

After scraping and sanding, the chair was assembled then given a light fuming in ammonia and finished with three coats of Danish oil.

25mm SQUARES

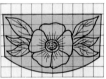

25mm SQUARES

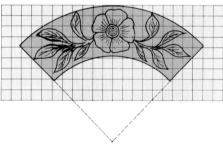

If you are seeking something different to display at local shows the spinning stool has a lot to commend it. Material cost is low and it is simple to construct. Yet there is plenty of scope for individual expression in the carving which distinguishes it as hand-made.

Spinning stool

Go back 200 years or so and nearly every cottage in rural England had a spinning wheel. To go with it there could have been a stool. Maybe just an ordinary, rough and ready one. Perhaps even a milking stool would have been pressed into service.

Later, specially made stools, with high backs, were introduced. Their style and shape varied through local custom. Some seats were round, some rectangular, others shield-shaped. All, though, were decorated with carving.

Last summer I had a charming couple from Aberdeen on one of my courses. Over a coffee break I happened to mention I had often thought of carving a spinning stool.

On their return home they sent me some photos of a stool dating back to the late 1600s. It is at Haddo House, near Aberdeen. Made of oak and heavily carved, it is of the style which seems to have been popular in Scotland.

The Spinning Stool is an attractive item of furniture. Apart from its obvious use, it makes a good decorative addition to any home. Being small, it can be used as an occasional chair. Or it can be used as a focal point in a hall or on a landing ●

Back ready for carving.

Seat design incised. Note extra leaves.

Routing seat background.

The beauty of a £5 offcut

The experienced eye of cabinetmaker Arthur Cross fell on an offcut of striped oak and he knew the wood had the potential to be an attractive piece of furniture. The wood cost him £5. From it he made this side table. Here he explains how you can make one just like it.

As usual, a visit to Whitmores, my local timber yard, saw me waiting for the lifting vehicle to arrive because the timber I wanted was at the bottom of the stack. Not that I mind waiting – I'm lucky to have a timber yard nearby which specialises in supplying the furniture trade and is happy to let me select the wood I want. While I was waiting I wandered over to the offcut shed. There I saw something that brought memories flooding back of my apprenticeship as a cabinetmaker with my father.

What had brought back the memories was a piece of striped oak left on top of a pile. It was just over 63mm (2½IN) thick and had clearly been cut off a wide board. A shake ran almost the whole length of it.

It had been quarter sawn and I could see the medullary rays running across the dark brown streaks that go with the grain and give the wood its name of striped, or tiger oak – wood that we used to know as spoilt oak.

The memories this wood evoked were of the days shortly after I left the RAF having completed my National Service. It was 1952. Len Ward, a fellow apprentice, and I

started making furniture out of prana pine and this striped oak, which was all we could afford. The public wasn't interested – in those days people were spending their money on washing machines, televisions and all those domestic appliances which most people now take for granted but which were novelties at that time.

I thought there would be enough timber in this offcut to make a small table, so, for nostalgia's sake as much as anything, I decided to buy it. At the office they charged me £5 for it – clearly there is still a limited demand for striped oak.

By the time I had cut out the shake and the sapwood I finished up with one piece 280mm (11IN) wide and another 200mm (8IN) wide. Both were still 63mm (2½IN) thick.

The narrower piece had the best figuring so I decided to use that for the top, cutting off two, 12mm (½IN) thick boards. I edge jointed these to make the top 840mm (33IN) long and 405mm (16IN) wide. By the time they were planed smooth the top was 10mm (⅜IN) thick.

The next most important parts of a table like this are the drawer

Arthur Cross

For more than 100 years an Arthur Cross has been cabinetmaking in Burbage, Leicestershire – the current craftsman's father and grandfather before him.

The previous two Arthurs faked antiques – and they did it so well that Arthur Cross III is convinced their work is to be found in many a museum and stately home.

The present Arthur Cross has three sides to his business. He still makes replica antiques using the tools and methods craftsmen of the 17th and 18th century would have used. He also restores antiques and makes furniture of his own design.

fronts and the front rails. These would be 20mm (¾IN) thick and could also be cut from the 200mm wide piece of oak. I cut it in half along its thickness to make the 20mm thick boards.

The ends would be 12mm (½IN) thick, cut from the wider piece of oak so I cut off a board 12mm thick. The rest I sawed out to 10mm (⅜IN) full – in other words slightly more than 10mm in order to end up with 10mm once the parts had been planed – to make the other parts of the drawers.

There was enough wood left from the 20mm thick board I used for the drawer fronts to make the drawer rails and kickers (the pieces

I then prepared the timber to the sizes you can see in the cutting list.

Your source of timber will inevitably be different from mine, but I have included the above to show you how there can be potential in pieces of wood which others have discarded and to give you some background to this small side table I made.

Making the table

Make the mortise and tenon joints to fit the ends into the

You will also need sundry pieces of oak for drawer stops, drawer slips, knobs and brackets.

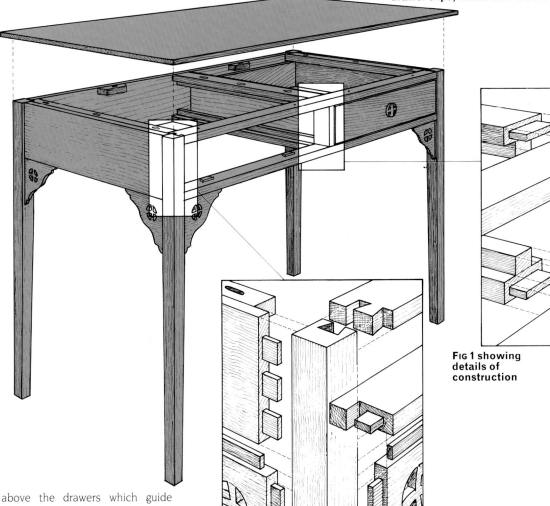

FIG 1 showing details of construction

above the drawers which guide them at the top).

There was not enough wood for the back of the table, so this had to come out of my stock. The legs also had to come out of stock. I had had an odd piece of brown oak nearly 75mm (3IN) square in my workshop for some time. I rip sawed this into four to make the legs. By the time they were cleaned up they came out to 32mm (1¼IN) square.

legs. I always use three tenons because the panels and legs will not move at the same rate. You can see what happens if you don't do this by looking at some furniture made about 10 years ago which has been in a modern, centrally heated house since then. The legs have shrunk on to a single tenon causing an unsightly bulge

where the tenon is positioned. Using three tenons makes a greater allowance for the movement of the legs. The back panel also uses three tenons.

Position the top tenons at the front of the sides 25mm (1IN) down from the top of the panel. This is to avoid a weak area at the top of the front legs when the top ▶

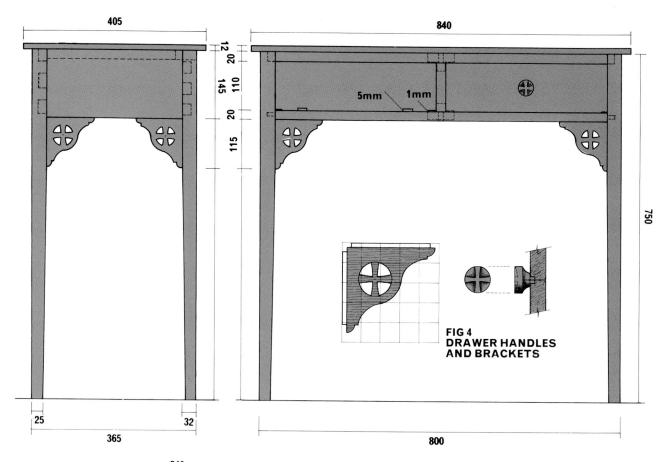

405

840

12
20
110
145
20
115

5mm **1mm**

**FIG 4
DRAWER HANDLES
AND BRACKETS**

750

25 **32**

365

800

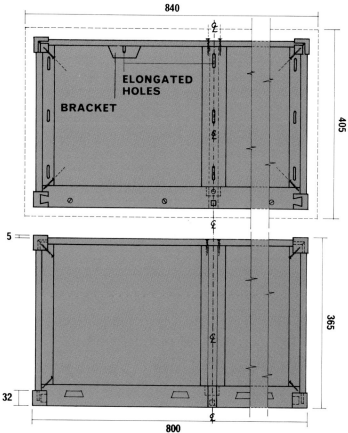

840

**ELONGATED
HOLES**

BRACKET

405

5

365

32

800

**The bottoms of
the drawers are
cut from the same
piece of wood as
the top of the
table.**

front rail is dovetailed in. The tenons at the back of the sides can come nearer to the top. Position the end panels so the outside edge is 5mm (³⁄₁₆IN) in from the outside edge of the legs. The mortises are 6mm (¼IN) wide and

20mm (¾IN) deep, mitred to accommodate each other. Fit the back in the same way as the sides.

Use mortises and tenons to join the top and bottom front rails with a central style.

The top rail is dovetailed into

the top of the legs. The bottom rail is mortised and tenoned into the legs.

Mortise the top and bottom central drawer bearers into the backs of the front rails only. They fit flush to the inside of the back of the table. Do not saw these bearers to length until the carcase has been glued up.

The legs look more elegant if they are tapered. I have put brackets underneath the table, as you can see. These are purely for decoration and can be omitted if you prefer. If you are going to include them – and they are a nice touch –

start the taper from about 6mm (¼IN) below the bottom of the bracket.

The taper is on the inside two faces of the legs only, bringing them down to a 25mm (1IN) square at the bottom.

Cut out the end drawer bearers. These should fit snugly in between the back of the front rails and the inside of the back of the table. They are not mortised.

Cut out six brackets (if you are going to add them), two for the front and two each for either end. Allow 8mm (⅜IN) for tenons. Chop out mortises on the legs and underneath the bottom rail and side panels to accept the tenons on the brackets.

The brackets at the end could be produced as part of the end panels, but I cut them out separately in order to get a better grain pattern.

In the past, brackets were merely glued and pinned into position, or were fixed with slim dowels, but done that way they are usually the first parts to fail. Mortises and tenons make them more secure.

The carcass is now ready to be glued up. Make sure it is square. And, before fitting the drawer bearers make particularly sure the front rails are not in winding (or twisted).

Getting the drawer bearers to line up takes some concentration, but it is important that they do line up. I always fit the end bearers first, holding them in position with G cramps. I then put a straight edge across them and draw a line for the position of the central bearers. You might like to use a spirit level. The bottom drawer bearers should be slightly higher than the lower front rail to give clearance to the drawer front.

Mark the position of the bearers on the back panel so you will spot any movement.

Before you glue the top bearers (or kickers) into position cut slots in them for the screws which will hold the top in place. In the top front rail, holes, rather than slots, are drilled for the screws. At the back, two brackets with slots in them are glued on to the back panel for securing the top.

When the glue has set, screw the drawer bearers into position. The central bearers are screwed through from the back. The side bearers are screwed diagonally into the legs.

Before fitting the top I used a filler on the underside and gave it a thick coating of lacquer. This will stop it going slightly hollow as the years roll on and the timber dries out, which has always been a problem with thin, solid tops.

The timber I used was kiln dried, so there should not be too much shrinkage. However, there is usually some and efforts to cope with it are never wasted.

After Jim Kingshott's excellent article on making drawers (**furniture**, Issue 1, page 46) I do not intend to go into detail about how to make the drawers for this table, but see the separate panel on the left for a few tips.

Glue drawer stops on to the bottom rail so the drawers are flush with the front of the table when they are closed and cannot be pushed in too far.

I decided to use wooden knobs on the drawers. I make these with a square on the back to fit into a stopped mortise in the drawer front (see FIG 4). I then screw into the back of the knob from the inside of the drawer.

I cut the Maltese cross device in to the brackets with a coping saw, then carved them. I carved the crosses on to the drawer knobs. This decoration is there for no other reason than that my name is 'Cross'.

To finish I used light oak grain filler followed by two coats of clear polyurethane, lightly sanded when dry and waxed with Wheelers Traditional Beeswax Furniture Cream. You could use French polish or oil if you preferred ●

Drawers

The drawers for this side table are of straightforward, traditional construction using lap dovetails at the front and through dovetails at the back. Make fine pins at the front to show off your skills.

On decorative pieces like this table I like to use timber for the drawer bottoms which matches the table top. Here I have used 8mm (⅜IN) thick pieces left over from the 280mm (11IN) wide piece of striped oak - one of the two pieces I started with.

The drawer bottoms are made up to 336mm (13¼IN) square by gluing the wood together edge to edge, but allow the bottom to stick out at the back of the drawer by 5mm (⅜IN) or so to allow for shrinkage (which there might well be with oak). The grain of boards used for drawer bottoms runs across the drawers, not front to back, for this very reason.

I have fitted the drawer bottoms into beading, or drawer slips, I made from the oak I used for the majority of the job. I glued the beading onto the inside of the drawer sides and front, as you can see from the illustration.

Again, because of the possibility of shrinkage, make the drawers a good fit into the carcass.

While you are not working on the thin parts of the drawers put them under weights to keep them flat. Never assemble a drawer with parts that have gone hollow. If this is a problem, dampen the concave side with a moistened sponge and the wood should straighten out in about 20 minutes.

Below. The drawers are made in the conventional way. The bottom is fitted into drawer slips cut from the tiger oak and glued to the sides and front.

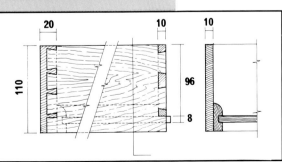

Routing Sheraton

After making the Sheraton dining table featured on pages 52-4, Robin Anderson decided to complete the suite with four side chairs and two carvers. Here he explains how he did it, using a router and radial arm saw.

Making this set of chairs presented me with a problem because most of the chairs of the period were beyond my skills. After much searching in vain, I contacted **Woodworking***today.* They came up with the plans for a Sheraton elbow chair. I then found a similar, but much less complex design by a manufacturer of reproduction furniture. My design is based on a mixture of the two – more the latter than the former.

The next step was to make a prototype to prove to myself I could make the chair and to obtain family approval for the design. I used sycamore for this. I achieved both objectives – made the chair and the family liked it.

I gave a lot of thought to the methods of manufacture. The chairs can be made by conventional means using mortise and tenon joints and hand shaping, but I came to the conclusion that, while reproducing the style accurately is important, consistency is essential. What I mean is that if an angle is 1DEG larger (or smaller) on one chair than another there could be as much as 13mm (½IN) variation in the widths of the chairs. And that would show.

So I decided to make jigs and fixtures wherever they would add to speed and consistency, and to use brass dowels in place of mortice and tenon joints. I chose brass rather than wooden dowels because the same strength could be achieved from smaller sections.

The jigs can be divided into three categories: dowelling; shaping and sawing; assembly. While you can get away without the dowelling and the shaping and sawing jigs, the assembly jigs are important. The dowelling jigs, which are simple to make, are shown here. The shaping and sawing jigs are shown on the facing page and the assembly jigs are on page 64. All are made from 13mm MDF.

What follows is based on the methods I used, which were appropriate to my equipment. That consists of a home-made overhead router, and a radial arm saw with a device for cutting angles.

The rear legs conform to a radius of 1,524mm (60IN) because that makes it easy to calculate the angles required.

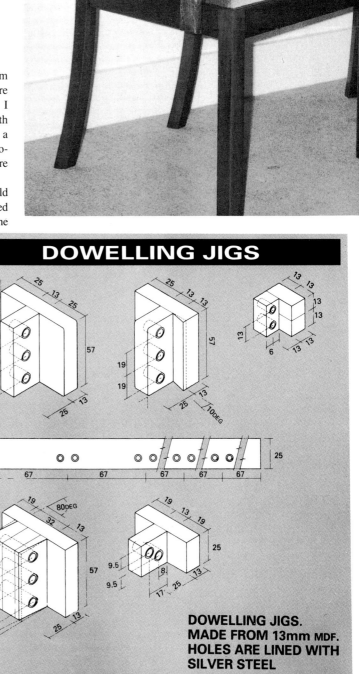

DOWELLING JIGS

DOWELLING JIGS. MADE FROM 13mm MDF. HOLES ARE LINED WITH SILVER STEEL

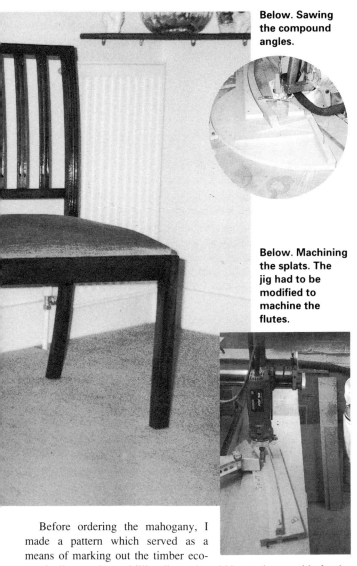

Below. Sawing the compound angles.

Below. Machining the splats. The jig had to be modified to machine the flutes.

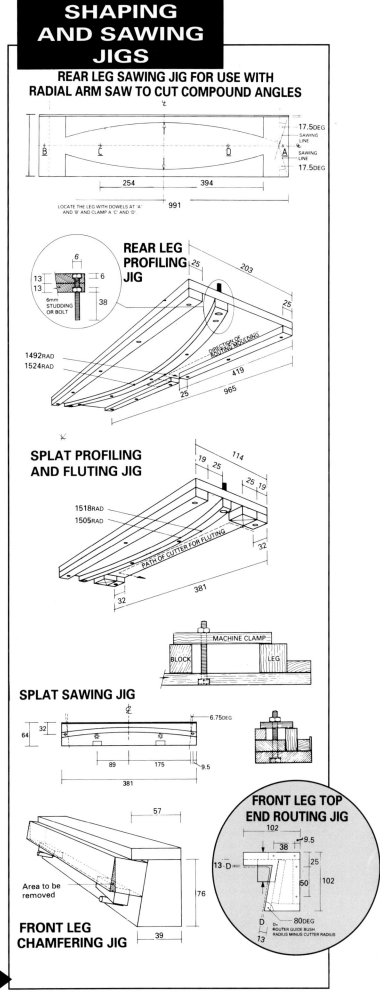

REAR LEG SAWING JIG FOR USE WITH RADIAL ARM SAW TO CUT COMPOUND ANGLES

17.5DEG SAWING LINE
17.5DEG
SAWING LINE

B C D A

254   394
991

LOCATE THE LEG WITH DOWELS AT 'A' AND 'B' AND CLAMP A 'C' AND 'D'.

REAR LEG PROFILING JIG

6
13
13
6mm STUDDING OR BOLT
6
38
25   203
25

DIRECTION OF ROUTING MOULDING

1492RAD
1524RAD
419
25   965

SPLAT PROFILING AND FLUTING JIG

19 25 114
25 19

1518RAD
1505RAD
32
PATH OF CUTTER FOR FLUTING
381
32

MACHINE CLAMP
BLOCK   LEG

SPLAT SAWING JIG

6.75DEG
64 32
89   175   9.5
381

FRONT LEG CHAMFERING JIG

57
Area to be removed
76
39

FRONT LEG TOP END ROUTING JIG

102
9.5
38
13 D
25
50   102
D 80DEG
13
D= ROUTER GUIDE BUSH RADIUS MINUS CUTTER RADIUS

Before ordering the mahogany, I made a pattern which served as a means of marking out the timber economically, acted as a drilling jig, and could be used as a guide for the profiling jig. I made it from 13mm (½IN) MDF using a portable router with a long radius arm. It has about 38mm (1½IN) extra at each end, through which 6mm (¼IN) holes have been drilled for positioning the legs.

The legs should be marked out including the extra length at each end, leaving about 1.5mm (¹⁄₁₆IN) all round machining allowance. Attach the pattern to the underside of the profiling jig and fit the studs in the holes.

The jig is designed to be used on the work table with a guide pin. The pin should be of the same diameter as the cutter. I use a separate work table secured to the main one and drill a 6mm (¼IN) hole with a router bit to make sure the guide pin and cutter are truly concentric. Both sides of the leg should be machined, taking several cuts. When that's done, machine the reeding. You can hand scrape it, but machining with a suitable cutter is quicker. I used a Titan MM-R10 cutter and a new 16mm (¾IN) DIA guide pin. By adding a stop, the reeding will start at the same point on each leg.

Now cut the compound angle at the top of the leg and remove the surplus at the bottom. The need for a compound angle arose because on all the chairs I examined the top rail sits on top of the legs – ie at 90DEG – but the reeding junction between vertical and horizontal is at 45DEG. Short of carving this manually, I could see no way of doing it without a compound angle. So, as I am no wood carver, I did it this way and made the rear leg jigs to cut it.

When you are making the sawing jig, drill a hole at each end of the base. Make sure they are both equidistant from the edge. Mark out

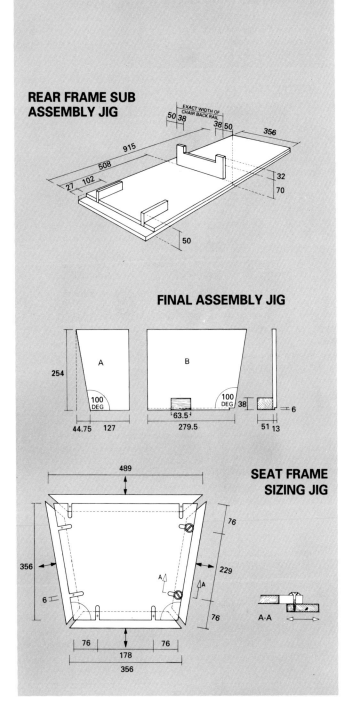

REAR FRAME SUB ASSEMBLY JIG

EXACT WIDTH OF CHAIR BACK RAIL

50 38   38 50   356

915

508

27 102

32

70

50

FINAL ASSEMBLY JIG

254

A

B

100 DEG

100 DEG   38

6

44.75   127   63.5   279.5   51 13

SEAT FRAME SIZING JIG

489

76

356

229

A

A

6

76

A-A

76   76

178

356

Radius the rear edges and drill 6mm (¼IN) diameter holes for the brass dowels.

The side rails are quite straightforward, although it is important to cut the 10DEG angle consistently. If you do not have a means of doing that, make part A of the final assembly jig (illustrated left) and use this whenever a 10DEG or 100DEG angle is required.

The side rails are longer for the carvers than for the other chairs. It would appear to have something to do with the proportions of the arms to side length. But why not make them all the same? Perhaps someone could tell me. Anyhow, who am I to flaunt tradition. Do not forget these rails are handed.

The front legs are handed but are fairly straightforward to make. It is important that the angle is consistent, so I made the front leg jigs and, having a depth stop on the router, was able to cut the legs identically.

The rebate at the top can be cut by hand but it is much easier to make the simple attachment for a router and use a 6mm (½IN) cutter. Remember to do six off right hand and six off left hand.

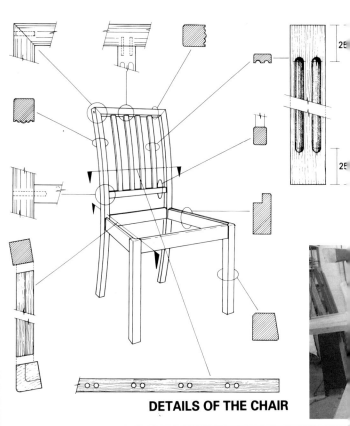

DETAILS OF THE CHAIR

the curved pieces to the base so they fit snugly against the leg. Two positions are necessary since the legs are handed. If you decide to carve the reeding, only the 72.5DEG angle need be cut.

Before clamping the legs to the jig, locate the hole at the bottom end of the leg with a dowel in the hole in the base. Clamp the jig to the saw worktable and cut all the top ends for six right hand legs, reset the jig for the six left hand legs.

When all 12 are cut, re-set the jig, locate the legs with the dowel, clamp and cut off the six right hand legs at 90DEG, and repeat for the left hand ones.

The splats are made using the profiling and fluting jig in a similar way to the legs. I used the Titan cutter MM-C02. The guide bearing is at the top and bottom, so part of the base has to be cut away to clear it.

After profiling all 24 splats, I added stops, refitted the splats to the jig and cut the top flutes. Re-set the cutter height and the process is repeated for the bottom flutes.

You need the splat sawing jig to cut the 86.5DEG angles and to make sure the splats are all precisely the same length. Again, the procedure is similar to that used for the legs, except the splats are not handed.

All other parts can be made to the drawings without further explanation, except that the front rail cannot be cut to length until final assembly.

Having made all the parts, I applied the first coat of stain and grain filler before gluing. I know from practice that any surplus glue seeps into the wood and inhibits staining if the bare wood is glued up. Do not, however, put grain filler into a joint or it will not stick.

To assemble the chair, start with the splats and the top and splat rails. It is not possible to clamp this without a complex jig since the pressure required cannot be applied in a single straight line.

I solved the problem by assembling each splat in turn to the splat rail using Superglue between

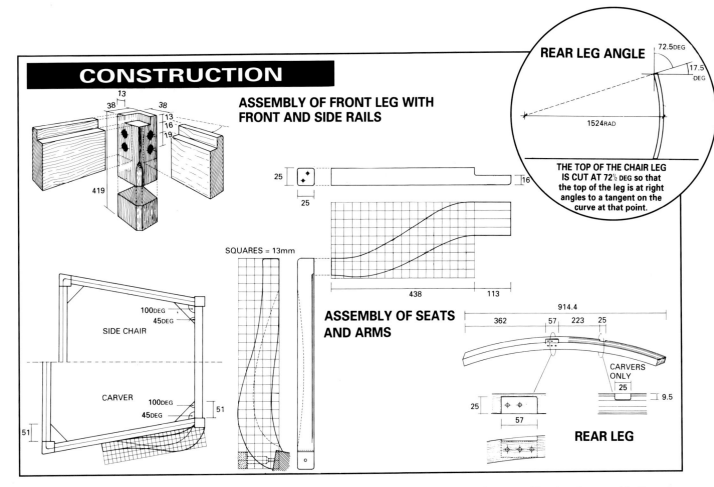

CONSTRUCTION

ASSEMBLY OF FRONT LEG WITH FRONT AND SIDE RAILS

REAR LEG ANGLE

72.5DEG

17.5 DEG

1524RAD

THE TOP OF THE CHAIR LEG IS CUT AT 72½ DEG so that the top of the leg is at right angles to a tangent on the curve at that point.

SQUARES = 13mm

ASSEMBLY OF SEATS AND ARMS

SIDE CHAIR

100DEG
45DEG

CARVER

100DEG
45DEG

CARVERS ONLY

REAR LEG

Clamping up the back and side rails and calculating the front rail length.

Left. A front leg being machined.

CUTTING LIST

finished sizes in mm, (inches in brackets)

In mahogany		
Rear legs x 12	1016 x 31 x 115	(40 x 1³⁄₁₆ x 4½)
Splats x 24	407 25 x 25	(16 x 1 x 1)
Top rail x 6	420 x 32 x 31	(16½ x 1¼ x 1³⁄₁₆)
Splat rail x 6	356 x 25 x 19	(14 x 1 x ¾)
Bottom rail x 6	356 x 58 x 25	(14 x 2¼ x 1)
Side rails side chair x 8	407 x 58 x 25	(16 x 2¼ x 1)
Side rails carver x 4	432 x 58 x 25	(17 x 2¼ x 1)
Front rails side chair x 4	483 x 58 x 25	(19 x 2¼ x 1)
Front rail carver x 2	508 x 58 x 25	(20 x 2¼ x 1)
Front legs x 12	432 x 38 x 38	(17 x 1½ x 1½)
Arms x 4 cut from	1220 x 77 x 25	(48 x 3 x 1)
Arm uprights x 4 cut from	1220 x 77 x 25	(48 x 3 x 1)
In beech		
Seat frame x 6 cut from 6 pieces each	1677 x 50 x 19	(66 x 2 x ¾)

front legs. When the glue has set, still using the assembly jigs, glue the final assembly together. A piece of wood is clamped under the bottom rail with the central clamp which extends sideways so the front leg assembly and side rails can be clamped to the rear assembly. All that remains is to fit the corner reinforcing fillets.

Up to this point, apart from longer side rails, the carvers are identical. Now you add the arms. The vertical support and the arm can be made in the same way as the rear legs and splats were, but as there are only four of each, you may not think it is worth it. After they have been cleaned up, the arm and the upright should be dowelled and glued together.

Screw the arm to the rear leg and clamp the upright to the side rail while the joint between the arm and the upright sets. When it has, remove the clamp and unscrew the arm. Refit them and glue and screw them into place. Finally, plug the screw holes.

UPHOLSTERY

Not having any experience of upholstery, I had this done for me on frames I made. The frames should be in hardwood, such as beech, say 50mm (2IN) x 19mm (¾IN). Leave a 1.5mm (¹⁄₁₆IN) clearance all round for the material.

Since there will inevitably be some difference between chairs I made an adjustable seat frame sizing jig, which is an oversize seat. The bolts on the jig are loosened so the sides can be adjusted. The jig then drops into the chair seat. Three pieces of veneer 75mm x 0.5mm x 1.5mm (3IN x ¹⁄₆₄IN x ¹⁄₁₆IN) are packed between the four sides of the chair and the jig is opened up to a tight fit. The bolts are tightened and the jig removed. Put the jig on the frame and the required size can be marked out. This worked extremely well and, when the seats were returned, they all fitted perfectly.

In conclusion, I was told and have read that sets of chairs are a job for the specialist. However, it presented a challenge and the result has been rewarding. Not only do the chairs look nice, but they are comfortable to sit on and have been well worth the effort □

the wood and the brass dowels and holding the joint in position until it set. On a trial, the wood broke, not the joint. I repeated the procedure for the top rail but as all four splats must be fitted at the same time I opened the holes up slightly to ease assembly.

Fit the back legs to the bottom rail and the splat assembly, concentrating on the joints between the top rail and the legs. These should be glued and clamped.

The next task is to determine the length of the front rail. Having established it and cut the rail to size, dowel and glue the rail to the

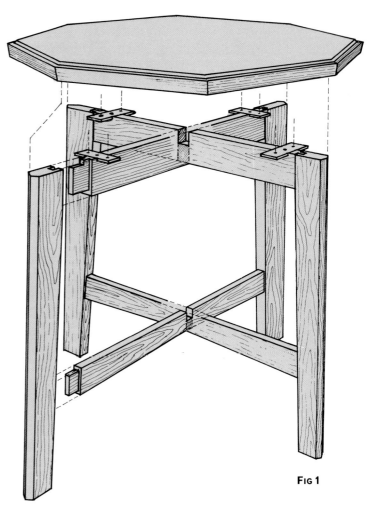

FIG 1

A marble top coffee table

Former Shoreditch College lecturer Jack Maynard (now retired) had a marble top which he wanted to use for a coffee table. Here he explains how he built the table.

If you don't have a marble top, don't worry. Afterwards Harry Levinson explains how to make a piece of MDF look like marble.

The design of this coffee table was primarily based on an octagonal marble top I had which had come from India. The height was determined by the size of the easy chairs in the lounge where it was going to be used and the wood from which it was to be made, iroko, was to match the teak furniture already in place.

Indian marble tops are not easily obtainable, but there are many alternatives which could be used. These could include man-made board finished with a marble effect (see next article). Solid wood could be used, but if so, allowance must be made in the metal holding plates for movement of the timber.

The amount of top overhang is also a matter for consideration. In the case of the heavy marble top, this was kept to a minimum for stability. With lighter materials it could be increased to give a larger working surface area.

The marble top is the most difficult part of the job and should be tackled first. The marble octagon will not be perfectly symmetrical and it is advisable to make a cardboard template first. The template should then be reduced in size by cutting 10mm (³⁄₈IN) off each edge to establish the basic shape of the multiple top. Trace this shape on to the ply and cut to size. Now mark both the marble top and ply

base so that there will be no doubt from then on how the one fits on to the other.

The ply base is lipped with iroko. I suggest the cross section of the lipping be formed as shown in FIG 4 and a total length of 1200mm (about 48IN) be cut. This enables the piece to be securely fixed at each end while ploughing or routing and also gives two spare pieces – just in case. After shaping the section it is ripped down the middle, giving two lengths of lipping. The next job is to produce a groove in the eight edges of the ply top ready to receive the lipping.

Because of the irregularities of the octagon the angles between the lipping pieces will not be the same and this causes problems.

Cut a piece of lipping to fit one of the eight edges and glue it in place. This establishes a firm base from which to fit the others. Plane the bevel on this first piece as indicated in FIG 3. Now cut pieces of lipping to fit each end of the first piece and glue and cramp in position, using the cramps on alternate sides of the ply. When the glue has set, bevel the edges to match the first piece. Continue in this way to complete the lipping process in five stages.

The supporting frames are relatively simple in construction, but the angle of the tenon shoulder of the lower rails should be established by cutting the upper rail joints first, cramping them together dry and then G cramping the lower rail in position and scribing off the angled joint line with a sharp knife.

The upper rail halving joint is quite straightforward, but the lower one needs some care on the underneath side of the joint due to the sloping edges. The top is held on to the supporting frames by four metal plates (FIG 1) and 12 screws – four into the upper rails and eight into the ply top. Before assembling the frames, cut recesses out of the top edges of the upper rails to house the metal pieces.

One of the supporting frames can now be glued and cramped. After the glue has set, taper the legs in thickness as shown in FIG 2. This enhances their aesthetic appeal. Glue the rail halving joints and allow them to set with the legs in position, but not glued. The second pair of legs should be tapered in thickness and glued to complete the frame.

When gluing, take care to ensure all assemblies are square and in the same plane. The outer edges of the legs should now be bevelled to line up with the octagonal shape of the top.

Test for the flatness of the ends of the legs and adjust where necessary. Finally, chamfer the bottom edges of the legs to prevent splitting when the table is in use and moved about on the floor.

At this stage, the top should be screwed to the frame structure and checked for a good fit. Note that the marble has not yet been placed in position. Remove the top and prepare for finishing with a polyurethane varnish. This means a final cleaning up with a fine grade of garnet paper and removal of all dust.

The first coat of varnish should be diluted with 10% white spirit and applied to the whole job, including the surface on which the marble top will rest. When dry, carefully rub it down with wet and dry abrasive paper. Apply at least three more coats of varnish except where the marble will be fixed, and rub down between each coat. The final coat may be rubbed down with 0000 wire wool and wax, and polished with a soft cloth. This should produce a lustrous matt surface which is smooth to the touch.

Now the marble top has to be fixed in place. Spread an even coat of tile cement on the ply base and run grooves over the surface with a plastic spreader. Place the slab firmly in place, ensuring that the marks made at the beginning of the exercise coincide. After the cement has set, any gaps round the edge of the slab may be made good with a filler, although very little should be needed.

Finally, screw the supporting structure to the top and the table is ready to use. ▶

MARBLE TOP TABLE CUTTING LIST

Finished sizes in mm (inches in brackets)

Ply top size as dictated by template x 16mm ($^5/_8$IN) thick

Lipping	x1	50 x 20 x 1200	(2 x $^3/_4$ x 47)
Legs	x4	40 x 22 x 420	(1$^5/_8$ x $^7/_8$ x 16 $^5/_8$)
Rails – upper	x2	50 x 18 x 370	(2 x $^{11}/_{16}$ x 14 $^9/_{16}$)
lower	x2	37 x 16 x 380	(1 $^1/_2$ x $^5/_8$ x 15)

You will also need:

Metal plates	x4	22 x 3 x 50	($^7/_8$ x $^1/_8$ x 2)
Screws CS	x4	20mm ($^3/_4$IN) No6	
Screws CS	x8	13mm ($^1/_2$IN) No6	

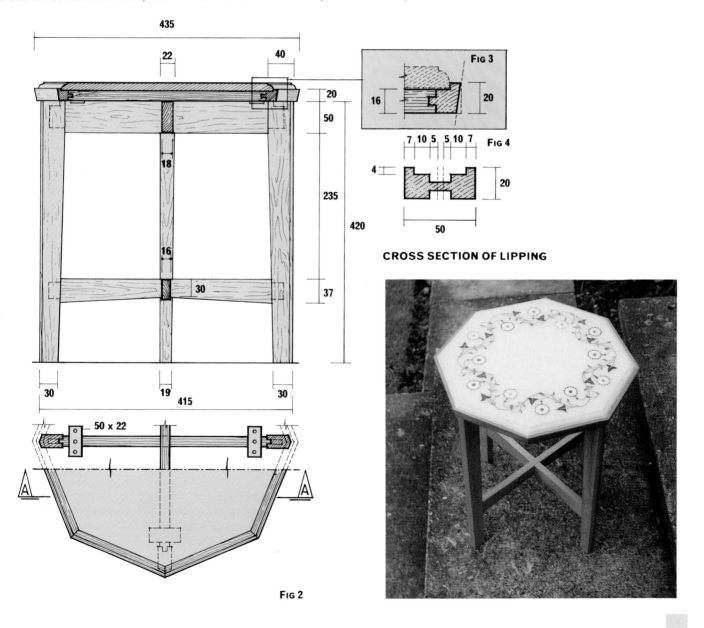

FIG 3

FIG 4

CROSS SECTION OF LIPPING

FIG 2

If you don't have a marble table top...

You can still make a table like the one Jack Maynard made even if you don't have a marble top. You can buy marble from a stonemasons, although a high quality green marble like verd'egypt costs about £300 a square metre. Alternatively you can create your own marble (or other) effect on MDF using the techniques explained here by Harry Levinson.

There are lots of different types of marble – a local stonemason has a selection of 85 in stock and can get others. The stone comes in all kinds of colours. They can all be copied using a technique similar to the one I explain here, but it is important to decide which stone you want to imitate before you start. Here I have chosen to reproduce verd'egypt – Egyptian green marble.

The verd'egypt marble effect, which can be achieved on MDF, with the tools used to create it.

The technique itself is fairly simple. Perfecting it so the work really looks like marble takes some practice, so try out your technique on something like hardboard before you tackle the table top.

Marbling can be performed on almost any smooth, solid substrate. A table top of MDF is ideal. Once you have cut the MDF to the shape you want and cleaned it up it should be filled and sealed – universal primer will do the job excellently.

The whole of the table top should be painted, using an ordinary paint brush, with black eggshell, an oil based paint of mid sheen available from good quality decorators' shops. You will need three or four coats, at least, and it will need to be left to dry (about eight hours) and cut back between each coat to get a really smooth finish. You can finish the final coat with 1000 grit wet and dry or 0000 wire wool.

Once this is ready, use a rag to wipe the surface with boiled linseed oil with a drop of liquid dryer in it. Then, without waiting for the oil to dry, dab on spots of the green. The green is an artists' oil colour called oxide of chromium. It is applied using a plastic dishwash scourer to give the basic pattern. I used to use a feather, but a student came up with the idea of using a scourer. It works and is easier.

Once the background has been prepared and a layer of linseed oil applied, green colouring (oxide of chromium) is dabbed on. Here I am using a feather, but you can use a dishwash scourer.

The green colouring, like the boiled linseed oil, should have a drop of liquid dryer added to make sure it will dry overnight. Once the work is dry, glaze it with linseed oil again before resuming. The oil adds a depth so that, as with real marble, you can see below the surface. This time add a touch of white artists' oil paint to the green, but do not mix them together thoroughly – you want a streaky effect. Using a goose feather cut to a serrated edge, apply the paint in random squiggles to

Once the green is dry, another layer of linseed oil is added and a touch of white paint is added to the green and applied using a goose feather to create a streaky effect.

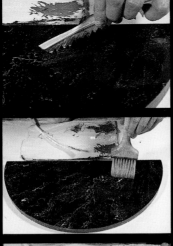

represent the veining in the marble. This adds layers of depth to the work so the finished piece does not look like a two dimensional painting on the surface of the material. The squiggles are made over the dabs put on by the dishwash scourer.

Now spot in touches of white and use a hog's hair softening brush or hake brush to soften the lines of the marbling. Just soften the painted surface. A hog's hair brush is the more expensive of the alternatives, but sometimes a hake brush loses hairs on to the work.

To finish, use at least three coats of varnish to recreate the hard, shiny look of the stone you are trying to emulate. After two coats of varnish cut back the surface with 1000 grade dampened wet-and-dry abrasive. Apply the third coat and cut back lightly with well soaked wet-and-dry.

Finally, if the table top is mainly for decoration you can finish off with beeswax, building up as much of a shine as you like. If the table top is going to be used a lot, do not use wax because it will mark. A hard polyurethane finish will protect the surface.

Bird's eye maple

An alternative to a marble finish for the MDF table top might be to create a bird's eye maple effect. This time the eggshell background is cinnamon.

Once the background is dry the graining is going to be added using a powder pigment called burnt umber moistened with a 50/50 mix of vinegar and water. But if the pigment is to adhere, the background must be completely free from grease. This is achieved by rubbing it with whiting.

When it is clean, a brush called a wavy mottler is just touched on to the vinegar and water mix and given the lightest of dabs on to the powder pigment. It is then dabbed and zig-zagged down the work to create the graining effect. On some parts the brush is dragged to give the clearer patches which are found in bird's eye maple.

To create the 'bird's eyes' which give the maple its name I use a pencil with a rubber in the end. I dig out some of the middle of the rubber to create a ring and dab the rubber over the still damp surface of the graining to create the circular markings of the wood. You have to work quickly – the water, vinegar and pigment mix dries in about 15 minutes.

The markings are brushed out lightly to remove hard edges and blend them into the background slightly. You have to use a badger bristle brush for this. Nothing else is soft enough to use with water and vinegar.

Again, finish the work with three coats of varnish, with the second and third coats cut back as before, and polish with wax ●

Touches of white alone are added.

A hog's hair or hake brush is used to soften the lines.

At least three coats of varnish are needed to recreate the hard, shiny look of stone you are aiming for.

For bird's eye maple the eggshell background is cinnamon. Once dry, graining is added using a mix of vinegar and water and burnt umber.

A brush called a wavy mottler is used to create the grain effect.

A badger bristle brush softens hard edges.

The eraser end of a pencil, hollowed out, creates the bird's eye effect of this distinctive graining.

Once again, the badger brush removes hard edges.

Finish with varnish and polish with wax.

The tools needed for the marbling and graining shown here – a hake brush, a pencil with an eraser in the end, a goose feather, a wavy mottler and a badger bristle brush. You can also use a dishwash pad for the first layer of green put on for verd'egypt.

Harry Levinson

Before becoming a specialist finisher, a mathematics degree had taken **Harry Levinson** into adult education for the BBC and on to directing programmes such as Horizon.

He also taught film and TV production at polytechnics and art schools and was senior lecturer at the **North East London Polytechnic** when, at 40, he decided he had to have a change.

He went back to college himself, to the **London College of Furniture**, as it then was, where he learnt about restoration.

Afterwards he set himself up as Hampstead Decorative Arts, putting marble and grain finishes on to chipboard, metal, wood and plaster in bathrooms, boardrooms and casinos.

Now he is teaching again, running courses to let others into some of the secrets he has learnt – and, he admits, still learning himself.

His courses are attended by all kinds of people – from professional furniture makers and carpenters (especially people fitting bathrooms and kitchens) to those who are just looking for an interesting hobby.

And all skill levels in all kinds of finishing are catered for, from gilding, antiquing and trompe l'oeil to the simpler effects like those of verd'egypt and bird's eye maple which he has talked about here.

Harry Levinson, 2/20 Highgate High Street, London N6 5JG. Tel: 081 348 2811.

One side of the back of this early 20th century reproduction of a Chippendale chair had been attacked by a dog, the other by a do-it-yourself restorer who did not know what he was doing. Graham Usher explains how the chair can be restored properly.

Back together again

People often come in hoping they have discovered a 'treasure' in the loft, or at an auction, or that has been bequeathed them. Rarely are the pieces what the owners hope they are. More often they are later reproductions, like the chair pictured here. It is a reproduction Chippendale chair from the early part of this century. Nonetheless, it is, generally, in good condition and is a nice piece of furniture in its own right, so it is worth restoring.

When it was given to me both sides of the top rail needed replacing. They could not be repaired.

I replaced them using Honduras mahogany in keeping with the original wood. I chose a piece close in grain structure to the original and lighter in colour – which is almost inevitable because the wood I was using was not as old as the original and wood darkens with age.

It is better to make repairs with a paler wood than the original if you cannot find a piece which is a perfect match because you can always stain it darker.

After gently reconstructing the chair, use stiff card to make templates of the damaged areas. Transfer the shapes to your chosen wood and roughly cut them out.

Glue the new pieces into position. I used pearl glue because it is what would originally have been used in the construction of the chair and with restoration it is good practice to use sympathetic materials.

Glue the joint and rub the surfaces together, holding the new pieces firmly in place with masking tape (clamping would be difficult). It is most important to have the grain of the new pieces of wood running in the same direction as the original work. Many a job has been ruined because this has been overlooked.

When the glue has set, drill through the wood blocks and into the original material so that the joint can be dowelled. I used 6mm (¼IN) dowel – enough to strengthen the joint but not so much as to weaken the wood. When you are drilling the holes remember that another one has yet to be drilled for the tenon dowel to secure it to the upright, so leave room for it.

Now the levels of each block must be cut. This is the most complicated part. Make sure you measure accurately by having the splat in place. Usually the top of the splat lines up with the top of the uprights. If it is different, measure it and mark out the appropriate lines on the blocks.

The front-to-back angle needs to be worked out if there is one.

This usually means using your eye to true up the piece. Always leave the block just a little oversize and shave it to fit. Now drill 10mm (⅜IN) holes for the tenon dowels. Mark the position of the holes using dowel points into the top of the uprights and drill the holes. Make sure they run parallel.

Once the top of the back sits properly on the uprights, scribe a line all the way round on the base of the blocks. You will have to judge it by eye, but make sure the line of the upright flows sweetly through the block to the top.

Mark this line, also by eye, then, holding the top firmly in the vice, shape the block down to the scribe marks, offering it up to the piece frequently until a minimum amount of wood is left to be removed.

Replace the top rail and hold it down firmly with a sash cord and a windlass, pulling it into the exact position that it will be when it is glued. Finish shaping the block except for the front where the

acanthus leaf and reeding design is going to be.

Mark the design on to the block. The reeding has to be carved after the block has been glued into position, but the rest can be worked flat on the bench. It is simple shallow relief carving which can

Subject:	A reproduction Chippendale style chair with ball and claw feet, fretted splat of typical design and top back with acanthus leaf carving. All of good quality.
Wood:	Mahogany – medium coloured Honduras.
Date:	Circa 1900-1920.
Clues:	The weight of the chair is an indication that it is a 20th century reproduction of an 18th century design – a period piece would be much heavier, using Cuban or Spanish mahogany.
	The colour also gives it away. It is plum red, which is very much a late Victorian and turn of the century colour. For an earlier chair I would be looking for a warm, medium to dark nutty-brown.
	The joints offer further evidence. They were dowelled, not tenoned. Dowelling tells me this chair is of later construction than the 18th century. However, the quality and colour of the chair put it not later than 1920/30.
	The screws holding the corner blocks completed the picture. They are definitely machine made, but the threads had late Victorian and turn-of-the century pitch (angle of thread). So 1900/20 will not be far out.
Problem:	The top back and splat were broken, with pieces from the top having been repaired before. One part had been chewed by a dog. The other had been filled with car body filler. They needed to be replaced.
Note:	This job is not beyond the ken of an amateur cabinetmaker with some knowledge, but is often botched because not enough attention has been paid to assessment or preparation.

be done with a veiner and a fine gouge. When you have finished the carving, sand it to finish quality.

I was taught by an old craftsman that whenever I could, I should put the workpiece in a vice or clamp it to a bench top. It is sensible to make the job as easy as possible.

The whole back is now glued up and clamped into place using the windlass method plus a few clamps to hold the splat together. ▶

In the photograph below you can see the splat after the clamps have been taken away. Note that the masking tape, which held the joint together while the glue set, is still in place. Give the glue at least 24 hours to set before cleaning up the joints.

With the repair made, the new wood now has to be stained to match the old. Use Van Dyke

Brown Water Stain, so if you do get the new wood too dark you can easily wash some off. This is the base colour and should be left a little lighter than the surrounding wood.

Van Dyke stain comes as crystals. Mix them with water in a container then heat that in a saucepan of water stirring regularly. If you live in a hardwater area, add a washing soda crystal. You can also add a couple of drops of ammonia, but if you do the wood will continue to darken down for two or three weeks, so allow for this.

Make up a strong batch and dilute it as necessary by adding more water to make it as light as the job requires. Apply with a brush or rag and wipe off the excess before it dries when the whole area is covered. When it is dry start to apply shellac polish (I used button polish).

Apply the first coats of shellac with a polisher's mop. This is a brush with zorino or goat hair bristles, which are exceptionally soft, making the mop ideal for laying on polish. When the first coat of shellac is dry, rub it down with fine glasspaper, dust it off and apply a second coat.

To have a chair like this restored would cost about £100, but the work is not beyond a competent amateur. Afterwards, as one of a pair, the chair would be worth about £500.

When the second coat is dry, clean the whole chair. I, like most restorers, use a cleaner I make myself. My particular formula is:

Boiled linseed oil 4 parts
Clear white vinegar 4 parts
Methylated spirit 2 parts

This is applied with 0000 steel wool.

Some points on the ingredients: do not buy raw linseed oil and try to boil it yourself (you will blow yourself up); you can use brown vinegar, but clear is better; you can add a drop or two of ordinary household ammonia if the piece is

really dirty, but you should wear a mask while applying the cleaner if you do this.

The polish is applied to the new wood before the chair is cleaned to mask the bare wood from the cleaner. If it is not masked a chemical reaction takes place between the steel wool and the vinegar which stains the wood a blackish colour.

If you do get a stain in this way you can remove it with oxalic acid, which is a bleach. Wear rubber gloves when using the acid. Clean a small area, such as a leg, at a time and wipe it clean with a rag.

Although a base colour of Van Dyke brown water stain was put on to the new wood, the difference between it and the original wood at this point is marked. This is as it should be, because more colouring will be added as the final coats of shellac are applied.

Before that, the brushed-on coats of shellac need to be rubbed down with 400 grit paper and grade 0000 steel wool, ready for the final coats of polish to be applied with a rubber.

A rubber in this case is a lint-free rag of cotton about 305mm (12IN) square wrapped tightly around a wad of cotton wool. The rag has to be lint free so it does not leave whisps of cotton in the polish.

To make the rubber you lay the rag flat on a surface. Take a handful of cotton wool and put it towards one corner of the rag and fold the rag tightly around it. Then twist the rag up to hold the cotton wool tightly. If you leave the part you are going to use slightly pointed it is easier to get into every

awkward corner of the job.

The shellac is put into the rubber by unfolding the rag and pouring it on to the cotton wool. This means the rubber is fully charged and a little squeeze every now and again will release some more polish. If you dip the rubber into shellac it will only soak up a small amount.

Using the rubber, apply 'bodying-in' coats of polish over the repaired areas. Feather out over the whole back with the rubber, but make sure you concentrate on the repaired areas.

Once the grain has been filled with polish and you are building up coats, you can start to work on the final colour match.

Spirit stain is applied to the repair to colour it. You may be able to see from the photograph that the colour of the repair is now slightly darker than the original wood. It needs to be because when it is sealed with a coat of polish the rubber will take off some of the colour.

It is best to add the colour in stages instead of trying to cover it in one. When you look at wood you tend to register one colour, but in fact it is made up of many colours all built up on top of and around each other.

I always start colour matching by using light hues and slowly build up to the matching tone, imitating the colour structure of the wood itself. This way you arrive at a more natural finish without getting that harsh, 'painted' look that can easily result.

Always remember when patching and colouring with dry colours or spirit stains to assimilate the surroundings rather than to copy them exactly.

People do not look at furniture with their noses touching the wood. Generally they are at least half a metre (18IN) away, so use that advantage to give depth and perspective to your colouring-in and gently layer it between coats of polish.

The chair is now almost finished. But before the final spiriting-off (cleaning the surface with the rubber charged with methylated spirit only) touch up the areas where the rubber could not quite reach. Use a fine pencil brush moistened with methylated spirit to take out the white lines made from polish-dust that would not come out when you brushed off the dust after rubbing down the polish.

Clean off the polish lightly with meths and leave it to harden for at least 24 hours. Then apply wax with 0000 steel wool to take away the brittle newness of the polish This is an old trick and worth doing, particularly with antiques. It mellows the shine and gives it more depth.

My customer was delighted by the appearance of his restored chair – and amazed that it looked as though it had been treasured and lovingly waxed for generations.

This is the secret of good restoration. It is a careful and loving process, coaxing the piece back into life. Good restoration cannot be hurried, which is why it is never cheap to have done.

You can do it yourself and it can be rewarding if you are prepared to devote all the time and loving care to it that successful restoration requires ●

Graham Usher runs short and long courses in furniture restoration, and can be contacted at: Fairhope Fine Furniture Restoration, 5 Rose Terrace, Mitchell, Nr Newquay, Cornwall TR8 5AU (Tel: 01872 510551).

Finishing materials are available from: M. D. Finney Timber & Wood Finishes, 66-68 Thirlwell Road, Sheffield S8 9TF (Tel: 0114 2588399), and Fiddes, Brindley Road, Cardiff CF1 7TX (Tel: 01222 340323).

Graham Usher

In spite of being persuaded to take an apprenticeship as a motor mechanic by his father, Graham Usher's first interest was always cabinetmaking. So, when the apprenticeship finished and Usher had passed all his engineering exams, he went straight into a job with Timothy Dewey, furniture restorers in Bath.

In the following years he learnt French polishing with Bob Cooke, an expert finisher, and eventually managed to persuade Frank Keevill, the man responsible for repairing the rood screen at Westminster Abbey after the blitz, to teach him carving. In 1975 Usher set up on his own.

Between 1980 and 1984 he worked in the USA, establishing a restoration workshop for an auction house in New Orleans.

Returning to the UK he set up in business as Fairhope Fine Furniture Restoration, teaching as well as restoring.

If you want to attend one of his courses, or you have something in need of restoring, contact him direct.

The great Windsor

Why are they called Windsors? Who first made them? Why are the people who turned the components called bodgers? There is a lot of mystery surrounding one of the most significant developments in English furniture. David Knell tries to unravel some of it.

I t is a pity the origin of the Windsor chair – one of the most important developments in the history of English furniture – is lost in the proverbial mists of time. Stools using the same basic construction technique – members wedged into a slab seat – were universal by the Middle Ages and the addition of a simple back is an elementary concept that may well be nearly as old. But it was an important development.

It is not even known precisely where or when the first examples of this revolutionary innovation were made. All that can be said is that it was *probably* somewhere around Windsor, Berkshire, and *probably* around 1700.

All the earliest Windsor chairs appear to have been made in the Thames Valley region and it is natural enough that they should be named after the local market town which acted as the collection and distribution centre.

Windsor was ideally situated on the Thames, at a time when the easiest transportation to London (the prime retail target for any goods) was by river. From London the chairs could also be shipped on to many other parts of the country by means of the efficient coastal trade routes.

It was evidently not long before Londoners and others were referring to these distinctive products as 'chairs from Windsor' or, simply, 'Windsor chairs'.

It is not surprising, then, that the early written references to Windsor chairs tend to be from places reasonably close to the town, either in advertisements by London retailers or by shops even closer to where the chairs were actually made.

It does come as a surprise, however, to find that the earliest known reference to a Windsor chair ▶

In the tradition of the Thames Valley Windsor chair makers, Stewart Linfold, in High Wycombe, still send their chairs to London, where they are sold by Harrods. They are, though, also more widely available. Prices for the lathback armchair start at £637 and for the rocker at £330.

mystery

VERNACULAR
FURNITURE

is not English at all but American. Three Windsor chairs are listed in the will inventory of John Jones, a Philadelphian merchant, in 1708.

Given Jones's occupation, it seems likely that his chairs were imported from England rather than being native American products.

One of the earliest English references to Windsor chairs occurs in a letter written by Lord Percival in 1724. He describes a visit to the garden at Hall Barn in Buckinghamshire and mentions that, since the grounds were so large, his wife "was carr'd in a Windsor chair like those at Versailles".

Any link between the humble Windsor chair and the grand palace of Versailles might seem rather odd. Certainly Lord Percival's allusion puzzled historians for years until it was discovered that it was an 18th century custom to place Windsor chairs on wheeled platforms in the same way that grander chairs were rolled on wheels and used to parade Louis XIV and his courtiers around the grounds of Versailles.

The earliest illustration of Windsor chairs, a drawing of about 1733, shows two of them mounted on wheeled platforms and being driven around the gardens of the Rotunda at Stowe. A steering column is connected to the front wheel of each platform, allowing the occupant to guide the contraption as he was pushed along by friends or servants. It seems the average 18th-century aristocrat would have been somewhat unimpressed by the joys of jogging.

The Windsor chair appears to have been almost inextricably linked with garden use throughout the 18th century. John Brown, of London, was advertising "all sorts of Windsor Garden Chairs of all sizes painted green or in the wood" in 1727 and their occasional appearance in 18th-century paintings is nearly always as outdoor seating.

No doubt the rustic nature of the Windsor form enhanced its popularity since it was ideally suited to the current vogue among the nobility for contrived pastoralism – a trendy urge to play at being peasants in an artificially bucolic setting.

There are exceptions to the garden rule. One painting of the 1730s, for example, shows a few Windsors ranged near the dining table in a baronial hall. There are also exceptionally high quality Windsor chairs in mahogany from the period which

A Thames Valley bow-back Windsor in yew with elm seat, circa 1790, flanked by (left) a yew and elm bow-back from north-eastern England, circa 1850, and (right) an ash and elm bow-back from the West Country, made about 1800 and still bearing its original dark green paint. (Courtesy of Sotheby's, Sussex)

were evidently intended for indoor use.

A bookish connection is suggested by the "Seaven Japan'd Windsor Chairs" listed in the library of the Duke of Chandos in 1725 and by the large set ordered by Oxford University for use in the Bodleian in 1766.

A 1765 inventory of the Duke of Cumberland's furniture at Windsor Great Lodge, on the other hand, includes "one mahogany elbow Windsor chair" in the butler's pantry.

There was apparently no social restriction on where the Windsor could be found. Nor, it will be noted, was its ownership by any means confined to the lower classes. The popular notion of the Windsor chair originating purely as 'country' furniture for the farmhouse or cottage must be seriously questioned.

It is quite possible that the first Windsors suddenly emerged fully formed (much like the first products of the printing press – an evolutionary process consistent with many other furniture types but entirely opposite to the one traditionally accepted for Windsor chairs.

The primary back members of 18th-century Windsors almost invariably consist of a series of vertical spindles. Sometimes included is a central splat, often of a vasiform shape – echoing those used in fashionable joined chairs – and occasionally pierced. In the earliest type, the comb-back, all these members are united at the top by a horizontal crest rail, the ends of which frequently flourish into rounded 'ears'.

Left. Ash and elm comb-back Windsor from the Thames Valley region, c1750. (Courtesy of Sotheby's, Sussex)

Right. Modern copy of an 18th-century Gothic Windsor. A lively interpretation but lacking the delicacy of the originals. (Courtesy Sotheby's)

As to whether the legs of the chair were united by stretchers or not appears to have been decided by regional conventions, economic considerations or merely the personal whim of the individual chairmaker or workshop.

There is nothing to support the view that chairs without stretchers are necessarily older then those with them. Indeed, the first wedged chairs that we would now recognise as being Windsors may well have been provided with stretchers. Examples without stretchers, on the other hand, were demonstrably still being made in some areas well into the 19th century. It is possible that the style may merely represent a less sophisticated variation rather than being an archaic retention of the prototypal form.

Since the first Windsors appear to have been made some three decades before the earliest surviving illustration of them, we simply cannot know for sure exactly what they looked like.

Where stretchers are incorporated in a comb-back Windsor they are typically aligned in an 'H' formation: a pair of stretchers connecting front and rear legs and tied together by a central one.

An alternative to the comb-back is the bow-back, which had developed by the middle of the 18th century. Here the horizontal crest rail was replaced by a bent hoop, the ends of which terminated in either the arm bow or the seat.

The same period also saw the introduction of a bowed front stretcher (the so-called crinoline type) as an optional form. Cabriole legs were occasionally used for front legs on better chairs.

The central splats of both comb-backs and bow-backs produced in the London/Thames Valley region during the second half of the 18th century were often pierced in distinctive patterns.

A bow-back with its splat pierced in the Chippendale manner has been noted bearing the trade card of William Webb, recorded as working in Newington, Surrey, between 1792 and 1808.

Perhaps the best known pattern, a pierced motif in the form of a wheel, is on another bow-back which bears an inscription giving directions on how it was to be shipped to Gateshead. The details suggest a transportation date between 1779 and 1783.

In the most striking style of all, however, the spindles are dispensed with altogether and, apart from

Left. Yew and elm bow-back with wheel motif incorporated in the splat, Thames Valley, c1780. An identical chair was one of six shipped to Gateshead between 1779 and 1783. (Courtesy Sotheby's)

Right. Cherry and elm Windsor with boxwood stringing, Mendlesham area, Suffolk, c1820. (Courtesy Oswald Simpson)

the arm bow, back bow and arm supports, the back is composed entirely of splats pierced to resemble medieval tracery. The back bow is normally formed as a pointed, or lancet, arch to complete the Gothic appearance.

To many, Gothic style represents the zenith in Windsor design. That such chairs were also highly esteemed by contemporaries is suggested by the fact that they were made from yew (except for the seat, which is elm), a more expensive timber than the ash or fruitwood usual in lesser chairs.

Windsor styles produced in the Thames Valley region diversified still further during the 19th century and the industry became particularly concentrated around High Wycombe, in Buckinghamshire. However this region was by no means the only one making Windsor chairs by this time and one of the most interesting challenges facing the historian is exploring the Windsor traditions that emerged in other parts of Britain. Regional types are often highly distinctive and can frequently be readily identified by their stylistic and constructional characteristics.

One of the most publicised regional varieties is the square-back design made around Mendlesham, Suffolk, during the first half of the 19th century.

Typically, these have a pierced splat flanked by spindles and a row of three turned balls below the top rail. Since they were regarded as special, rather than everyday chairs they nearly always have arms.

Oral tradition attributes their invention to father and son Daniel and Richard Day. No contemporary record of a local chairmaker named Daniel Day has so far been traced, although one named Richard Day was born in Mendlesham in 1783 and died there in 1838.

The chairs are something of an enigma since they appear to represent an entirely isolated tradition of Windsor chairmaking in East Anglia.

A significant Windsor chair industry also emerged in the West Country during the 18th and 19th centuries and some of the most distinctive designs were made in and around the village of Yealmpton, in Devon, from the early 1800s to about 1850. These include bow-back armchairs, in which the arms are bent from flattened sections of ash, and examples of the continuous-arm Windsor, in which the back bow and the arms are formed from one continuous strip of wood.

The continuous arm Windsor is a style once thought to have been peculiar to North America, and is still thought by some to have developed there. But that the continuous-arm Windsors found in Devon are not merely American imports is indicated not only by the slight differences in style, but also by an examination of the timber. American Windsors of this type and period tend to have chestnut, pine or whitewood seats, but the seats of the English versions are made of elm or sycamore.

The constraints of a brief survey have allowed me to speculate on the origins of the Windsor chair in the 18th century and to touch fleetingly on only three of the regional traditions which it spawned.

There was also a profusion of variations of the Windsor in the Thames Valley and beyond during the 19th century, the Celtic and North American traditions, the West Country types and the diverse industries of north-eastern England ●

Select bibliography

COTTON, BERNARD D. *The English Regional Chair.* Antique Collectors' Club, 1990.

CRISPIN, THOMAS. *The English Windsor Chair.* Alan Sutton, 1992.

KNELL, DAVID. *English Country Furniture.* Barrie & Jenkins, 1992.

ROE, F GORDON. *Windsor Chairs.* Phoenix, 1953.

SPARKES, IVAN. *The English Country Chair.* Spurbooks, 1975.

A handy table for the hall

This semi-circular occasional table is neat enough to fit in a passageway or small hall. Kenneth Bramley shows how he made it.

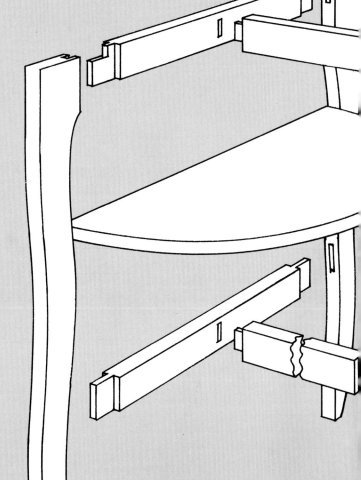

This table was made from well seasoned Japanese oak which is good to work and has a good colour and grain pattern. Quarter sawn planks show off the grain to its best. Use pieces finished to 25mm (1IN) thick for the framework and 15mm (⅝IN) thick for the top centre panel and shelf. I always set out working from the face side and face edge.

The top. Make a plywood template for the top using the dimensions in FIG 1 and mark on it the positions of the boards and joints, working from a centre line. Using the template, mark out the positions for the mortises in pieces A and B and the tenons on pieces C and D.

Before cutting them out, mark and cut grooves 8mm (⁵⁄₁₆IN) wide and 10mm (⅜IN) deep round the inside edges of each board to take tongues on the centre panel. The grooves should be 8mm (⁵⁄₁₆IN) down from the face side.

MEASURING

Cramp the frame together dry, making sure the joints fit together properly, and check it is square by measuring the diagonals. Make a template to the size of the centre space for the panel. Use the template to mark out the centre panel, making the panel 10mm (⅜IN) larger all round to allow for the tongues.

Cut out the panel and cut the tongues all round to match the grooves in the top frame. After fitting the top together dry to check, it can be glued and cramped. When the glue has cured, plane and sand both sides with the grain.

Make another template to the finished size and shape of the top and mark on it the position of the three locating dowels (FIG 2). Cut out the top, clean up the edges and fix an oak edging strip round the outside circumference. Round the edges to merge the grain with the top. Use the template to mark the dowel positions on the underside of the top. Mark the centres with a bradawl and drill the holes 10mm (⅜IN) DIA x 17mm (¹¹⁄₁₆IN) deep.

The frame. Mark and cut out the pieces for the back frame using

CUTTING LIST
finished sizes in mm, (inches in brackets)

Top pieces	x 1	685 x 75 x 25	(27 x 3 x 1)
	x 1	535 x 100 x 25	(21 x 4 x 1)
	x 2	355 x 100 x 25	(14 x 4 x 1)
	x 1	510 x 190 x 15	(20 x 7½ x ⅝"
Shelf	x 1	510 x 255 x 15	(20 x 10 x ⅝"
Legs	x 3	760 x 50 x 25	(30 x 2 x 1)
Back rails	x 2	522 x 45 x 25	(20½ x 1¾ x
Front rails	x 2	318 x 45 x 25	(12½ x 1¾ x

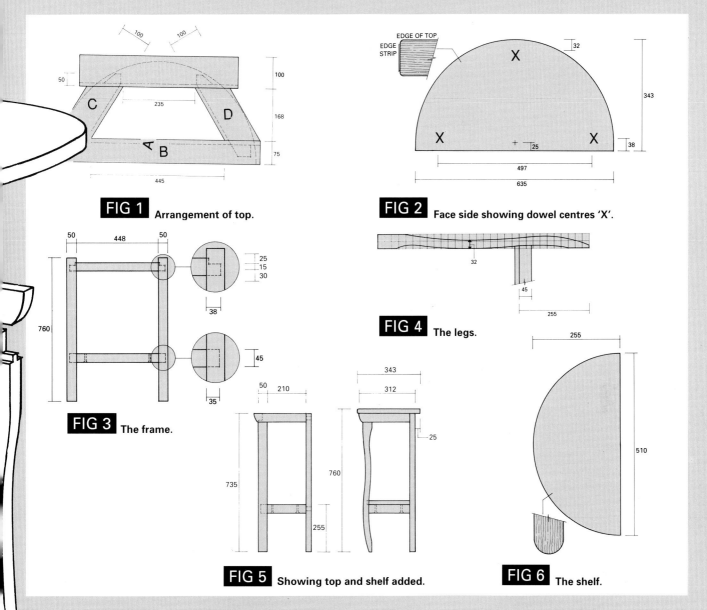

FIG 1 Arrangement of top.

FIG 2 Face side showing dowel centres 'X'.

FIG 3 The frame.

FIG 4 The legs.

FIG 5 Showing top and shelf added.

FIG 6 The shelf.

FIG 3. Clamp the legs together to mark out the mortises for the tenons in both legs at the same time so they match, then chop the mortises out. The top mortises are 38mm (1½IN) deep and the haunches 10mm (³⁄₈IN) deep. The bottom mortises are plain, 35mm (1³⁄₈IN) deep. Mark and cut out the top rail tenons.

Make a template for the shape of the legs using FIG 4. Mark and cut out the legs and clean up the edges. Cramp up the legs and top rail dry and mark out the bottom rail to fit between the legs. Mark and cut out the tenons to fit the mortises in the legs. Cramp up the whole frame dry and check that it is square by measuring the diagonals.

Before gluing the frame together drill two countersunk screw holes up through the bottom rail, each one 50mm (2IN) in from each leg. These are to allow the shelf to be screwed on later. Now glue and cramp up the frame. When the glue has cured, cut off the horns at the top, plane and clean up the whole frame.

Mark and cut out the third leg and two remaining rails using FIG 4 and 5. Mark and chop out the through mortise in the top rail, allowing the tenon shoulder to be set in by 20mm (³⁄₄IN). Put a circumference on the front end of the rail.

Mark and cut out the tenon at the top of the leg and chop the 35mm (1³⁄₈IN) deep mortise in the back of the leg. Cut out the shape of the leg using the same template as for the other two, and clean up. Mark out and cut the tenon on the bottom rail.

Mark out and cut the tenons in the two short rails to fit into through

mortises in the back rails. Mark and chop out the mortises in the centre of the back rails. The through mortises should be wedged.

Drill two countersunk screw holes up through the bottom rail, one 25mm (1IN) in from the front leg and the other 50mm (2IN) in from the back rail. These are for screwing on the shelf later.

SQUARENESS

Assembly. After cramping up dry to check for squareness, glue and cramp up the front leg and rails to the back frame. Use the previously cut template of the top to mark the positions for the three dowel holes on the top of the frame, allowing the template to overhang the back of the frame by 25mm (1IN). Drill the holes and glue in the 10mm (³⁄₈IN) DIA dowels.

Mark and cut out the semi-circular shelf (FIG 6), and round the circumference edge using a router or spokeshave. Clean up all edges and surfaces. Mark and cut out the shelf to fit round the back legs so the back of the shelf is level with the back of the frame. Screw the shelf to the frame with four 50mm (2IN) countersunk screws through the pre-drilled holes in the bottom rails. Finally, glue the top to the frame using the locating dowels.

Use fine grit paper to clean up the completed table and clean with white spirit. I used three coats of interior Ronseal hardglaze clear gloss varnish, cutting back between coats, to finish. □

PROJECT

Inspired by the land of the Pharaohs

When designer-maker Nicholas Chandler was commissioned to make some unusual dining furniture, he looked to the land of the pharaohs for inspiration. In this two-part project he describes how he designed, then made, the chairs and table. First, the chairs.

When I was commissioned to make this dining set the client said he wanted a pedestal leg table and six chairs in a blonde coloured wood in a surreal or Egyptian style.

I had great fun on the surreal theme, using the Belgian surrealist painter Magritte for inspiration, with bowler hats, sausages and pipes. But I could not really see my sketches coming off the page into real life. If I cannot visualise the finished article, I know it hasn't got a future. I also thought the novelty would soon wear off.

The Egyptian theme really caught my imagination as it is a subject that has always fascinated me – pyramids, tombs, gold, the beautifully stylised depiction of events in hieroglyphics. And, of course, those rich, lovely colours.

I started by drawing a steep pyramid form, but with a broad flat top, like the pylons of the temple of Isis at Philae. This was the basis for the chair back shape. By making the shape a frame rather than a solid board I could span it horizontally with 'rungs' coloured a rich turquoise, as on Tutankhamen's gold funeral mask.

The wood therefore needed to be as gold coloured as possible and I settled on Canadian rock maple, which would be finished with Danish oil or lacquer.

The shape made a powerful image when viewed from the front or back and next I had to design the side view shape. I wanted to make the chairs as comfortable as possible – dining chairs are so often extremely uncomfortable, particularly when sitting on them for hours at a time.

When designing a chair you have to begin by setting yourself four basic dimensions – the height of the seat from the floor, the width and depth of the seat, and the angle of the back. After this you have great freedom in terms of form.

I began by drawing round a ⅛th scale model man with moveable limbs in a sitting position. I accepted that the height of the seat would be around 405-430mm (16-17IN) and the back to lean at 5DEG. I made the back shape to follow the contours of the model's back.

The side rails and front legs were to have a 'four square' appearance. I could see from the front view drawing of the chair back that the back of the seat would be narrow, so I splayed the side rails to the front legs. The feet of the front legs would then line up with those of the back frame.

I hate using stretchers on chair legs unless they are aesthetically necessary, so I didn't.

With the design drawings approved by the client I next made a full

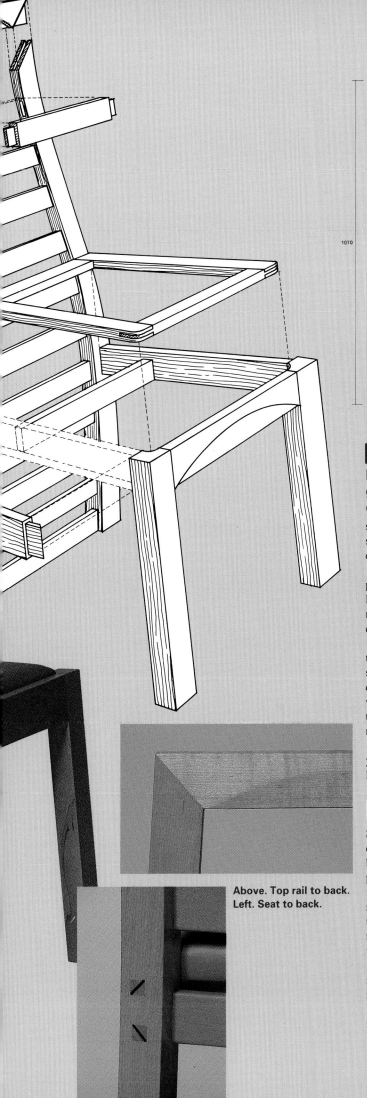

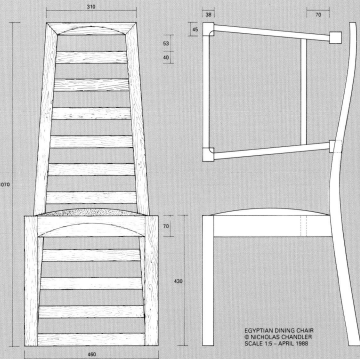

310

38 70

45

53
40

1070

70

430

70

460

EGYPTIAN DINING CHAIR
© NICHOLAS CHANDLER
SCALE 1:5 – APRIL 1988

FIG 1

Front view of the chair giving overall dimensions.

FIG 2

Side and top view of the chair.

sized chair in pine. This not only produces templates and jigs and shows the best way of going about the job, but also shows up any design faults that may not have been apparent on the drawing board.

I was surprised by the model. The chair had looked so majestic on paper but the model resembled a souped-up deckchair. There were line errors – the back legs needed to be tapered towards the top and reduced in width; the rungs in the back needed to be narrower and curved to improve comfort.

When sitting at a dining table many people tuck their legs under the chair or even curl their ankles round the legs. When I tried this sitting in my chair I found the lower edge of the front rail cut into my calves. This was corrected by cutting out a hyperbolic arch in the rail with a compass plane. Having created the feature, I repeated it on the top back frame member and the back of the bottom frame member to make it look less chunky.

It is better to do all your thinking at the drawing board and make your mistakes on a mock-up rather than trying to think through problems and rectify mistakes while you are making the finished article.

Making the chair

Start by cutting out all the pieces, preparing them to size using the cutting list and Figs 1 and 2, and cleaning up. When cutting out the back legs (Fig 3) keep the waste pieces as they will be useful for packing when sawing and mortising later.

There are 204 mortises to be cut in six chairs (34 per chair) so I recommend the use of a mortiser or router for this. Using a power tool also means you need only mark the start and stop points of the mortises as the side fence controls the position from the edge of the wood.

Cut the mortises in the front of the back legs to receive the side rails first. The leg will have to be held with tapered battens for machining as it is tapered.

Tenons can be marked out and cut by hand but, again, a spindle moulder makes the job a lot easier.

Above. Top rail to back.
Left. Seat to back.

Because of the shape of the back frame, each rung is a different length. Accurate marking out and cutting is essential or a glue line will show on this light coloured wood. I used a full-sized frame fixed to a back board as a jig so each rung could be accurately marked out and tested for a perfect fit.

With all the rungs cut out they are covered with leather, which is carefully trimmed back to the tenon shoulder line and glued on. There is a special adhesive for leather called Tenaxatex. It is recommended for use watered down 10 to 1, but I found five parts water to one part glue better. Or else PVA watered down 50/50 is fine.

The top rail of the back frame is a mitred bridle joint to the legs. The angles of the mitres are not 45DEG, but 46DEG and 48DEG to allow for the splay of the legs. The bottom rail is a straightforward stopped and shouldered tenon.

I marked out the arched depressions on the front rail and the two back rails by bending a steel rule. It was held at each end and at a third point in the centre of the arch. The depression can be cut out with a compass plane or spokeshave.

CRAMPING UP

Fit the whole back frame together dry and cramp it up so you can see where the cramp blocks will go and that the cramps are set in the right positions. When you are ready, glue it up and cramp.

Now make the front leg frame. The front rail is fitted flush with the front legs. I hate shoulders there as they catch the backs of the legs. Fit the legs and rail together dry as before, then glue and cramp up.

The side rails have angled tenons at each end (FIG 4). Where they meet the back frame I used twin through stub tenons wedged diagonally with ebony (FIG 5). This is a feature which is not only mechanically strong at a critical point on the chair, but also provides a visual 'pull' of the side rails into the back frame. The ebony gives an impression of leather thongs that would have been used by the Egyptians for binding furniture together at joints.

Apply the finish now, before making and fitting the leather seat. The

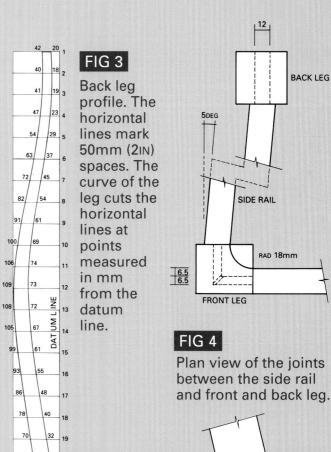

FIG 3

Back leg profile. The horizontal lines mark 50mm (2IN) spaces. The curve of the leg cuts the horizontal lines at points measured in mm from the datum line.

FIG 4

Plan view of the joints between the side rail and front and back leg.

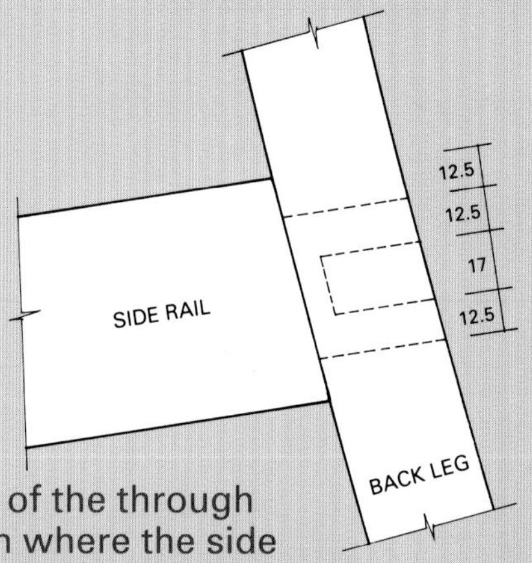

FIG 5

Side view of the through stub tenon where the side rail joins the back leg.

leather cladding on the rungs must be carefully masked off when applying finish to the back frame, so make sure it is. I have experimented with various finishes from Danish oil to pre-catalysed lacquers and water-based cellulose. Your choice will depend on personal taste and the use or abuse your chairs are likely to get. A waterproof coating is advisable if sticky fingers are likely to come into contact with them.

The seat frame is made from beech, using bridle joints at the corners. It should be made 5mm (³⁄₁₆IN) smaller than the space it fits into. The frame is upholstered using hessian webbing which is tensioned tightly over the frame and tacked underneath. On top of the webbing use 38mm (1½IN) upholstery foam, or 25mm (1IN) of upholstery foam topped with 12mm (½IN) of soft foam if you prefer a softer seat. Cut the foam to size and chamfer the top edges. The seat is covered in the same blue leather as used on the frame rungs. It is tensioned evenly over the foam and tacked to the underneath of the frame.

It rests on a rail fitted between the side rails, 70mm (2¾IN) forward of the back frame. The rail is fitted flush with the undersides of the side rails and 20mm (¾IN) down from the tops of the rails. The seat is supported at the front by recesses cut in the inside corners of the front legs (FIG 2) ☐ Part Two (matching table) is on page 86.

Nicholas Chandler, Woodpeckers, Rackenford, Tiverton, Devon EX16 8ER. Tel: 0884 88380.

CUTTING LIST

finished sizes in mm, (inches in brackets)

	mm	inches
Back legs x 2		
cut from	1200 x 200 x 45	(47¼ x 8 x 1¾)
Top rail	310 x 40 x 20	(12¼ x 1⅝ x ¾)
Bottom rail	410 x 50 x 38	(16¼ x 2 x 1½)
Rungs x 10		
various lengths		
up to	460 x 40 x 20	(18 x 1⅝ x ¾)
Front legs x 2	420 x 45 x 38	(16⅝ x 1¾ x 1½)
Side rails x 2	425 x 70 x 20	(16¾ x 2¾ x ¾)
Front rail	460 x 70 x 20	(18 x 2¾ x ¾)
Seat frame		
cut from beech	50 x 25	(2 x 1)

Leather supplier: Connelly Bros (Furriers) Limited, Wandle Bank, Wimbledon, London SW19 1DW (Telephone: 0181 542 5251).

Make yourself a show piece

This low table in rosewood was made by cabinetmaker Adrian Parfitt as an exhibition piece. Here he explains how to make it.

People can be reluctant to buy furniture when it is just a drawing on a piece of paper. They want to touch it, which is why, occasionally, I produce pieces which have not been commissioned. This low table in rosewood was one of them.

Such pieces are always good for exhibiting – and you have to attend shows when you are in business to get your name known and to keep yourself in front of potential customers. I like to have new pieces to exhibit because I think there is nothing worse than

Adrian Parfitt in his workshop

LOW TABLE CUTTING LIST		

Finished sizes in mm (inches in brackets)

ROSEWOOD

Legs	x 6	535 x 75 x 22 (21 x 3 x $^7/_8$)
Bottom rails	x 6	230 x 55 x 40 (9 x 2 $^1/_4$ x 1 $^5/_8$)
Laminated edgings	x 24	460 x 25 x 3 (18 x 1 x $^1/_8$)
Veneer	x 6	380 x 342 x 3 (15 x 13 $^1/_2$ x $^1/_8$)

CHERRY

Laminated edgings	x 6	460 x 25 x 3 (18 x 1 x $^1/_8$)
Inlay	x 6	405 x 3 x 3 (16 x $^1/_8$ x $^1/_8$)

MDF

Top	x 1	760 DIA x 18 (30 DIA x $^3/_4$)

The finished table showing construction details.

going to an exhibition and seeing pieces of furniture that have been on show for the past five years.

There was a show coming up and I'd had a piece of rosewood in the workshop for some time. I had seen it during a visit to a timber supplier and I just could not resist it, although I had no immediate use for it.

With the exhibition imminent I decided I could afford to spend some time designing something which would show off the full beauty of the wood.

I like to use flowing curves in my designs – which is completely opposite to how my work used to be. A few years ago it was all squares.

After playing around with several ideas on paper I settled on this light, airy design which would be just as appropriate in a modern home as in a period setting.

Making the table

Because all the curves of the legs and the bottom rails have to be the same you need to make templates of them to follow. I cut them out of MDF.

The top is made up from 18mm MDF with 3mm ($^1/_8$ IN) rosewood veneered on to it. There is a laminated edging made up of four strips of rosewood with a strip of cherry on the inside edge to match the stringing between the rosewood veneer.

Use the MDF templates to mark out the six legs and six bottom rails (you can make templates by scaling up the drawings over the page). Cut out the legs and rails just full of the line.

Plane the legs down to 22mm ($^7/_8$ IN) and clean them up.

The rails are fixed to the legs with slotted dovetail joints. Rout the slots into the bottom of the legs using a piece of MDF as a simple jig.

Mark the dovetails on the bottom rails and cut them out. Clean up and dry assemble the legs and rails to shape them using a combination of saw, spokeshave, rasp and glasspaper.

Cut the tenons at the tops of the legs and glue the rails into the legs. You can clamp them using a band clamp or some home-made variation you can devise for yourself. ▶

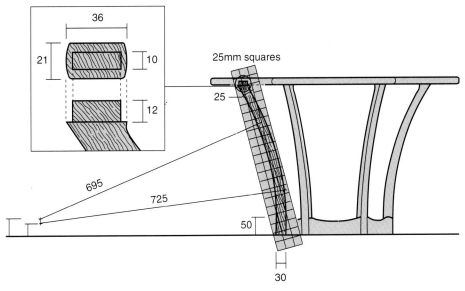

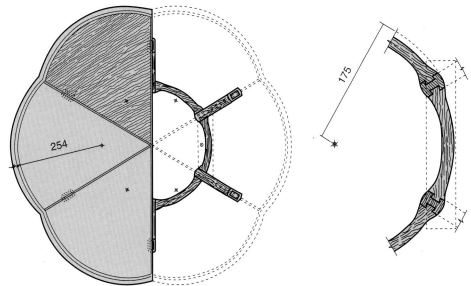

Once the glue has set, run the rails into the legs so the assembly follows smooth lines.

To make the top, cut a circle of MDF slightly larger than the 760mm (30IN) DIA you will end up with and divide it (but don't cut it) into six segments.

You can probably remember from your school days how to work out the size of each segment. You can either set the angle at the centre at 60DEG or use the formula for the circumference of πD divided by six (there being six segments).

The curve on each segment of the top is easily achieved by putting a trammel bar some distance in from the centre of the table and describing an arc. I did not measure the distance in, I used what looked right, which turned out to be about 254mm (10 IN). Do not make the curve too tight or the legs will look as if they are not curved enough. The fixed end of the trammel bar must be on a line which bisects the angle at the centre of the table.

At the same time as I was marking out the table top I marked out the mould for the laminated lipping, which is made up from scrap MDF, two thicknesses being glued together to give the mould the thickness you require. You can then use the inner part of the laminating mould as a template and use a router with a template follower to shape the top of the table as required.

The laminated lipping is made up in six separate parts from four, 3mm (1/8 IN) strips of rosewood and one strip of cherry on the inside. I used Cascamite to glue them together in the mould and then clamped the mould up.

Adrian Parfitt

Before moving to Elsworth, Cambridge, 18 years ago Adrian Parfitt served his apprenticeship as a bench joiner in London, working on shop and hotel fittings.

In Elsworth he worked for two companies making high class joinery, fitted furniture and restoration work. He made some cabinets for hotels and museums and realised that was what he wanted to spend his time doing.

Gradually he became more interested in cabinet-making and realised if he wanted to produce good quality furniture, as often as possible to his own designs, he would have to work for himself. So, 10 years ago he set up his own business.

Then, as now, most of the jobs he gained were local and were domestic. But then they were mostly for built-in furniture or pieces copied from magazines such as 'Homes and Gardens'. As his reputation has grown he has been commissioned to produce more of his own designs.
Adrian Parfitt, The Brick Barn, Dear's Farm, Fardell's Lane, Elsworth, Cambridge. Tel: 0954 7312.

When the glue is dry, plane the mouldings down to the 21mm (7/8 IN) thickness that the top will be (18mm [3/4 IN] MDF plus 3mm [1/8 IN] veneer).

The top is veneered using the traditional method of veneer hammer and Scotch glue.

Let in cherry stringing between the segments after routing out the grooves for it.

Glue the edging on (again, I used Cascamite for this), flush it off and round over the edge with a router.

Chop out the stopped mortises for the legs on the underside of the table top and fit the top on to the legs.

Clean it all up and glue the top to the legs. As the top is MDF there should not be any movement in it so it does not need to be allowed for in construction.

Finish is a matter of preference. I used three coats of lacquer cut back with 0000 wire wool and waxed ●

Inspired by the land of the Pharaohs ②

In his previous article (page 80) Nicholas Chandler described how he designed and made dining chairs inspired by the Egyptian pyramids. Here he explains how he made the table to go with them.

The style of this dining table had to reflect the design of the chairs I had made to go with it. It had to reflect their tapered back frame, which it does because the shape is repeated on the four sides of the pedestal base, making a truncated pyramid.

I increased the proportions of the frame dimensions on the table because I wanted something that was solid, both visually and physically. The rungs are similar to those in the chair backs, although they are flat, not curved.

The pyramid shape created two problems – the top of the base would be too small by itself to support the table top and the base would be too wide, halving the footroom at the sides. Diners would be constantly kicking it.

I solved the first problem by designing some substantial bracing rails. The top needed strong bracing anyway, and following the maxim 'make a feature from a fault' I beefed it up even more and curved up the ends. This shape looked wing-like – similar to the wings of the Egyptian god Osiris, further emphasising the Egyptian theme. I wanted to paint wing feathers on this feature, but the client wouldn't have it.

again. Fresh eyes can see what tired ones may miss.

A favourite trick of mine is to turn the model upside down. I discovered this by accident when I had been labouring for hours over a piece of calligraphy. I knew it didn't look right but couldn't work out why. In anger and frustration I threw it across the table. It landed upside down and I could see at once what was wrong – I couldn't read the writing but I could see the shapes and spaces in between which gave the game away.

I now look at all my designs upside down – if it looks this good upside down just think how good it must be right way up! I also ask my wife. She is no artist or designer, but I have come to trust her gut feeling about a design. If she doesn't like it, but doesn't know why, it usually reflects a tiny doubt I had about the design anyway.

Someone I knew once commented on my 'fetish' (as he put it) for model making. "I never make models," he said, "I just seem to know what's right." Which is probably why he never made a living at cabinet making. His prices were ridiculously cheap, the finishing was awful and the construction decidedly suspect – it probably got in the way of his ego. The rest of us make models to test the physical appearance of our designs.

There are two transverse rails angled to fit snugly either side of the base top and two wings running down the length of the table. The wings butt join the base top and are cut to fit round the transverse rails. The result is an extremely sturdy and heavy structure.

The second problem, the wide base, was solved by narrowing the end frames and making the base rectangular in plan, reflecting the fact that the top is longer than it is wide. The angle of the side frame members was also adjusted to 5 DEG. The ends are 10DEG off vertical. This meant the area at the top of the base would not be too small. If both angles had been 10DEG the top of the pedestal would only have been 150mm wide – not much on which to rest a table 1200mm wide.

Next I made a ⅛th scale model of the table with hardboard and a hot glue gun. I hate model making for its own sake, but sometimes it is necessary to prove that the theory of the drawings will work in 3D reality. Does it look good as you walk round it, or are there any awkward areas to be reworked?

When designing you can become bogged down in the details without looking at the design as a whole. You need to stand back and look at it, or even put it away for a few days before looking at it

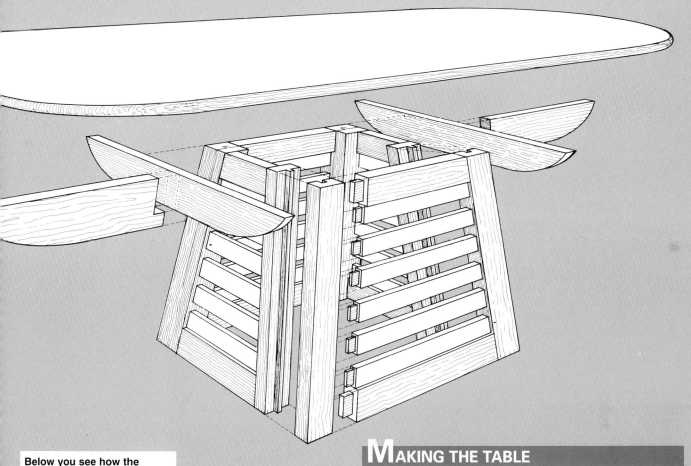

Below you see how the design elements of the chair, featured in the article on page 80, are carried through into this table to make a distinctive and attractive dining suite.

MAKING THE TABLE

Whenever I make a table I always make the top first, because no matter how long the wood has been in my heated workshop there is always some movement or shrinkage once it becomes a table top. As the top is the most important part of a table you need to spend some time getting it absolutely right.

In this case it is 40mm (1⅝IN) thick maple, so I didn't want to risk any glue lines opening up. Some makers simply butt join the edges of the boards or use dowels in the edges, but I prefer to over engineer, just to make sure. I work loose tongue and groove joints 6mm (¼IN) down from the top surface and 6mm up from the underside. This gives near perfect alignment which saves much time in levelling down.

The text books say you should align boards with the growth rings turning alternatively upwards and downwards to minimise the effect of shrinkage. Others say this can cause rippling, and it is better to have the growth rings facing all the same way, even if this does lead to a bowed or cupped shape.

I prefer to avoid the problem altogether by using quarter-sawn boards. That way the growth rings are at right angles to the top surface and there is no cupping, warping or twisting.

When gluing up the top boards make sure you work on a large, flat surface. Check for twisting with winding sticks and correct with wedges under the appropriate corner. When dry, clean up the top with a thicknessing sander or use a try plane to take off the high spots. Use sharp blades as maple is a close grained hardwood and any tears will show. I keep two spare honed blades handy so when the one I am using begins to show signs of losing its edge I can pop a spare one in without losing rhythm or momentum.

Plane the top at a 45DEG angle to the long edge so you take a shearing cut. Check the surface with a long wooden straight edge. Rub bright coloured chalk along the straight edge and mark across the grain every 300mm (12IN) along the length of the top. You will see any high spots left. Repeat this along the grain and diagonally.

When both sides are flat, finish by sanding. A pad sander will take ▶

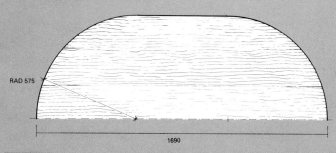

FIG 1

Half plan view of the table top.

RAD 575

1690

CUTTING LIST
finished sizes in mm, (inches in brackets)

Pedestal base		
Side frames		
Top rails x 2	400 x 90 x 45	(15¾ x 3½ x 1¾)
Bottom rails x 2	620 x 90 x 45	(24½ x 3½ x 1¾)
Sides x 4	750 x 90 x 45	(29⅝ x 3½ x 1¾)
Rungs x 2	505 x 50 x 20	(19¾ x 2 x ¾)
x 2	468	(18¾)
x 2	435	(17³⁄₁₆)
x 2	402	(15¾)
x 2	370	(14⅝)
x 2	336	(9¼)
End frames		
Top rails x 2	255 x 90 x 45	(10 x 3½ x 1¾)
Bottom rails x 2	360 x 90 x 45	(14³⁄₁₆ x 3½ x 1¾)
Sides x 4	750 x 90 x 45	(29⅝ x 3½ x 1¾)
Rungs x 2	285 x 50 x 20	(11¼ x 2 x ¾)
x 2	265	(10⅜)
x 2	250	(9¾)
x 2	235	(9¼)
x 2	220	(8¾)
x 2	205	(8¼)
Table top		
make up to	1690 x 1150 x 40	(66½ x 45⅜ x 1⅝)
Bracing rails		
Transverse x 2	975 x 100 x 40	(38⅜ x 4 x 1⅝)
Longitudinal x 2	520 x 130 x 40	(20½ x 5⅛ x 1⅝)

the drudge out of this job. I use aluminium oxide paper which lasts longer than ordinary paper. Start with 80 grit and work down to 180. Finish with 240 grit when the final shaping is done.

Mark out the D ends of the top (FIG 1) with large compasses set to 575mm (22⅝IN) radius. Cut off the waste and clean up the profile with a compass plane or spokeshave.

Radius the edge of the top with a router and 20mm (¾IN) radius cutter. It is a good idea to have help and spread padding on the floor when working on the top as it is heavy and you do not want to risk damaging it.

Cut the bracing rails to shape. The rails going the length of the table are shaped to butt up to the pedestal and are cut around the two transverse rails, which are angled to fit snugly against the pedestal. Clean up the rails with a compass plane or spokeshave and sand down to 120 grit.

Smooth the edges with 150 grit paper wrapped around a block. Position the rails accurately and evenly on the underside of the top so they fit up against the pedestal and screw them to the top through slotted holes to allow for movement.

The pedestal (FIGS 2 and 3) is made in much the same way as the chair backs described in the previous article, only this time the work is easier because the frames are straight, not curved. I cut the compound angle by setting my saw blade at 5DEG and the mitring fence at 10DEG, but it would be easy enough to set out using a sliding level.

The frames and the rungs are mortised and tenoned together – it saves time and effort if you can use a mortiser or router for the mortises and if you can cut the tenons with a spindle moulder, but it can be done by hand.

Once the frames of the pedestal have been cleaned up and glued together the rungs are clad in leather. There is a special glue called Tenaxatex for sticking leather on. It is recommended to be used 10 parts water to one part glue, although I have found ration of 5:1 better. Otherwise you can use PVA watered down 1:1.

The four frames of the pedestal are glued together to make the truncated pyramid. I cut a groove down the back face of the side members to take a tongue I cut out on the edge of the end frames for greater strength.

Use tapered battens cut at the same angle as the frames to cramp up the base squarely. When the pedestal is cleaned up you can hardly see the joint.

Finish the wood as you did for the chairs, using Danish oil, pre-catalysed lacquer or water-based cellulose. Remember to mask off the leather clad rungs when you apply the finish. I now use an airless spray gun for finishing, but remember you will need good ventilation and a respirator mask if you decide to spray.

To assemble the table, put the top upside down on to some padding, screw brass fixing plates to the top of the pedestal, place the pedestal on the top between the bracing rails and screw the fixing plates to the top. The fixing plates should have slotted holes to allow for movement. I made my own fixing plates out of 6mm (¼IN) brass plates because those I could find commercially available were made from thinner brass and I wanted to be sure the top and pedestal had a strong joint.

Turn the table the right way up and the job is finished ☐

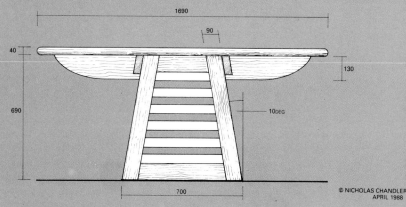

1690
90
40
130
690
10DEG
700

FIG 2

Side view of the table.

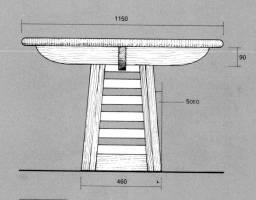

1150
90
5DEG
460

© NICHOLAS CHANDLER
APRIL 1988

FIG 3

End view of the table.

Mending a mortise and tenon

A common problem in antique furniture is the failure of a frame because of damage to the mortise and tenon joints. Here Ian Hosker starts restoring an 18th century gate-leg table by mending the damaged frame.

There is a fundamental difference between conservation, restoration and renovation. Conservation is concerned with carrying out repairs but allowing the difference between old and new to remain obvious – in other words the conservator allows the original craftsmanship to stand alone. Restoration returns an item to the condition that is appropriate to the age of the piece. This means all repairs are unobtrusive, coloured and polished to match the original work. Renovation is about repairing without any particular regard to maintaining authenticity.

Of the three approaches to the repairing of furniture, restoration is the one that concerns us here. Conservation is very much the realm of museums and galleries. Restoring allows us to live with the furniture after the repair. Renovation – without being too snotty about it – has no place in the restorer's workshop.

This little tour has been made because there are occasions when you look at a piece and wonder how it has managed to get into such a state. How far to go in carrying out the repair becomes critical because over-restoring can devalue the piece both in monetary and authenticity terms.

The subject of this article is a case in point. The general overriding principle in furniture restoration is: do nothing but, if you must do something do the absolute minimum. Unfortunately the minimum on this table was quite a lot. However, the aim remains the same: to restore in such a way that the piece looks as though nothing has been done to it.

There are three steps to restoration:
1) identify the problems
2) assess additional problems – eg will there be any difficulties in effecting a repair because of some structural constraint

3) set priorities and order the repairs, taking into account anticipated problems and certain conventions.

The photograph shows the table, which can only be described as a wreck. But the photograph only hints at the scale of the problem. The top was badly marked and the polish was peeling off as a result of years of abuse. In fact, the top looked as though it had been given a coat of varnish over an already degrading surface. The gaps that are clearly evident are the result of the boards of oak having separated. As for the underframe, every joint was loose and the whole table rocked in every direction.

The table dates from the 18th century and FIG 2 shows an old

FIG 2

repair to one of the gate legs (one that was repeated on the second gate). The wooden laths were nailed on to support the mortise and tenon joint. In fact, every tenon in the gate legs was severed from its respective rails so the laths were the only means of support. And this is where things become really interesting because those laths were the result of a

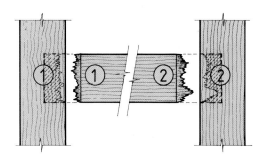

FIG 3

FIG 4a

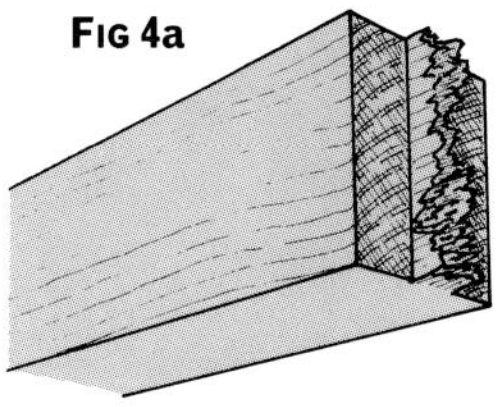

FIG 4b

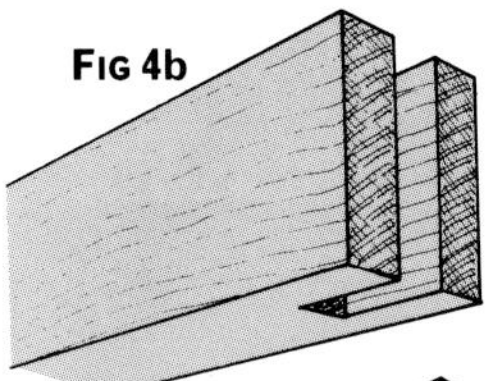

FIG 5

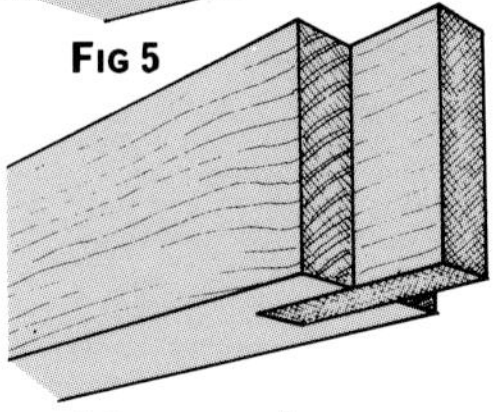

Above and below. How a broken tenon is mended.

FIG 5a

19th century repair. How can I deduce this? The nails that held them to the frame were hand wrought. So, here I had a table with history. It was clearly a genuine early 18th century piece – the old, bodged repair provided evidence of this. The provenance of old items is difficult to chart in the absence of written records (such as bills of sale or inventories) but it was possible to imagine the rough ride this table had endured in its lifetime.

The assessment of the damage led to the following priorities: repair the structural damage to the severed tenons; separate and glue the joints in the underframe; remove the top and glue the boards together; strip the flaking finish from the top, stain and repolish while attempting to retain as much of the old surface as possible (no mean task).

This scheme follows a pretty conventional order of priorities. As far as possible, repair structural damage first then tackle polished surfaces. The reason is a matter of common sense; if you repolish before repairing structural damage you run the risk of damaging the newly restored surface.

Repairing the gate legs

Once the laths had been gently prised away, both legs easily disintegrated into individual members. In one sense the severity of the damage made life easier as there were no problems in trying to

FIG 6
Where a frame cannot be taken apart the loose tenon is fitted into the mortise, slots are cut into the rail ends and the rail is gently tapped into position after gluing.

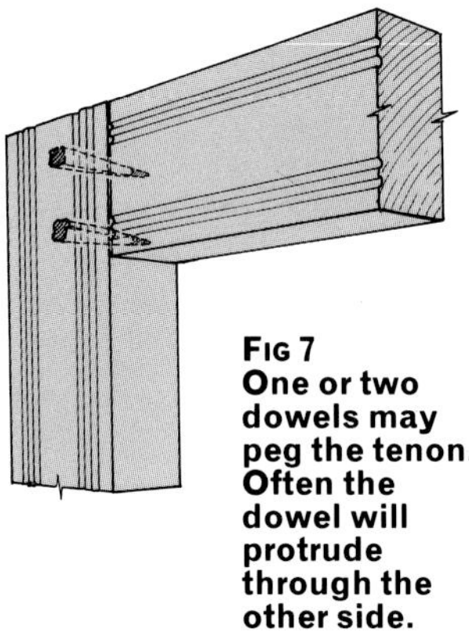

ease joints apart by straining sound joints – always a tricky scenario. As I said, each tenon of both legs had been severed, leaving tiny stubs on the rails and the mortises filled with the severed tenons. Before beginning repairs on structures that have been taken apart, label each part (FIG 3) and cross-reference it so you are not left scratching your head when you are putting them back together again.

While it is relatively easy to clear out the tenon stubs from the mortises, the rails appear to present a rather difficult problem.

In fact there are two options. You can either make new rails (which contravenes the principle of maintaining as much of the original craftsmanship as possible) or you can repair the tenons. Repairing the tenons is the preferred option and it is not as difficult as it seems. The standard technique is to make loose tenons (FIGS 4 & 5). Essentially, you are letting in a tongue of wood to replace the old tenon. FIG 6 shows a variation on the theme where a frame cannot easily be taken apart. The loose tenons are fitted to the mortise and a slot cut into the rail which is slid on to the tenons. The frames are then assembled in the normal way.

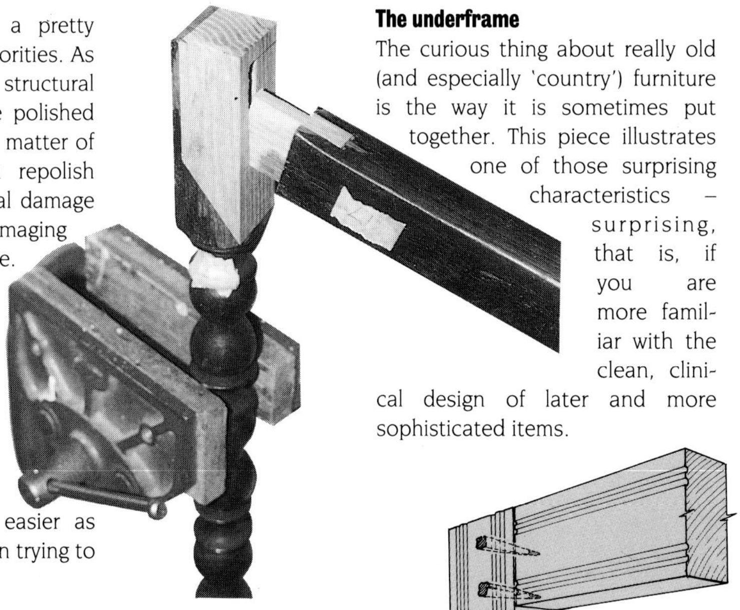

The underframe

The curious thing about really old (and especially 'country') furniture is the way it is sometimes put together. This piece illustrates one of those surprising characteristics – surprising, that is, if you are more familiar with the clean, clinical design of later and more sophisticated items.

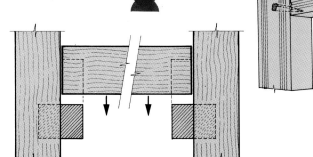

FIG 7
One or two dowels may peg the tenon. Often the dowel will protrude through the other side.

You are probably familiar with the good practice methods of attaching tops to underframes by slot screwing and the use of buttons or metal brackets that allow for movement of the wood. In this case the top was nailed to the frame, which is not all that unusual in a piece of this age. You have to remember that 18th century craftsmen, especially those in country areas, did not have the tools available to us today.

They did not have power tools, of course, but neither could they just pop out and buy the relatively simple tools we take for granted. They would make their own planes, chisels and most of the other tools they needed. They might employ the skill of a blacksmith in their toolmaking, but the blacksmith's skills varied from village to village. You also have to remember that screws and nails had to be hand made by the blacksmith, which meant they were expensive, and screws were more expensive than nails.

To repair the frame it was necessary to remove the top by gently (read carefully) prising it off in order to dismantle the frame. It seems reasonable to expect joints which are so loose to come apart without too much difficulty, and so they would if I had been dealing with a modern (or relatively modern) table. Unfortunately, these joints were pegged. That is to say, a dowel was driven through the joint as shown in FIG 7. Again, this was standard practice in 'country' furniture up to the early 18th century. As an aside, the shape of these dowels is an indicator of

FIG 8

Dowel pegs in old furniture are rarely round and they often taper.

authenticity. Modern dowels are round in cross section – machine made – but early joint pegs were hand made and so were rather squarer (FIG 8).

The way they are removed from the joint is important as replacement dowels need to be of similar size and shape. I drilled them out using a bit of smaller diameter than the peg (ie giving the peg a hollow core) and then gently ▶

tapping them out with a mallet, which usually led to them disintegrating, leaving the original hole unscathed. Once the frame had been taken apart and reassembled, new square pegs were made using a bandsaw, receiving final hand shaping before being driven back through the joint.

As with the gate legs, each member of the frame was labelled to ensure that reassembling was in the right order. In this case, the gluing up presented no problems but it often happens that the looseness of a joint is exacerbated by shrinkage of the tenon or widening of the mortise. It is then necessary to pack the joint. One of the best ways of doing that is to glue a piece of veneer on to one cheek of the tenon before reassembling (FIG 9). This is usually enough to fill the gap in the joint. It is important to do this as no amount of gap filling with glue can hope to produce a strong joint – especially an old and possibly worn one.

The top

I will dwell for a moment on the nails that have been mentioned. They are a clear indicator of age in that they were hand wrought wire nails. FIG 10 illustrates the general shape. Later copies of this table would almost certainly be constructed differently and there would be evidence of machining.

Let us now look at how the common problem of parting butt joints in tops is caused and, in this case, tackled. To a great extent, the problem was a function of the method of construction. Every serious cabinetmaker knows that if you do not allow for movement in wood you will regret it. With this table, the nailing down of the top prevented free movement as the boards expanded and contracted with fluctuating environmental conditions. Coincidentally, this also presented a small but ethically important dilemma that I shall refer to later.

When this table was made, of course, there was no central heating reducing the relative humidity of air to single figures. Timber was air dried – kilns were for pots, not wood. Furniture, therefore, was subjected to a wider variation in environmental conditions than it is today. Consider, also, the hermetically sealed environment of mod-

ern homes. Relatively high temperatures coupled with the low relative humidity of the air conspire to cause old timbers to shrink and release a range of in-built tensions with sufficient strength to split wood along lines of weakness. If, as was the case here, the joints open up completely life is a little easier.

It is necessary to plane the edges true before gluing the boards back together again. FIG 11 shows how this is done. Edges which butt against each other are planed as in (a). That is, the boards are book matched. This allows for

FIG 11a

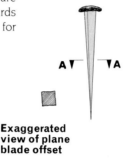

PLANE SOLE

T=topside
U=underside
B=butting edges

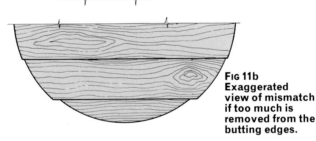

FIG 11b
Exaggerated view of mismatch if too much is removed from the butting edges.

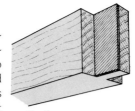

FIG 9

If the tenon is loose a strip of veneer is glued to the cheek to improve the fit.

FIG 10
Hand made nails are a sign of authenticity.

A ▼   ▼ A

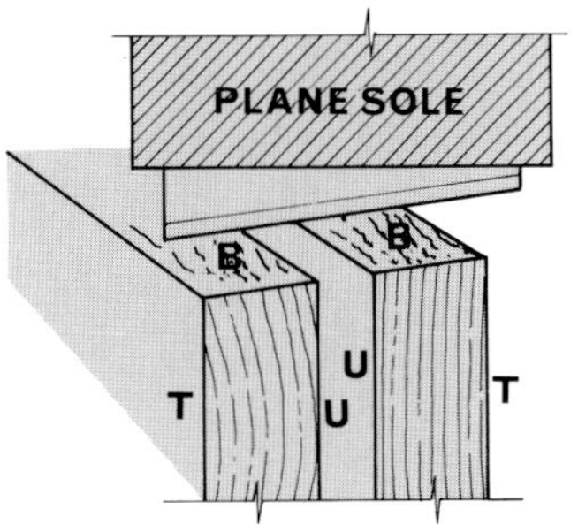

Exaggerated view of plane blade offset

the problem of off-set in the blade alignment so that when the edges are brought together the two errors cancel each other out.

A problem that can occur with tops that are shaped rather than rectangular is that the reduction in width of each board leads to a slight mismatch when they are glued up (FIG 11b) so it is important to remove as little wood as possible. In other words, you need to be accurate and get it right first time. Apart from that point, the process is no different to preparing butt joints in new timber. Don't try to glue up without re-truing the edges – it rarely works and definitely will not work if the joint has been open for a long time.

The really tricky part is the gluing up. With a new joint it is normal to shape and plane the top after gluing to level and equalise but you can't do that (or, rather, it is not ethical to do it) when you are restoring old joints. Joints up to about half a metre (18IN) can often be successfully 'rubbed' using animal glue, but longer joints are more difficult to manage, especially if the boards are slightly bowed, which they usually are.

FIG 12 illustrates the technique for jointing longer boards. The boards are placed face down on a thick ply base (a sheet of newspaper between the base and the top) and heavy weights or cramps are used to flatten the boards against the base. PVA glue and sash cramps are used to make the joint. If this has worked (and it's too late afterwards if it hasn't) the edges of the boards should be well aligned, ie there will not be a ridge, or, if there is, it will only be a tiny one.

Replacing the top

Here is the dilemma I referred to earlier. I knew the nails used to fix the top to the frame had led to the split in the first place, but is it legitimate to change the method of fixing? To my mind the answer is 'no' because, again, this goes against the basic principle of preserving as much of the original craftsmanship as possible. So I nailed the top back on to the underframe using the original nails. This constitutes restoring so the piece looks untouched. ●

IAN HOSKER

Trained by his grandfather from the age of 14, Ian Hosker now runs his own furniture restoration business from Sidmouth, Devon, as well as teaching the craft in community education (evening classes, summer school, etc).
After four years learning cabinetmaking, restoration and French polishing with his grandfather, Ian Hosker went to college to learn to be a teacher. In 1976 he started working for West Cheshire College, teaching physics, chemistry, biology and maths, although by 1980 he was teaching furniture restoration again and had started his own restoration business.
Lately he has been working on his first book, which is about wood finishing and finishes.

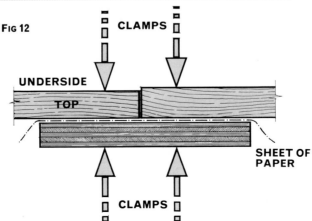

FIG 12

CLAMPS

UNDERSIDE

TOP

SHEET OF PAPER

CLAMPS

Using Sam Maloof

American David Donnelly uses fellow countryman Sam Maloof's innovative dado-rabbet chair joint to solve the problem of designing a chair with a solid seat that has the front and back legs continuing above the seat.

When you decide to build your first chair it can be a daunting thought. All those curves and rounded parts. But take the plunge. You will be pleasantly surprised to find your fears are unfounded and that most of the joints in a chair are marked out and cut before the shaping of the curves.

I wanted a chair that had some unusual features. To make it comfortable to sit in I made the seat deeply contoured and sculptured, and shaped the splats to fit a person's lower back. I wanted each part to blend and curve into each other with the front and back legs continuing above the seat to become the arm supports and the back. Doing it this way does away with the need for stretchers as the arms give the structural strength.

The seat is made from four pieces, each 407mm x 121mm x 48mm (16IN x 4¾IN x 1⅞IN). If you can't find wood 48mm thick, 38mm will suffice. Traditionally, the pieces would be glued together and the top would be contoured by carving it out with an adze. We're going to use a better method, pioneered by Sam Maloof. Before the pieces are assembled, position them together and mark them with the four templates shown in FIG 1. Template 1 outlines the inner and outer shape of the seat. Templates 2 and 3 mark cutaway views of the contouring, and

template 4 marks the front edge.

Before contouring the seat, mark and bore dowel holes in the edges for joining the parts. Make sure the dowel holes remain in the solid portion. To reduce the stress created by gluing dowels across the grain, use extremely short, 10mm (⅜IN) dowels – about 25mm (1IN) long. Biscuit joints would also be satisfactory. Don't glue the pieces up yet, because they need bandsawing first. By supporting the wood diagonally on one edge you'll be able to cut between the lines you've drawn.

At this stage, the purpose of bandsawing is not to cut a perfect line. In fact. it's almost impossible to cut the line perfectly because of the constantly changing plane of the surface. This bandsaw technique is not easy, so practice on scrap wood first to get a feel for how the saw wants to pull the wood.

After bandsawing, assemble and glue up (with dowels) the four seat pieces. The result may not be very attractive, but you've already removed 90% of the waste.

solutions

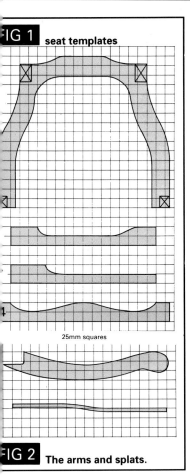

FIG 1 seat templates

25mm squares

FIG 2 The arms and splats.

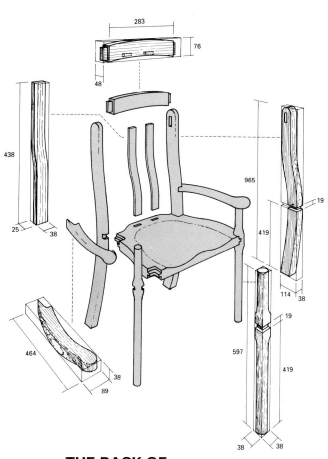

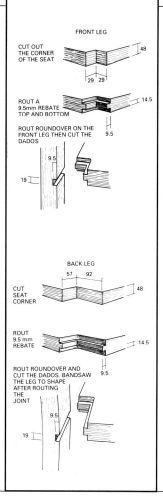

FRONT LEG

CUT OUT THE CORNER OF THE SEAT — 48

29 29

ROUT A 9.5mm REBATE TOP AND BOTTOM — 14.5

ROUT ROUNDOVER ON THE FRONT LEG THEN CUT THE DADOS 9.5

9.5

19

BACK LEG

57 92

CUT SEAT CORNER — 48

ROUT 9.5 mm REBATE — 14.5

ROUT ROUNDOVER AND CUT THE DADOS. BANDSAW THE LEG TO SHAPE AFTER ROUTING THE JOINT 9.5

9.5

19

To clean up and shape the seat contour I used a 178mm (7IN) sander. Start with 24 or 36 grit abrasive on the sander and sculpt away. Sandpaper this coarse cuts wood like a knife through butter, which is what you need to clean up the bandsaw cuts and round everything out. Check the shape by sitting on it and seeing how it feels. After roughing out, finish off with a 100-grit abrasive.

To join the legs to the seat I used the half-lap dado rabbet (groove rebate) joint perfected by Sam Maloof in the USA. This joint allows for exciting design applications, but once again I recommend testing it on scrap wood before attempting the real thing. Taking it one step at a time, this joint's really quite simple and it looks attractive.

Mark out the front and back legs, but do not cut the joints yet. It is important to keep the material square at this stage while you mark where the grooves go, two on each leg. As you can see from the illustrations, the right and left back legs are mirror images of each other and require grooves on opposite

THE BACK OF THE SEAT IS CURVED, SO CUT THE JOINTS BEFORE SHAPING THE SEAT.

sides. Mark them carefully, then go ahead and cut the grooves 19mm (3/8IN) wide by 10mm (3/8IN) deep.

The back of the seat is curved and narrower than the front. Again, mark and cut the joints before cutting the outer seat profile so you work with square reference edges. Refer to the drawings for the seat joint measurements. Mark out and notch the corners. Note that the front and back joints are cut differently.

To make the L-shape rebates on the top and bottom of each seat joint, use a router with a 10mm (3/8IN) rebating bit. Set the depth of the bit by testing it on scrap wood. The tongue on each seat joint must fit snugly into the groove on the corresponding leg.

After routing the corner of the L in the joint it is round and makes the joint fit snugly. With a roundover bit in your router that matches the arc in the L-shaped rebate on the seat, round the inside corner of each leg. If your joints don't fit tightly in the corners, correct them using hand tools until you have a perfect fit – I used a carving gouge for this.

Before bandsawing the back legs to size, and while the wood is still square, mark and cut mortises for the crest rail, 19mm (3/4IN) wide and 19mm deep.

Cut the back legs to size on a bandsaw. Take care not to cut within 25mm (1IN) of the rebates in order to keep the joints square. Sand the sides smooth to remove the bandsaw marks. Round over the edges and the top with a 13mm (1/2IN) roundover bit, but avoid the areas that will touch the outer corners of the seat joints. These are blended together later by hand.

The front leg stock should be 597 x 38 x 38mm (23½ x 1½ x 1½IN). Cut grooves on ▶

two adjacent sides of each front leg for the seat joints. They should be exactly the same dimensions as the back leg grooves.

Round over both the front outer corner and the inside corner of each front leg with a 13mm (½IN) roundover bit in your router. Do not round over the corners that touch the exposed edges of the joints. Dry fit the legs into the seat joints. Once again, you may need to modify the corners of the joints with a gouge to make a snug fit.

Mark the legs where they meet the seat. Since you will not turn the legs where they join to the seat, these marks will serve as visual references on the lathe. Now mount the legs on a lathe and turn them above and below the seat joint until they are round.

The crest rail is curved. While the wood is still square, cut tenons to fit in the mortises in the top of the back legs. The final thickness of the rail is 29mm (1⅛IN). Offset your tenons towards the front of the rail.

Mark the top and bottom of the crest rail to indicate the inside and outside curves. Also mark mortises for the two splats in both the bottom of the crest rail and the top of the seat. Be sure they line up. Chop out these mortises, which are the same size as the width and thickness of the splats.

Cut the curves for the crest rail on your bandsaw, maintaining a thickness of 29mm (1⅛IN) after finishing the curve. Sand the faces smooth, then round over the top and bottom edges with a 10mm (⅜IN) roundover bit. Be careful to avoid routing into the mortises for the splats.

"WHILE THE SPLATS LOOK AS IF THEY HAVE BEEN BENT, THEY WERE IN FACT BANDSAWN."

Finally, bandsaw the splats to size. While they may give the appearance of being bent, you can accomplish the same effect much more simply by bandsawing the bends into them. After cutting, hold them against your back. If you don't like the way they fit or support the small of your back, make new ones and modify the shapes accordingly. Round the edges with a 6mm (¼IN) roundover bit, but stop just short of the ends so the housed ends of the splats will fit square in the mortises.

With most pieces complete, try a test assembly. If you're gentle, it should even support your weight. Double check the lines you drew for the outer profile of the seat to be sure they line up with the outside edge of the back legs. Disassemble the chair and

bandsaw the outer profile on the seat.

To continue the rounded theme of the chair, round over the bottom sides and back of the seat. Once again, avoid areas that are housed in joints. Since I wanted to round over these areas to a deeper and wider degree than a router bit would allow, I turned to a rasp.

With every piece except the arms now cut to size, glue and assemble the chair. The work that remains – making the arms and fine-tuning the joinery – can only be completed when the chair is assembled.

The splats can be housed in their mortises without glue. With that exception, glue all the remaining pieces together – front and back legs, seat, and crest rail.

Clamps are especially important on the seat joinery since the structural soundness and aesthetic appearance both depend on the joints being secure. Take care that all four legs touch the ground when you glue up the chair or it won't sit flat. If it rocks, check your clamps to see that the pieces are not racked out of square. You can also apply clamps downward from the seat to your benchtop to force it to sit flat.

The arms (FIG 2) require a certain finesse and some hand-and-eye co-ordination. It is easiest to do this after the rest of the chair is assembled so you can combine measurements with hand craftsmanship.

The measurements provided for the arms are only rough sizes. Through trial and error, cut and modify the joints at the back of each arm with chisels and gouges so they fit flush against the back legs. In addition to rounding the corner of each joint, bevel them where they meet the back legs since the legs are slanted.

Round the upper and lower edges of the arms with a 13mm (½IN) roundover bit. Avoid the area around the joint at the back. Attach the arms by screwing the front ends to the front legs and the back ends to the back legs. I used 76mm (3IN) screws in front and 50mm (2IN) screws at the back. The screws will be covered with 13mm (½IN) oak plugs, so drill both pilot holes and short inset holes for the plugs before screwing.

For additional support you may also add reinforcing screws to the seat joints. Apply one 76mm (3IN) support screw (with pilot holes, inset holes for plugs, and plugs) through each leg and into the seat from the sides – not from the front or back.

Your chair is finally together. But before you finish it or show it off, let's fine tune our joinery with rasps, rifflers, files, and abrasive paper.

The back of the arms and chair backs

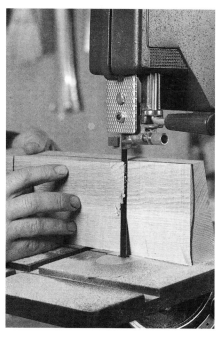

Much of the wood removal for shaping the seat can be acheived on the bandsaw before the boards are joined together.

CUTTING LIST
finished sizes in mm, (inches in brackets)

Back legs x 2	966 x 115 x 38	(38 x 4½ x 1½)
Seat x 4	406 x 121 x 48	(16 x 4¾ x 1⅞)
Front legs x 2	597 x 38 x 38	(23½ x 1½ x 1½)
Arms x 2	464 x 89 x 38	(18¼ x 3½ x 1½)
Crest rail x 1	321 x 77 x 48	(12⅝ x 3 x 1⅞)
Splats x 2	438 x 38 x 10	(17¼ x 1½ x ⅜)

Note: a smaller thickness of 38mm (1½IN) is acceptable for the seat and crest rail.

Try a test assembly – it should look like this.

And the best part is using them.

David Donnelly – thoughts on design

My growing interest in chairs culminated in a two-week period I spent with Sam Maloof. I was impressed in different ways by Maloof's design, construction techniques, joinery, and working style. From a design perspective, these are all interrelated.

Later, when I began designing my own chair, I was afraid I would be too strongly influenced by Maloof to the point that my design would mimic or, worse, plagiarise his ideas. Eventually I convinced myself that these concerns were unwarranted. Of course, his influence is evident. But that's as far as it goes. After all, everyone is influenced by the world around them and their experiences. Nothing can be designed in a vacuum.

Once I have realized that Maloof has solved an age-old problem of designing a chair with a solid seat that allows the front and back legs to continue uninterrupted above the seat to become the back and arm supports, can I ever turn my back on that realization? It would be like scientists ignoring the work of their predecessors. If they did, we'd still be living in the stone age. If I use or modify Maloof's innovative dado rabbet chair joint, is that a form of plagiarism? If the answer is 'yes' then we could never again use any joint that had ever been invented. Taken to the extreme, even designing a chair with four legs and a back could be a form of plagarism of somebody, whoever that poor forgotten soul may be.

There are conceivably so many questions you could ask yourself before settling on a design: do you want a rectilinear or rounded form; should the seat be built in or added on; what shape should the splat, arms, crown rail, back and legs take; how do you unify the elements; should the joinery be functional or aesthetic; does the design address the problem of wood movement; should the back flair outward; how do I hold it all together. And so on.

Once I began toying with ideas and mocking up joints and shapes with some scrap Douglas Fir that was lying around, I was amazed how things eventually began to flow into a cohesive whole.

In spite of my best efforts to throw up mental road blocks and blanket myself in insecurity, a chair began to develop. Problems persisted, however, and to answer these I turned to my training in creative behaviour.

There are five steps to the creative process: problem definition, preparation, incubation, illumination, and evaluation. Simply put, to recognize a problem or need, know your craft and study the alternatives, let the ideas ferment while you go on to other things, come to a decision about which path to take, and then test your results to see if they work.

To me, the most important step is incubation. This is where I can forget about a problem by turning it over to my subconscious. If I just try hard to be creative it doesn't work. The greatest resource we'll ever have for new ideas is in our subconscious. It's a great relief to know that I can let go of a problem, and that eventually the answer will come to me out of the blue, even if it's just in bits and pieces. But if I know it's OK to have a blank mind and let my subconscious earn its keep, then it can be a great relief. Once I stop trying so hard, ideas will often gush forward.

Another key component to incubation is visualization. Visualization is being able to see pictures in your mind. It can work either consciously or subconsciously. Since wood projects are visual and new designs are original, we need to be able to see it in order to create it. I don't have a very well developed sense of visualization, but it is strongest at night when I'm either asleep or half-awake. On a couple of occasions, I've had real breakthroughs when a picture would come to me at night showing me just what I needed. Then I would either sketch it out or just turn to my tools and hack away.

On the chair I made, I was having a real problem with the arms. Nothing seemed to work, including the first pair I made. So I let go of the problem and about a week later the answer came to me in my sleep when I visualized the arm design that I needed.

Sam Maloof once said: "One design begets another." I realized what he meant when I was working on my chair. Every time I resolved a problem – such as turning a vague concept for a splat into reality – new ideas for designs would come to me. Then this new design might lead to another idea for the profile of the seat, the crown rail, or something else.

In short, agonizing as it may be, the experience of designing provides an intense sense of fulfilment. It is originality in its purest form and almost enough to reconcile the cruel irony when the skill of our hands doesn't do justice to the vision in our mind.

should blend together. Because of the irregular angles and shapes involved, this requires hand shaping with a file or coarse sandpaper. Round over the back of the arm until it blends into the chair back. Watch your grain direction as you file to avoid tearing the fibres.

The legs should flow smoothly into the seat. File down any hard corners or edges on the legs that your router or lathe may have missed near the seat joints. Take off any exposed corners on the tops and bottoms of the splats in the same manner.

Sand the seat all the way round on the edges – front, sides, and back. A belt sander or palm sander should do the trick. Pay particular attention to the smooth fit of the joinery. The legs and seat should blend smoothly at every corner.

Before applying a finish, your chair needs to be sanded smooth. With fine furniture, sand all the way down to 220grit. Then wet the wood lightly with a damp sponge to raise the fibres. When it is dry, sand the fibres off.

> **"I LIKE THE LOOK OF TUNG OIL AND THE DURABILITY OF POLYURETHANE, SO I MIX THEM"**

Each variety of wood has unique qualities that affect how it needs to be finished. Oak, of course, is hard, open-celled, and has prominent annual rings. Because it is so porous, I always use a paste filler before applying the finish. Paste filler mixes very nicely with stain, so I usually use a combination of paste filler and stain in one step, then wipe it off.

A lot can be said about finish techniques, but I will be brief and just mention how I do it. Your own method may be better. Since I like the hand-rubbed look of tung oil and the durability of polyurethane, I mix the two together 50-50 and wipe on three coats by hand. Rubbing it in and wiping it off creates thin layers that do not drip or run. Since chairs take a lot of abuse, I feel the polyurethane is necessary for hardness.

I made four of these chairs (all with arms) and I use them around my breakfast table. I hope they give you as much pleasure as they've given me □

ADULT'S ROCKING CHAIR

This chair, by Nigel Halliday of Beaversdam, is designed for adults while nursing a baby or reading the children a bedtime story.

Inspiration for the designs of our nursery range of furniture comes from the Arts & Crafts movement of the last century. We like the clean, simple lines of the work of this period which often reflected the way of life of the craftsmen and the honesty of production.

We usually make this rocking chair in American red oak (as illustrated) to match the rest of our range. But it would look particularly attractive in English oak and would, perhaps, be more in keeping with the Arts & Crafts movement.

In the end, of course, your choice of timber is a matter of personal preference.

In the design shown here we have used a flat, solid seat. It can be softened with a loose cushion if required. But if you have a flair for upholstery, the seat – and, indeed, the back panel – could be upholstered.

If you do decide to upholster the seat, remember to make four corner brackets for it as it will be loose and work a rebate on the seat rails. This rebate should be about 6mm wide and the depth of the loose seat frame (or plywood base) to be used.

The rebate does afford extra support, but its main function is to prevent a gap being formed between the seat frame and the loose seat through which daylight can be seen. Alternatively, supports about 10mm square could be glued and screwed on to the inside of the seat rails.

Having prepared the timber from the parts list, remembering that the widths and thicknesses given are the finished sizes, glue and cramp the seat. You could make the back panel from a few nice scraps if you wanted to, but the solid piece is fine if you have it.

Make the seat from three or more pieces joining them together with the heart side alternately up and down. This will minimise any movement there may be if the moisture content is still a little high. Once glued and cramped, these can be left overnight and planed or sanded flat and squared off at a later stage.

The back legs and rockers should be cut out and shaped. Shaping the rockers will be easier if, using FIG 2 and graph paper, you make a full-size drawing of them and take a template from that.

Mark out all the pieces in four groups – the legs and the back panel, the back rails, the front rails, and the side rails and arms. When gauging remember that, in this design, the outer face of the rails all round are flush with the outer faces of the legs, but the back panel is central within the top and middle rails.

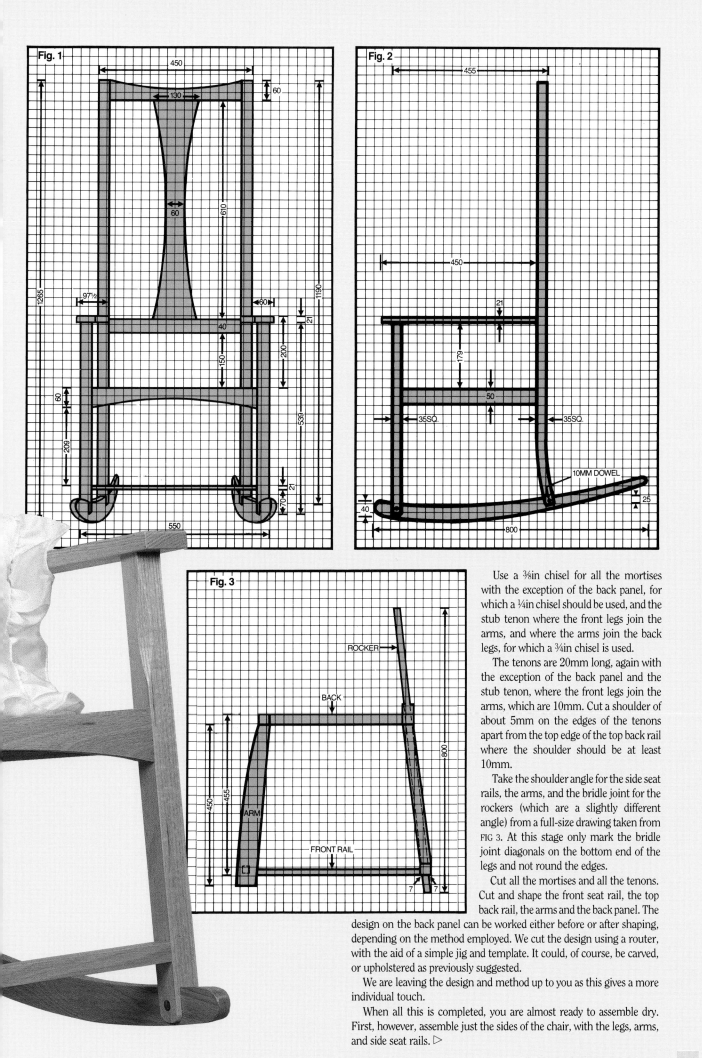

Fig. 1

450
130
60
60
610
40
97½
60
1265
150
200
21
209
60
539
1190
21
70
21
550

Fig. 2

455
450
21
179
50
35SQ.
35SQ.
10MM DOWEL
40
800
25

Fig. 3

ROCKER
BACK
800
450
455
ARM
FRONT RAIL
7   7

Use a ⅜in chisel for all the mortises with the exception of the back panel, for which a ¼in chisel should be used, and the stub tenon where the front legs join the arms, and where the arms join the back legs, for which a ¾in chisel is used.

The tenons are 20mm long, again with the exception of the back panel and the stub tenon, where the front legs join the arms, which are 10mm. Cut a shoulder of about 5mm on the edges of the tenons apart from the top edge of the top back rail where the shoulder should be at least 10mm.

Take the shoulder angle for the side seat rails, the arms, and the bridle joint for the rockers (which are a slightly different angle) from a full-size drawing taken from FIG 3. At this stage only mark the bridle joint diagonals on the bottom end of the legs and not round the edges.

Cut all the mortises and all the tenons. Cut and shape the front seat rail, the top back rail, the arms and the back panel. The design on the back panel can be worked either before or after shaping, depending on the method employed. We cut the design using a router, with the aid of a simple jig and template. It could, of course, be carved, or upholstered as previously suggested.

We are leaving the design and method up to you as this gives a more individual touch.

When all this is completed, you are almost ready to assemble dry. First, however, assemble just the sides of the chair, with the legs, arms, and side seat rails. ▷

Holding a rocker on each side in turn against the housing depth mark on the front edge of the front leg and the rear edge of the back leg, mark the housing depth for the curve of the rocker on the internal edges of the legs.

With a mortise gauge, continue the lines marked on the ends for the bridle joint round the edges of the legs. Cut the housings and round off the corners.

Now assemble the chair dry, clean up, cut off the waste on the front of the arms and round off the top edges. Using a spokeshave work a hollow chamfer on the top inside edges of the front legs.

Glue and cramp up the front and the back of the chair and leave these overnight. At this stage plane and sand the seat.

Glue the whole chair together. Once in the cramps, and if you have room, the chair could be up-ended and the rockers glued in and G-cramped.

You could bore the holes and put the dowel through the bridle joint now, but we prefer to G-cramp and put the dowels through the later. The dowels are both for strength and a decorative element.

Once the rockers are glued and doweled, the next step before a final clean-up is to glue and screw the seat supports on to the front and side seat rails and fit the seat, which should be screwed at the front and slot-screwed at the sides. ☐

This is the range of nursery furniture designed and made by Beaversdam.

Beaversdam design

Beaversdam is a partnership between Nigel Halliday and Dennis Smith. Halliday, who is from Northern Ireland, served his apprenticeship in various branches of the joinery trade, including cabinet making, boat building, shop fitting, and housing joinery. Later he went into guitar making. In between times he attended Bible College in England where he met his wife-to-be.

Smith, who is from London, spent the first part of his working life as a civil servant in the Lord Chancellor's offices, although both his father and his grandfather were foreman-joiners. In 1979 he moved to Lincolnshire and trained at Lincoln Technical College. He has since worked in housing joinery, furniture restoration, and furniture making. He now lives with his wife and their three children in Alford, Lincolnshire.

The two men met at a Christian Fellowship, to which they still both belong. It was during a period of unemployment that they discussed and put together their idea of launching a small business venture. They decided to specialise in nursery furniture, making quality, hand-made pieces. Their designs are their own, being inspired by the Arts & Crafts movement.

The name Beaversdam comes from the works of C S Lewis, in his *Chronicles of Narnia*. These books had become favourites with both partners' families, and it was decided to use this name from *The Lion, the Witch, and the Wardrobe*, the second of the *Chronicles*.

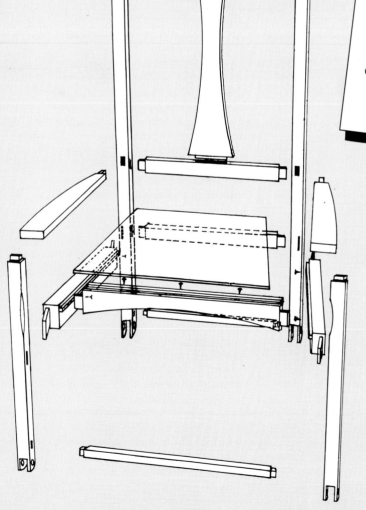

Rocking Chair cutting list (finished sizes in mm)			
Description	length	width	thickness
Back legs (2) from	1500	80	35
Front legs (2)	560	35	35
Rockers (2) from	820	160	21
Arms (2)	490	60	21
Side seat rails (2)	440	50	50
Back middle rail (1)	430	40	21
Back seat rail (1)	430	40	35
Back stretcher rail (1)	430	21	21
Top back rail (1)	430	60	21
Front seat rail (1)	530	60	21
Front stretcher rail (1)	530	21	21
Back panel (1)	650	130	15
Seat (1)	500	425	20
Seat supports (3)			
10mm dowel			

One of the best

Manhar Savla

We were going to call this "six of the best", it being to do with cane, but there is not enough room for six projects and one should be enough to give you a feel for the material.

Cane furniture is ideal for the conservatory. It fits in well with the idea of a sun room and is both attractive and durable. Working it should present no great problem.

This project for a cane table should answer most of the questions which are likely to arise about working in cane. Using the same principals it should be possible to design and make a variety of cane furniture.

The cane used for this coffee table is natural manau grade 1, which is probably the finest cane available. It will give a good natural finish. If you want a stained or painted finish use skinned rattan. This is smoothly skinned so that the outer layer is completely removed and the material is sanded down to the core until it no longer contains the rings which are usually considered the hallmark of cane. It looks almost like dowel.

You could make the table any size, but remember to cut the glass top ⅛in smaller on the length and width than the actual inside size of the table top. Instead of glass you could use cane webbing, as for the magazine shelf.

Cutting the cane

It is best to cut the cane with a hacksaw using a fine tooth blade. Simply hold the cane in a vice and cut the cane to size.

Making the jigs

At each fastening stage you will need the jigs in figures 2, 3 and 4. The jigs are made by fastening pieces of wood 1in thick by 1¾in wide on to board. Only three pieces of wood form the construction ▶

jigs, one piece 36in long and the others 12in. They can be formed as required simply by part nailing the batons into a board as they are required.

The jigs for the ends (figure 2) require the 36in long baton to be fixed parallel to the edge of the board and 21in up from the edge. Leaving a gap of 3½in between the bottom of the 36in baton, fix the 12in batons at right angles at an equal distance from the centre of the 36in baton. The distance from the outside edge of one 12in baton to the inside edge of the other should be 13¾in.

The jigs for the shelf and for fixing the top and the shelf to the sides are similar, but to the dimensions in figures 3 and 4.

The jigs for bending the bracing cane on the sides and the ends require formers for bending the cane around. These are made from 1in thick squares of timber with a radius to suit your own taste. A radius of 2½in produces a good curve. They should be positioned just over the width of the cane in from the top and side batons.

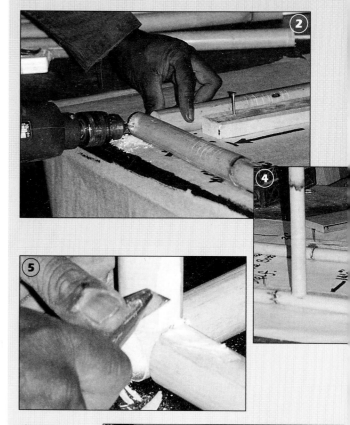

Making the shelf

Cut a piece of ¾in plywood (or you could use chipboard) 16in wide and 18⅛in long. Soak a piece of close woven cane webbing 18in x 24in in luke warm water for about an hour to soften it. Apply a thin layer of PVA adhesive all over one side of the plywood.

The webbing has two distinct sides, one smooth and the other rougher. Remove the webbing from the water, shaking off excess moisture, and place it on the board, smooth side up. Flatten the webbing and press it tightly down against the board. Place grease proof paper over the webbing and put another board on top of it. Put a weight on top and leave it to dry.

When the webbing is dry, turn the board webbing side down on

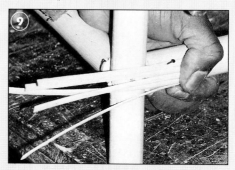

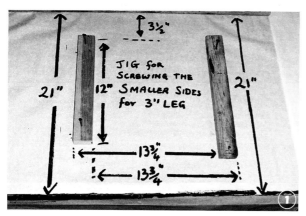

the bench and trim the webbing around the board.

Fastening the ends

Using the jig in Fig 2 position two end pieces along the batons which are at right angles to the top baton. The leg goes along the bottom. Drill a hole through the leg and into the end piece. Position the hole slightly to the top of the end piece because another hole and another screw will be required to secure the side. Countersink the hole and screw in a 2½in screw to fasten the leg to the frame. Repeat for the bottom part, again drilling slightly off centre to allow for the bottom shelf assembly fixing. Turn round and fix the leg the other side. Complete the other end in the same way.

Constructing the shelf

Using the jig in Fig 3 construct the shelf frame following the procedure for the construction of the ends.

Joining the ends

Using the jig in Fig 4, fix the ends to the side pieces (Pic 3), positioning the holes slightly towards the bottom of the side piece. Countersink the holes and fix with 2½in screws.

Turn the table on to its side and, using a 3in length of cane cut from scrap to position the shelf assembly 3in from the bottom of each leg, fix the shelf assembly into position (Pic 4).

The table is now ready for binding.

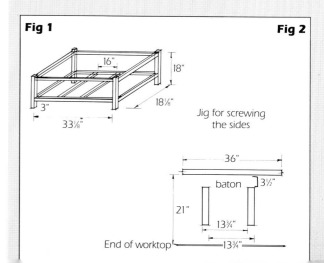

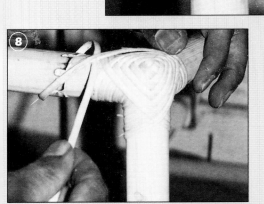

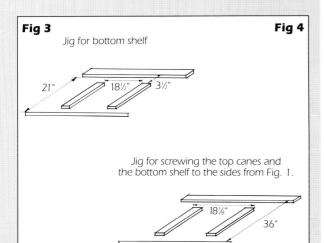

Binding

The distinctive binding on cane masks the basic construction and gives a pleasing decorative finish.

Begin by slicing off some of the cane at the joints using the knife. The cut should go up about two inches from the joint and be about 1/16in deep (Pic 5) on the insides where the glass and the magazine shelf are going to be. For the four top corner bindings slice off the outside of the joint at the top of the leg (Pic 6).

Cut 40 x 7in strips from the binding. These will be used later. Soak the strips and the remainder of the binding material in cold water until soft.

Top corner binding

Using the soaked reel of binding, feed one end through the gap formed where the side and the end join the top of the leg. Take it

in 1½in and tack it in position with a gimp pin (Pic 7).

Take the binding over the top so it is flush with the top corner. Keep it to the left of the point which you formed when you shaved the top of the leg. Take it round to the right, around the leg and bring it back on to the point on the right. Follow the line of the previous binding and continue with this figure of eight pattern until the joint is complete.

To finish, tuck the binding under itself (Pic 8) and tack it into position using a gimp pin.

T-joints and lower corners

You have already cut 7in strips of binding. Use four or five of them to cover the lower corner joints and the T-joints. Pin the strips side by side (Pics 9 and 10).

Feed the end of the roll of binding under the strips close to the leg and pin it in position (Pic 11). Wind it round the strips working out from the leg. Finish off by wrapping it back under itself and tacking it in position as with the top corners. Pic 12 shows a finished bottom corner.

Making and fastening the braces

Using the jigs in Figs 5 and 6, take the two pieces of 60in long ¾in rattan and mark off 15in from one end. This will be the approximate bending point.

Have a big bowl of water and a rag nearby. Wet the rag and use it to wet the cane at the bending point. Light the blow torch and pull the cane where it is to bend, directing the flame on to the inside of the bend (Pic 13). Keep the cane moving so that the flame is not directed in one spot for too long. Wet the area occasionally. The cane will soften and give a little. Keep going until the cane is slightly overbent.

Put the bend into the jig while it is still hot. Wet it again and let it cool down for a few minutes (Pic 14).

Leave the cane in the jig and mark off where the bend the other end will come. Remove the cane and repeat the process, replacing it in the jig to achieve the final shape. Do the same, using the appropriate jig, for the end braces.

The braces will need to be cut off at 11¼in from the top to fit into the table frame. The braces are nailed into the frame using 1½in wire nails (Pic 15).

Fastening the webbing for the bottom shelf

Put the board with the webbing on it into the gap created for it.

Fig 3   **Fig 4**

Jig for bottom shelf

21"   18½"   3½"

Jig for screwing the top canes and the bottom shelf to the sides from Fig. 1.

18⅛"

36"

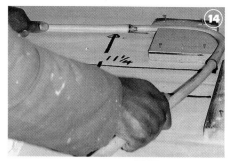

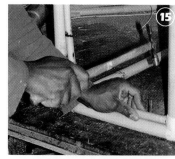

Fasten it with 2in wire nails (Pic 16).

Cut two lengths of koboo cane 20in long. Split the koboos straight through the centre using the razor knife. Split a few inches at a time, always cutting away from you. If the knife wanders off the centre it can be angled back on true.

Use these four pieces of koboo to bead the groove between the webbing board and the main cane. Gimp pins are used to secure the koboo (Pic 17).

The table top

Turn the table upside down on to the workbench. Use a small piece of ¾in board to mark a line round the four sides where the glass will fit. The piece of board is held flush against the cane and a pencil mark drawn on the cane.

Turn the table on its side and pin the koboos to the cane using the line as a guide. Keep the koboos below the line.

Finishing

You will find some whiskers sticking off the binding. To remove them, simply run a flame from the blow torch swiftly over them. Clean the frame with luke warm water and finish with a varnish or lacquer (Pic 18).

Parts List
Legs   (4) 1¼in manau cane x 18in long
Sides   (4) 1¼in manau cane x 33⅛in long
Ends   (4) 1¼in manau cane x 18⅛in
Ends for magazine rack
              (2) 1¼in manau cane a 18⅛in
Arch braces   (2) ⅝-¾in rattan x 60in
Beading for magazine rack and glass supports
              (2) 8-10mm koboo canes x 8ft
Binding cane ¼kg x 5-5½mm natural lapping cane
For magazine rack
              (1) ¾in plywood 16in x 18⅛in
              (1) close weave rattan weave 18in x 24in
Top   6mm glass 33in x 18in

For fixing
Woodscrews   (20) 2½in No10 flathead countersunk
Black gimp pins 30gm x 13mm/½in
A small bottle of PVA adhesive
A small can of varnish or lacquer

Tools
Drill, hammer, screwdriver, pilot countersunk drill bit for No10 screws, ruler, razor knife, propane torch, large pan or bucket, hacksaw. ☐

Cane & Able

In a converted stable which once housed the horsepower for barges working the Regent Canal it overlooks can be seen some of the very little cane furniture still being made in the UK.

It is being produced by a company called Cane & Able, whose proprietor is Manhar Savla.

The cane is displayed among other furniture being made out of old Indian windows and doors which Savla imports. They become available through demolition work being carried out in Rajastahn and Gujerat. Some of the doors are 12ft square – and heavy.

On the cane side of the north-west London business much of the work is contract business, for shops and restaurants, although Savla also has domestic work usually from people who want something of a particular size or shape.

"Normally I will sit down with a customer and we will design something together."

Cane is available, even if it is difficult to find, and Cane & Able will supply the raw material as well as the finished furniture.

They will supply it ready for use, too, which is important because raw cane is not always straight. It is drawn through a steel pipe to iron out the kinks.

There are not only many different varieties of cane, there are also many different sizes. Savla has used up to 55mm to make coffee tables.

It's amazing what people want in cane, though. Savla was once commissioned to make a giant bird cage, 48in in diameter and 8ft high, hand painted yellow (it was going to be spray painted but it was too big to get into the paint shop). It was the brainchild of an advertising agency.

A stool for STANDING on

Reader Nigel Smith wanted a stool that was stable and sturdy enough for his small daughters to stand on safely. This is what he designed and made.

This little stool was made because I needed something for my two daughters to stand on to reach the bathroom hand basin and toilet. They have long since outgrown it, but the stool remains as tough and sturdy as ever.

The stool needed to be of suitable height for a three-year-old and not take up much space when not in use. I also designed the legs to taper outwards towards the bottom so the top could over-

hang slightly, yet the stool would remain stable if a child stood on the edge.

Any two contrasting timbers will look well. I used recycled wood – the top was part of a mahogany veneered Victorian table and the legs and rails came from old fence posts.

Cut out and square the top to measure 310 x 210mm (12¼ x 8¼IN) and plane and thickness it to 20mm (¾IN). Round the corners to 25mm (1IN) radius. Soften all the edges and sand the whole top to 280 grit.

Cut four legs 250mm (9¾IN) long and square them to 42mm (1¹¹⁄₁₆IN). Mark the positions of the mortises for the rail tenons. The tenons are haunched for extra strength. If you select the grain of the legs carefully you can give the impression that the legs taper on all four edges, when in fact they taper only on the two outside faces. Mark and cut the tapers (FIG 1). I used a saw and plane, finishing by sanding to 280 grit.

Cut and square the rails from wood 68 x 20mm (2¹¹⁄₁₆ x ¾IN). Two rails are 250mm (9¾IN) long and two 150mm (6IN). Cut decorative beads on the outside bottom edges, and grooves 10mm (⅜IN) wide x 6mm (¼IN) deep round the inside top edges 8mm (⁵⁄₁₆IN) down from the top. These grooves are to take buttons for fixing the top to the frame (FIG 2).

Test position the legs and rails on the underside of the top and mark the rail tenons and shoulders. Cut the tenons, haunches and shoulders, cleaning up with a shoulder plane if necessary, and dry assemble the legs and rails to make sure everything fits together properly.

Sand all pieces smooth to 320 grit. After this I raised the grain with a damp cloth and, after drying, sanded again.

Glue up both end pairs of legs and rails first, using PVA adhesive. Make sure all is square and true. When the glue has dried, complete the underframe by gluing in the two long rails, again ensuring that all is square.

While waiting for the glue to dry, apply the first of two or three coats of well thinned polyurethane varnish to the top.

Make eight buttons (FIG 2) ensuring that the tongues are not an overtight fit in the grooves in the rails. Make sure that when the buttons are screwed to the underside of the top they will apply a firm cramping pressure. Drill and countersink the buttons to take 25mm (1IN) No 8 screws.

After final cleaning up and finishing of all the parts fit the top on with the buttons and screws.

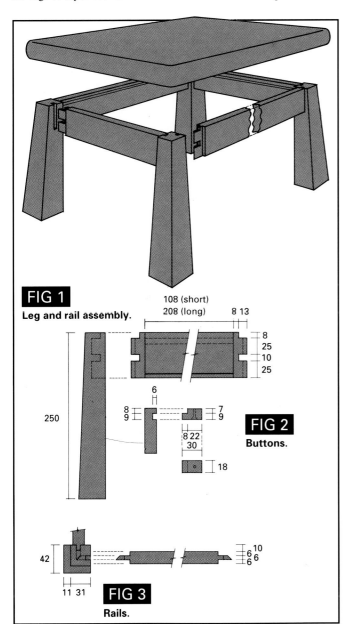

FIG 1
Leg and rail assembly.

108 (short)
208 (long)   8 13

8
25
10
25

6
8 7
9 9
8 22
30

FIG 2
Buttons.

18

250

42
11 31

6 10
6 6
6

FIG 3
Rails.

Windsor chairs are still being made in High Wycombe. These from Ercol Furniture may look a little different from those made 200 years ago, but they are part of a recognisable heritage.

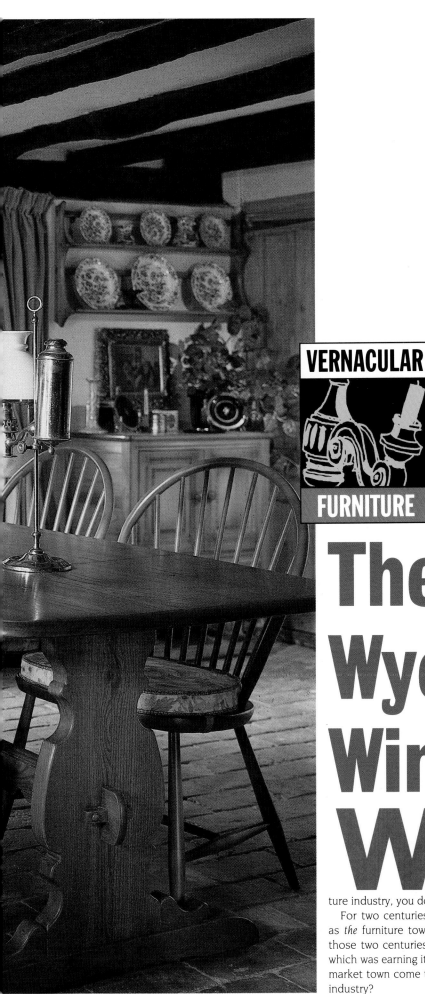

To many, vernacular furniture is epitomised by the Windsor chair. In spite of the name, Windsors are more closely associated with Wycombe, once the 'Chairopolis' of England. Windsors are still made in Wycombe, but they no longer dominate the town's economy, as John Mayes explains.

VERNACULAR FURNITURE

The Wycombe Windsor

Windsor chairs are still made in High Wycombe, Buckinghamshire, but it is no longer true to say of the people of the town, as it used to be said, "if you don't work in the furniture industry, you don't work".

For two centuries High Wycombe has been known as *the* furniture town of England, and for the first of those two centuries it was almost nothing but chairs which was earning it its reputation. So how did a small market town come to be so important in the furniture industry? ▶

Bodgers at work in the beech woods. They produced the legs and stretchers – and were paid 9/- (that's 45p) for a gross (144).

Sawing logs into lengths for chair legs.

A draw knife being used on a shaving horse to shape the billets before turning.

Below. The 'bottomer' used an adze to shape the seat.

There are wonderful stories as to how it all started. The most popular is that local farmers, when their labourers could not get out on to the fields because of bad weather, set them to make chairs, using the barns as makeshift workshops. Utter drivel, of course.

The earliest known reference to a chairmaker in Wycombe is an entry in the parish records – "Paid the chairmaker as was ill, 5/-". That was in 1793.

A year later a man called Samuel Treacher was sworn a burgess of the borough. He was described as a chairmaker. There were only 50 burgesses in the borough at that time and since a qualification for burgess-ship was the occupation of property with a rateable value of at least £8 a year it is reasonable to assume that Treacher was a fairly wealthy man employing others. A benefit of burgess-ship was that it entitled you to vote. Receiving such an honour must have meant Treacher was one of the borough's elite.

Progress seems to have been slow at first since, when the great county role was made for military purposes in 1798, only 33 out of 395 men listed appear as chairmakers.

The start of the industry was due to several causes, chiefly the availability of materials, primarily beech, the 'Buckinghamshire weed' – that tree which seeds itself, grows quickly, produces a timber which is easy to use, can be used green for some purposes and, when seasoned, is quite stable.

Then there are two other local trees, elm and ash, each with its own special value.

Wycombe was also close enough to London to make it possible to obtain skilled instructors, and a network of villages and small towns supplied a ready market for simple chairs.

It was probably the small size of the local market that caused the initial slow growth, but the industrial revolution changed that.

The introduction of machinery into agriculture and into the only local established trade, papermaking, meant that a good pool of labour was available. At the same time the railway arrived, making it possible to send chairs in quantity all over England.

The crying need was for someone to provide a link between the Wycombe chairmakers and the new and ever expanding artisan market – and a man called Benjamin North appeared and did just that.

As well as the domestic market, mass markets began to arise. The London pleasure gardens and the great revival meetings all wanted continuing supplies of cheap but sturdy chairs. For these and other purposes the answer was the Windsor chair, a simple chair with a wooden seat; a chair that could be mass produced without machinery and of which the turned parts – legs, underframing, backs – could be made in the beechwoods themselves.

A race of men grew up known – and no-one really knows why – as 'bodgers'. These men worked in pairs. They bought at auction a stand of trees, had them felled and then moved their simple workshop along-side. They worked the green beech, following a series of operations which are illustrated in the accompanying photographs.

The seats were elm. Elm trees were felled, the top removed and the trunks sawn into planks over a saw-pit, using a huge, stiff pit saw some 2.25 metres (7FT 6IN) long. Pit saws have a steel cross handle at the upper end, the tiller, so called because the top sawyer

stood on top of the log and did the steering. The bottom sawyer had a handle that could be detached when the blade had to be withdrawn to avoid cutting through the bearers over the pit.

The planks, like the turned stuff, were brought into the factory yard to season before use. A large bow saw was used to cut the seats from the plank and the traditional hollowed shape was chopped out with an adze.

For bow-back chairs the grown or sawn bows were steamed or, more usually, boiled, bent round a wooden former, tied across the ends and hung for as long as possible to set.

Other men, the 'sawyers out', cut out tops for comb backs, arms, back splats, plain or ornamental and any other sawn parts required.

All these parts came together into the hands of the framer – because you never made a Windsor, you framed it. He bored the holes for the legs, stretchers and back parts, tennoned all the round stuff, finished the dished seats with curved shavers and scrapers, and glued all the joints using wedges wherever extra strength was needed.

The chairs were coloured by dipping in a tank of dye made from wood chips. They were then polished. For common work button polish was brushed on. Better class chairs might be finished with oil and wax.

Beech was also stained and grained to imitate rosewood, dyed to simulate ebony or

A rocking Windsor – part of the modern range from Ercol.

For nearly all his working life John Mayes was employed in the Public Library, Museum and Art Gallery in High Wycombe. Most of the time he was curator of the museum. He worked there from 8.30 in the morning until 9.30pm, but was not expected to work between 1pm and 5.30pm. He spent this time seeking out the men and women of the town's furniture industry.

After a while a breakthrough came with the first tape recorders. "At first there was just an office Dictaphone," says Mayes. "It only ran on mains but I converted it to run on a battery. I used to walk miles with a motor car battery in one hand, the Dictaphone in the other and across my back an apparatus to convert the 12 volt output of the battery to 240 volts to operate the beast."

In 1960 he used his research to write the *History of Chair Making in High Wycombe.* In 1971, at the age of 60, he retired, but he still works at the museum as an unofficial honorary member of staff.

The Wycombe History and Chair Museum now has its own separate premises in Priory Avenue, High Wycombe. It is open to the public.

The bow back of a Windsor is bent in a former after being boiled to make it supple.

The bodger was paid 9/- (45p) for a gross (144) of Windsor chair legs – and that had to include three stretchers free with every four legs.

even dipped in nitric acid to produce a reddish colour sold as 'mahogany'.

Windsors were the chief, but by no means the only, chairs made. There were delicate cane seated bedroom chairs, sturdy rush seated chairs much favoured in churches, and chairs seated with willow strips dyed in many colours.

From the beginning caning was women's work. Initially rush matting was done by men but gradually that, too, went over to the women. Rush matters were paid rather more than caners but the work was harder, dirtier and smelly, "You could tell a matter a mile off by the stink of the rushes on her clothes," I was once told by an old furniture worker.

Here's some idea of wages and prices at around the turn of the century. The bodger delivered legs and stretchers into Wycombe at around 9/- (that's 45p) a gross (144) – and a gross was, in fact, a gross and three quarters since for every four legs, three stretchers had to be included free.

Cutting out seats from the elm plank paid 1/- (5p) a dozen, adzing about the same, framing, 4/6d (22.5p) a dozen and common polishing about 2/- (10p) a dozen.

Common cane seats paid 1¾d to 2d (less than 1p) and rush matting, 3d to 5d (1.25p - just over 2p) each.

An illustrated price list of a good manufacturer shows ordinary Windsors on sale at 23/- to 27/- (£1.15 - £1.35) a dozen, while cane seat chairs went down as low as 16/- (80p) a dozen.

Money could buy a lot more in those days, but it was still a low wage for hard work and a low price on the finished product.

Even shortly before World War Two Windsor chairs were produced in much the same way as they always had been and the people producing them were still paid very little, as someone had graphically pointed out with a piece of graffiti I saw in 1936. It was added to a placard outside the Town Clerk's office which announced that the wages of sin are death. The addition read: "and the wages in Wycombe are a bloody sight worse."

It was a hard trade for the master as well as employees. One master told me: "I drove my men to the very limit of what experience told me they would stand. But no master could have driven me to work the way I did, for I did my own travelling, going by train to London and walking untold miles in search of business. Then back to Wycombe, a hasty meal and out into the factory till midnight and after, preparing work for the men to finish next day.

"I was strong and healthy, but it was as well that I met with such success as I did in the course of a few years. No man could keep that up much longer."

There were many things employees resented apart from the low rates of pay. For example, the custom of the trade was that the men paid 2d a week for their essential grindstone and 2/- a week for 'benchroom'. They provided their own oil lamps and when gas lighting became common 6d a week was the usual deduction from their earnings to pay for it.

In some factories men had to stack planks and arrange the turned stuff in racks to season – "and you weren't earning money with your tools lying idle on your bench".

There were other oddities. Early photographs of chair factories often show the windows with no glass, just oiled calico. "Oh yes, you could have glass if ▶

A chair framer drilling holes for the legs. Although the brace is cushioned against his chest with a leather breast bib, youngsters starting this job would go home with their shirts glued to their bodies with blood until they hardened to the work.

you paid for it. But did you really want it? You have glass, only natural that you should sometimes want to stop and look out. You don't earn money with a straight back," one old chairmaker once told me.

Trade unions arose to deal with particular local problems, but they tended to die out when the problems had been resolved. In 1872, for example, the men's union put forward a list of suggested payments for no less than 250 processes, and the copy of that list used in the preparation of this article is so altered and revised that it could never have had a chance of being accepted by the chairmasters who, in turn, combined.

Confrontation led to strikes, not least about the amount of notice to terminate employment, which was fixed at one hour. If that seems hard to believe in the 19th century, take a leap to 1913 when a major strike took place. One item of contention was the period of notice the men demanded – not for the 9,000 or so ordinary workers, but for about 100 top grade carvers and cabinetmakers. They wanted two hours' notice instead of one. They didn't get it.

Right up to the end of the 19th century 'common' chair work predominated, although a few firms did strike out for a higher class of trade.

As early as 1851 Edmund Hutchinson had a great success when the richly carved and upholstered chair which he submitted was judged 'Champion Chair' at the Hyde Park Exhibition.

Other firms – notably those of Cox, North, Skull and Birch – began to produce not only chairs, but furniture, cabinets in rare woods, richly carved, suites of upholstered furniture, fine pieces in mahogany, rose-

In 1874 one-and-a-half million chairs left Wycombe, many stacked on to horse-drawn carts. They were selling at that time for an average of 3/- (15p) each.

A Windsor chair-making shop from about the turn of the century.

wood and satinwood, pieces painted with flowers and even miniature landscapes and portraits.

For this sort of development three things were needed: machinery, skilled workers to train local men, and (and it was a very big 'and') an acceptance on the part of the big retailers that Wycombe could produce anything other than common chairs.

By the 1890s furniture was being produced, albeit in small quantities. One maker, Birch, sent a wonderful collection of fine upholstered furniture to the great exhibition in St Louis, USA, where it won several gold medals.

If the beginning of 'Wycombe, Furniture Town' was dawning, it must be remembered that it developed on the back of chairmaking, which was still the major trade.

Statistics are available for the year 1874, when 1½ million chairs were produced at an approximate value of £250,000.

Such a volume of output needed at least some machinery, not necessarily to speed up production but to make it possible for unskilled labour to do the same work as had been done by the limited number of skilled hand workers.

The prime mover would be a steam or oil engine driving overhead shafting. Pulley after pulley added to that shafting to drive machines by belts.

So a typical mill developed with whirling belts in all directions; belts with the most horrific type of fastener, enough to give a modern factory inspector nightmares. Injuries were commonplace.

Inevitably, the big grew bigger, often by amalgamation, and the small grew fewer and smaller, although they were still of great importance in the struggle to lift the town out of its chairs-only reputation.

As early as 1893 the town had acquired a properly equipped and staffed technical school and, in later years, local men were connected with the design side.

All this time chairs were still the bread-and-butter providers for the town, but even here changes were taking place and manufacturers identified and catered for different tastes.

New designs appeared. An outstanding example of this is the range of the modern Ercol furniture, based on the traditional Windsor theme and made in a fully mechanised factory with only the fine finishing done by hand.

Take a chair so made and stand it alongside a good hand-made one – yes, there is a difference, but the lineage immediately shows through and the new is as easy on the eye and on the anatomy as the old.

In 1935 the *High Wycombe Furnishing Trades Official Directory* had been published. Even at that comparatively late date over a hundred firms, large and small, were listed. They made every conceivable kind of furniture. The Second World War was to change that.

Technical advances in the use of materials such as plywood and synthetic adhesives had been made over the years and this made the town an obvious place for the manufacture of aircraft components. Some firms went almost wholly over to such work.

Wycombe was an official reception area not only for individuals, but for firms engaged in important work and too vulnerable to remain in or around London. Demand for factory space was acute.

Some small firms sold up. Later, a compulsory system was enforced under which certain small firms were made to share premises to provide room for incomers. The furniture industry of Wycombe never returned to its pre-war prevalence.

For many years furniture was normally sold under the name of the retailer, which meant the great retail firms could and did dictate design and price range and, even more importantly, demand constant changes of style to fit in with trade shows.

What was needed was advertising by the makers on a national scale coupled with a trademark to identify their work. Parker Knoll, Ercol and Gomme were among the first to take the plunge.

It was a bold step but eventually many firms, from Wycombe and nationally, joined in. Advertising became much more informative and the simple catalogue gave way to today's elaborate and colourful brochures.

Sadly, the current recession has hit the trade badly. Several of the fine old firms are no longer with us. Some have gone completely, others have left Wycombe, perhaps to rationalise their production in other localities.

But still, if good furniture is needed, Wycombe can supply it ●

For almost three hundred years woven webbings in different forms have been used as the support material for upholstered furniture. In the production of modern furniture today woven webbing has largely been replaced by elastic webbing and a number of different metal suspensions. However, the traditional web is still widely used for reupholstery and in the restoration of antique and period pieces.

Good furniture deserves good materials when it is to be restored and refurbished, and best 'English' webbings have changed very little since the mid 19th century. Their strong black and white yarns of jute and cotton and the easily recognised twill weave with a chevron pattern are a sign of good quality web.

The very earliest webbings used in furniture were plain woven, heavy, girth webbings made from hemp and flax, which are both very course, very strong, natural fibres. Since the introduction of jute as the main ingredient in the making of upholstery webbings, plain woven 'common' webbings have been made as a strong, though less attractive, alternative to the black and white web.

Two widths are manufactured for use in upholstery, 50mm and 90mm (2IN and 3½IN). The 50mm is generally used in Britain and the wider web is preferred in mainland Europe.

Webbings can provide us with useful evidence of the age of a chair when its authenticity is being researched. The varying compositions, colours, weaves, and widths can help the historian or conservator to identify and date period upholstery. Auction houses will often use such evidence to confirm the age of important and valuable chairs which are to be offered for sale.

Chairs have a distinct and often colourful history in a way that is more personal to us than much of our other furniture. Throughout history our chairs and settees have reflected social change and need, and our way of life. Everyday the upholsterer is discovering small pockets of history when chairs of any age are being stripped and reupholstered or just recovered.

Upholstery webs must stand up to extremes of use from the moment they are fixed into a chair. Their quality is governed by their weight, the fibre composition and the construction or weave pattern. In addition, a webbing needs a strong and reliable edge which is called the selvedge.

Webbing weights are still measured in the traditional pounds per gross yards. For example, 2IN x 9LBS is one of the lightest grades used for upholstery and 2IN x 12LB is a top grade webbing. The heavier the weight, the closer and tighter will be the weave structure.

In the all-jute 'common' webbings the weave is plain – a simple over and under construction. 'English' black and white webbings, however, are twill woven, which gives strength and just a little flexibility. These 'English' types are made from dyed jute and cotton with white cotton edges. The same webbings are available in undyed jute, which has a pale brown and white appearance. The edges are still principally cotton.

A third version of the 'English' web is black and white in appearance but contains a small percentage of synthetic yarn – either nylon or rayon – for added strength. Some makes also have a distinguishing coloured thread running along their length, either at the edge or, more often, down the centre.

Conventional webbing techniques follow a traditional pattern. They are used basically to support hessian and stuffings or springs in chair seats and backs. They need to be stretched (especially in seats) and well fixed to the centre of timber rails. The 16mm (⅝IN) improved upholstery tack is the traditional fixing, although the 16mm or 10mm (⅜IN) staple is preferred where rails are delicate or where non-intrusive methods are adopted so as to preserve particularly old and rare pieces.

The 12mm (½IN) improved and fine tack is also suitable for small work and when rails are new and in good condition. The choice is a matter for careful consideration and, of course, depends mainly on the subsequent use of a chair or settee.

The secret of good web foundations is to have the web tight with well supported (but not over strained) edges. Unsprung upholstery seats, particularly, should be well webbed with spaces between webs less than the width of the web itself. It is better to err on the side of over webbing rather than under.

Research has shown that a chair seat generally supports about 80% of a sitter's weight, and that at the

Tacking 3 and 2.

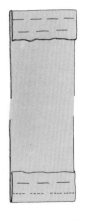

Stapling 4 and 3.

Webs & webbing

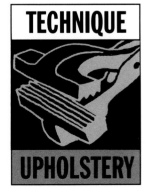

Much upholstery begins with webs and webbing, and this is where David James, one of the UK's most respected upholsterers, begins, in the first of three articles on upholstery techniques.

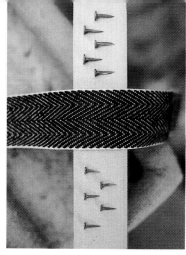

and a web strainer. The strongest fixing is produced by turning the end of the webbing up so a flap of about 25mm (1IN) provides protection in the form of a washer immediately under the tack heads. Tacks should be set at the rail centre with the folded edge of the webbing set back from the outer edge. This is vital to ensure a clear, uninterrupted line along a seat edge. Any sharp ▶

moment of impact a sitter's weight can be almost doubled.

Sprung seats depend very much on a good webbed base, although the springs themselves absorb and spread the weight applied. A sprung seat is, therefore, much kinder to the webbed base so the base should last for many years if it is well stretched and fixed.

To offset some of the punishing use webbings are subjected to, the top-stuffed unsprung seat is webbed on the top of the rails. This in itself is a stronger fixing than webbings tacked under the rails, as they are in sprung work.

For webbing work you need a tacking hammer, a pair of scissors

Left. A selection of Edwardian and Victorian webbings.

Below. Examples of stretchers.

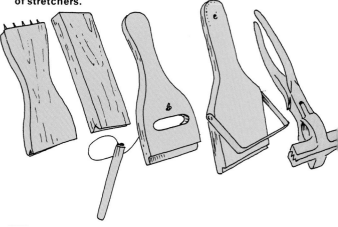

edges or arrises on the inner edges of the rails should be removed before work begins so the webs will not be chafed.

Start fixing by putting five tacks in a 'dog trot' formation into the end of the folded web. The two outer most tacks should be placed well up the webbing selvedge so that each edge is strong and well supported. After the centre tack is driven in the two intermediate tacks are set just forward of the first three. This formation means the rails will not split. If the rails are obviously delicate or narrow you can use 13mm (½IN) tacks.

Now the webbing has to be stretched, for which you will need stretchers. Webbing stretchers are basically simple tools and are designed to make straining relatively easy without exhausting the upholsterer. All the different strainers are made from wood (usually beech) with the exception of one which is steel and is traditionally known as the 'iron hands', perhaps because the user needs a grip of iron to use them successfully. However, they do have special uses where short webs are to be strained and also where access is difficult. The most common of the wooden stretchers is the bat and peg type, a tool which is very effective and produces a lever action to stretch and hold a 50mm (2IN) webbing while the second fixing is made.

Once the webbing has been stretched across the frame, the other end has to be fixed in place. Drive in three tacks while the web is under tension. Take care not to allow the tacks to go in at an angle. They have to be driven in straight and with the minimum amount of hammering. This avoids fracturing the web.

Release the strainer and cut the web, leaving a 30mm (just over 1IN) flap which is flattened and fixed down with two more tacks. This completes the second fixing.

If you want to use staples instead of tacks it is wise to use six or seven at each end in two rows of four and two or four and three.

With a few exceptions, webs in upholstered seating are interwoven to form a strong platform of support for the stuffings and springs that follow. Spacing and layout will vary to suit the frame size and design. A square or rectangular

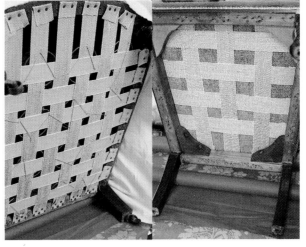

Above left. A webbed and sprung seat.

Above right. A stuffed seat on webs.

Bottom. Finishing – three tacks hold the webbing, it is folded over and two tacks go on top of the fold.

Centre. Starting – five tacks hold the webbing in place.

Below. Examples of webbing on various shapes.

David James

It used to be said of High Wycombe 'if you don't work in the furniture industry you don't work'. It is no wonder, then, that David James, being born and brought up in High Wycombe, should have gone into the furniture business. And the part of it he chose to specialise in right from the time he left school was upholstery.

For many years he was in business as an upholsterer, but more recently he has been passing on some of his considerable experience by lecturing (in fact, he has been senior lecturer in the subject since 1971) at Buckinghamshire College of Further Education. He is an honorary member of the City and Guilds Institute and has been awarded their licentiateship.

| Square frame | Splayed | Circular | Oval |
| Sprung | Stretcher | Backs | Curved (concave) |

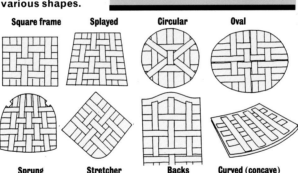

frame, for example, can be webbed with equal spacing throughout. Some typical examples are shown in the drawings.

This technique has to be varied for upholstering curved frames. A good example of this is the drop-in seat for a dining chair, which has a concave surface and curves from side to side. In this case the webs are fixed and strained on to the curved rails first. Then run the cross webs under all the first webs. Do not interlace them. Use the same procedure on a curved chair back. To maintain the concave design the second rows of webbing are only lightly strained. A scroll end on a sofa, for instance, is treated this way. The first webs are tightly stretched from side to side to maintain and support the upholstery, and the secondary rows run under two and over four, as shown in FIG 4.

Fig 4

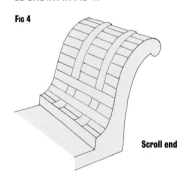

Scroll end

Webbing is a versatile and interesting material which has many uses and will often find its way into some unusual places. To give added strength in chair frames it can be folded double along its length and used in place of short stuffing rails. Webbings were traditionally used as hinges on a variety of wooden frames used for domestic purposes in houses. The three-fold screen which was an essential draught excluder in large houses and halls had webbings used as hinges to hold the fabric-covered sections together.

It is interesting to note that in the suppliers catalogues we use today, traditional upholstery webbings are still listed and graded in inch widths, pound weights, and rolls are made and sold in 18 yard and 36 yard lengths. Webbings have a strong sense of history, so perhaps we upholsterers should thank the saddle makers whose girth webbings we took and began using in the first upholstered chairs in the late 16th century ●

TECHNIQUE
UPHOLSTERY

Before most lounging furniture incorporated springs, squabs, or hair-filled cushions, provided the added comfort. They are still used, for new furniture as well as restoration work. David James explains how they are made.

Squabs and seats

Right. Opening up the past with a look inside an early 19th century squab. The outer covering of wool has been unpicked along the piped edge to reveal two earlier layers of covering over the inner case.

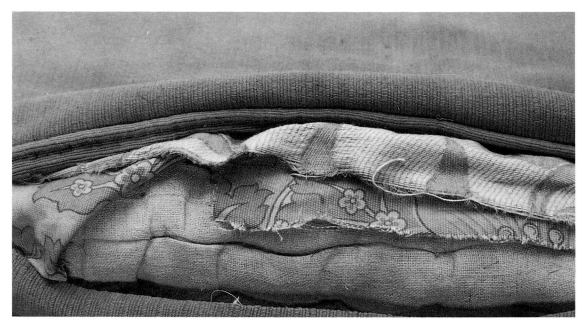

An Art Nouveau patterned weave, jacquard woven was found beneath the top cover. Much of the original colouring has vanished with time.

The innermost covering of the three is a heavy cotton floral print, typical of the late 19th century and still retaining some of its warm colour.

The inner case, made from flax canvas shows the hand sewn edges, the surface tufting and the mattress stitch.

The squab, or small hair cushion used in seating and chairs, is basically a miniature version of the mattress (see separate panel). It contains all the elements of materials and construction of the traditional unsprung mattress.

Good quality, curled hair is carded (combed) and then teased by hand and arranged to the right thickness and density inside a sewn-up case. Cases can be made up from jute or linen scrim (an open weave material) or cotton.

The case is cut and sewn up in a box shape with an open lid. It is made up from a top and bottom panel with a border, or wall, running all round.

Subsequent stitching and tufting reduces the overall size of the case, so it needs to be oversize in the first place by about 5%. An average sized seat squab or pad,

for a Windsor chair, say, or a window seat needs to be 32mm (1¼IN) to 38mm (1½IN) larger overall than the finished size.

The stuffing sequence of the cushion is important and allows a controllable build up of filling. Corners are firmly filled first, followed by the outer edges. Now the

centre is gradually filled by pushing small handfuls of hair to the far end of the case and slowly working back towards the opening. The thickness or height of the filling is controlled with the flat palm of the free hand placed on the case as stuffing progresses. This stops the case ballooning.

**FIG 1
A corner seat showing the use of squabs (or hair-filled cushions).**

Taking a close look into an interesting piece of period upholstery in the form of an early 19th century window seat with three squab cushions providing the comfort.

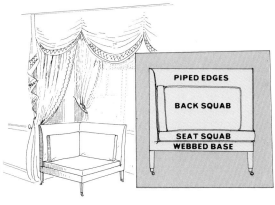

PIPED EDGES

BACK SQUAB

SEAT SQUAB
WEBBED BASE

Good density and evenness of the hair is vital. With a good, dense, tight and even filling completed, the open end, or lid, of the case is closed and pinned down. Fig 2 shows the ideal finished shape of the squab and the pins in place.

Fig 2
The ideal finished shape of the squab showing pins in place.

Before closing permanently with a fine slip stitch, the edges can be lightly regulated (Fig 3) and the tufting stitches put in place. The tufts are simply single, through stitches placed in a regular pattern. Sometimes at either end of the stitch a piece of fabric or wool is used to stop the stitch pulling through. The tufts do two jobs, they compress the squab to a flat, even thickness all over and at the same time will reduce any movement of filling during use.

Two typical tufting patterns are shown (Fig 4) along with the upholsterer's slip knot, which is used to squeeze and adjust down the surface to the level required. As many as 25 to 30 stitches is average for a small seat-size squab.

Having decided on a suitable pattern for the tufts, the positions are marked on both sides of the case and tufting can begin, starting at the centre and working outwards to finish with the outer rows. Each tuft is left tight, but still on a slip knot so the depth can be adjusted later if needed before locking off with two half hitches.

The case is now ready for closing, using either a fine slip stitch or by over sewing before the pins are removed (Fig 5).

Edge stitching with a mattress stitch

A mattress stitch is made with a two point needle (ie it has a point at each end) threaded with flax twine. The stitch is used around the border of the squab to pull small amounts of the filling into the edges. This technique produces a firm, upright edge and gives the squab shape and support. When the first row is complete, the work is turned over and

Fig 3
Above is a regulator. It is 200-330mm (8-13IN) long. The flat end is to hold and, while it contains an eye, this is just to hang it up. It is not threaded. It is poked through from the outside of the cushion, twisted and pulled out again to drag the filling right up into the corners and the edges.

Fig 4
Above. Typical tufting patterns. Below. Two kinds of tufts (although tufts are not always used, the twine sometimes simply forming a stitch through the fabric). The upholsterer's slip knot and two half hitches are also shown.

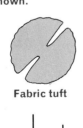

Fabric tuft

Wool tuft

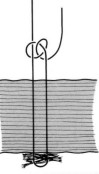

UPHOLSTERER'S SLIP KNOT

TWO HALF HITCHES

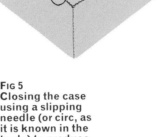

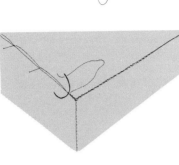

Fig 5
Closing the case using a slipping needle (or circ, as it is known in the trade) to produce fine slip stitches, or over sewing.

What you will need

Mixed curled animal hair (approx ½kg (1LB) per sq foot at 75mm (3IN) thick.
Fine linen scrim or canvas, or cotton ticking.
Medium or fine linen twine.
Cotton wadding, slip cotton felt, or wool felt.
Squabs may be lined with cotton calico cases when loose covers are preferred.

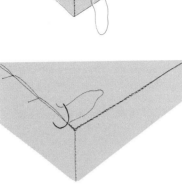

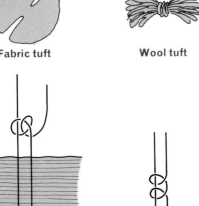

Fig 6
The two edge stitching techniques.

the adjacent edge is stitched in the same way.

The mattress stitch seems to have been one of the very earliest stitching techniques used by cofferers (coffin upholsterers) and upholsterers. The stitch is a basic zig-zag formation with the needle being pushed and pulled through the work edge.

There are two edge stitching techniques (Fig 6). The first runs along the border or side of the squab. The other is a top stitch which runs right through the corner of the edge and appears on the top of the case as well as the border. Both are in common use but apparently the first became widely known as the English mattress stitch. However, both stitch types do a similar job in holding together and supporting the edges of mattresses.

With the tufts tied off and the corners regulated, our squab interior is now complete and ready for covering. Although not essential, a layer or two of soft cotton wadding wrapped around the case gives an even and well filled finish and also stops any stray hair filling from penetrating the outer cover.

The covering treatment for this kind of very traditional cushion upholstery will depend on the style and the period of the work being created or re-upholstered. Seams may be plain or piped, or deco- ▶

With covers removed the tufting pattern is clear. It has a diamond formation.

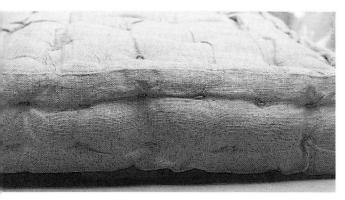

Border stitches hold the edges in shape at 40mm intervals.

The most recent top covering is a faded green wool repp, a tough furniture cloth, with piped edges entirely hand stitched. The ends of the piping are neatly hand finished into the border corners.

The needle returns into the case and pivots along the border by about 40mm (1½IN). After each stitch the twine is tightened to form the edge.

rated with cording or ruche. There are many variations. Covers can be fixed or loose. If they are left loose they can be removed for regular cleaning.

Loose covers, or slip covers, were quite common for upholstered furniture in the early part of the last century.

A variation

A firmer but more comfortable squab cushion can be made by adding a second stuffing of loose, curled hair to both sides of the ordinary squab.

If you do this, the tufts in the centre of the work are pulled down and tightened a little more than the outer rows. This will give the case a concave surface, with a shallow well in it.

The well on both sides of the work can be filled with an even layer of hair to reform the original thickness. Carded wool felt can be used as a second stuffing instead of hair.

These second stuffings will need to be lined and covered with cotton calico, which is turned-in all round the edges and pinned and slip stitched to the outer top edges of the squab case. Finally, the work is placed into its top covering with a wrap of two layers of cotton wadding.

Squabs of this kind were quite common during the Regency and early Victorian periods.

Thistle down, cats' tails, straw and cattle hair have all found their way into mattresses as fillings at one time or another in an attempt to provide somnolent comfort.

I remember reading, as an apprentice, that in 1953, or thereabouts, legislation went through parliament regarding the cleanliness of fillings used in articles of furniture and bedding.

It seems that up to that time almost anything that was soft and fibrous could be used in the stuffing of chairs and the filling of mattresses.

When I was a child my grandmother used to cut up what she called rags and make all sorts of things from them – rag dolls and rag rugs leap to mind. Rag dolls and rag rugs can still be bought today, but they are no longer made out of necessity. The terms are more of a romantic description for things made by hand from soft materials.

Quite clearly I remember as a small child asking why grandma was cutting up all her rags into tiny pieces. The answer was that new cushions were being made for the suite in the front room and the tiny bits of rag would provide the stuffing. What a difference 40 something years can make.

The cushions Grandma was making were top stuffed upholstery in unsprung furniture. This, basically, sits on top of a firm, traditional webbed base. Until springs for furniture came into general use in the middle of the 19th century, all upholstered and stuffed articles for sitting and sleeping on were simply top stuffed or, in some cases, deep stuffed.

Variations of feel and support were achieved by the use of different types of filling. Course, firm stuffings such as grasses, seaweed, woodwool, and straw provided the foundations, or first stuffings as we

call them today. Other, finer and softer materials were layed on or tied in over these. Examples such as animal hair, wool fleece, raw cotton and rags were typical. These were called second stuffings. When warmth as well as comfort was important, then uppermost fillings, especially those for bedding, could be feather, down, fine fleece or wool flock.

In this country we experience in any one year quite a range of temperatures, but during the summer months it is not always healthy or desirable to be surrounded by very warm soft fillings to sleep on. Today, the modern mattress contains a carefully engineered combination of curled fibre or hair, topped with a thick, cool layer of cotton and often a fine quilt of a synthetic filling such as polyester.

During most of the 19th century the hair filled mattress provided the answer. Providing the hair (which was a mixture of horse, cow and pig) was curled, it gave a good degree of resilience, was air permeable and had good thermostatic properties, making it cool in summer and warm in winter. At least, it behaved relatively well compared with the other fillings that were available.

The feather or wool filled overlay was carefully stored away in summer until needed as a winter topping over the hair mattress. Luxury, I'm sure, for those who were able to make such provisions for themselves.

A glance back at the history of bedding and upholstery fillings in this way gives a reasonably clear indication of the way in which natural materials and fibre fillings are selected and used for different purposes.

TECHNIQUE

UPHOLSTERY

The loose upholstered seat on dining chairs dates back to the Queen Anne period, although it is still being used today. Here David James demonstrates how the seat is upholstered as he restores a set of Victorian chairs.

Drop in for dinner

I n one form or another, dining chairs, in singles and in sets, appear in virtually every home in the country. They may simply fill corners or majestically stand in rows in grand dining halls. They are very often taken for granted until wear and tear takes its toll and they become noticeably uncomfortable.

The loose seat is typical of the upholstered part of many a traditional or modern dining chair. 'Pallet', 'slip seat', 'drop-in' are some of the names used to describe the detachable wooden frame which is upholstered and fitted into a dining chair.

Some of the earliest seats of this type were produced during the reign of Queen Anne, early in the 18th century. Since then they have drifted in and out of fashion and, of course, have been adapted and styled to suit current vogue.

During the Regency period (early 19th century) the loose seat appeared as a pegged frame surrounded on three sides by a mahogany or rosewood frame but with an open front. The Victorian version was designed as a drop-on seat and sat squarely on top of the show wood surround. Again, pegs or dowels held the seat secure. During the middle years of this century the rebated 'drop in' dining chair frame became popular once again.

This set of six, late Victorian mahogany spoon back chairs provides an excellent example of the upholstery on a drop-on dining chair seat. In this case the seats were on pegged beech frames.

The original seats were in poor condition. They were covered in black horse hair fabric typical of the period. Since much of the fabric was still in evidence you can see how tough a covering it is – and I say 'is' rather than 'was' because upholstery fabrics made from horse hair are still made today. The long strands of mane and tail hair are carefully laid and woven into a cotton base to produce a specialised narrow width upholstery fabric. Plain and patterned versions are made.

The chair without its seat.

Dining chairs of this period were strong and well made. Those that remain have survived 100 years of domestic use often practically unscathed. The set I chose for restoration was the KD (knockdown) type. Heavy, 10mm (⅜IN) bolts secured the back frame to the seat rails, an interesting design feature which made transporting them easier – important especially as many dining chairs of this type were produced for export.

Six new loose seat frames were made up from 78mm x 28mm (3⅛ x 1⅛IN) thick beech. The chair frames

The old seat frame.

themselves have been well cared for and exhibit a mature and colourful patina.

A new frame in position.

Loose seats and drop-in seats for dining chairs have to be adjusted and fitted to each individual chair in a set. Each frame is then stamped and numbered to correspond with its main frame. Three 13mm (½IN) pegs hold the upholstered seat frame in place.

A dowel and its location hole in the seat are marked to identify pairs.

Fitting the seat carefully to its chair is important. Our three peg holes were aligned and drilled first to achieve a snug push fit. Then, with the seat in place, the two back corner cuts are eased so a good allowance of 3mm (⅛IN) around each back leg makes room for the upholstery coverings and a small amount of filling. This softens the back corners of the seat and allows the covering to lay

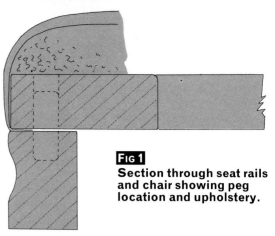

FIG 1
Section through seat rails and chair showing peg location and upholstery.

neatly against each leg upright.

With the inner fitting complete, a sharp pencil is run around the outer edges of each seat to indicate by how much the frame is oversize. Any overhang on the front, sides and back edges is planed off, plus 1-1½mm (¹⁄₁₆IN) to allow for the thicknesses of calico and top covering to be used.

Finally, the seat frame is removed so all the outer arrises can be planed off.

Before starting to upholster the chair, a rasp is used to make a small radius on all four inside top edges of the frame. Seat webbings are vulnerable to wear and fracture at this point because they flex when the seat is in use. Rounding the edges protects them.

The tools needed for the upholstery are pictured below. They are the basic range of tools required for a set of seats of this type, which use traditional methods and materials. They are:
Trimming scissors
Tacking hammer
Ripping chisel
Trimming knife
Web strainer
150mm (6IN) half round mattress needle
200mm or 255mm (8 or 10IN) regulator
12mm (½IN) and 10mm (⅜IN) fine tacks. ▶

Best English webbing (see article, page 109) 50mm (2IN) wide is used, fixed in a 3 x 3 pattern using 13mm (½IN) fine tacks. In the conventional way, the frames are webbed front to back first and the cross webs interwoven. For all the chairs, 14½ metres (47½FT) of webbing was needed. It cost £8.12.

Webbing the frame.

The seat is lined by laying 283.5g (10oz) of upholstery hessian over the webbing. Hessians are stretched hand tight and tacked with the edges turned out. If you prefer, a 340g (12oz) grade hessian may be used. Hessians are available in several different widths – generally, the most economical for chair work are the 915mm, 1220mm and 1820mm (36IN, 48IN and 72IN) widths. Our six seats used up 1½ metres (60IN) of 915mm (36IN) wide hessian at an approximate cost of £2.

FIG 2
The calico and cover are cut and worked into the back corners.

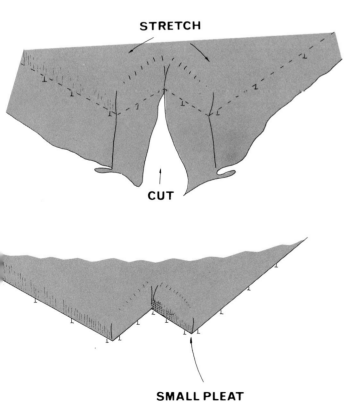

STRETCH

CUT

SMALL PLEAT

Hessian tacked on.

The main stuffing used in the seat is grey curled hair mixture. You need about 450g (1LB) of it for each seat of this size. The original upholstery contained a wool flock mixture which had compressed and become quite uncomfortable. Curled hair is better because of its resilience and durability. New curled hair costs about £3 per 450g (1LB), although the price can vary quite a lot from one supplier to another.

Curled hair stuffing.

The seat is gradually filled by pushing small handfuls of the hair mixture under stuffing ties of twine stitched into the hessian, working around the outer edges and finishing in the centre. The seat should be tightly stuffed. Push a small handful under the twine, sliding it along to make room for at least the same amount again. Aim to make the seats about 38mm (1½IN) thick, building up to 50mm (2IN) at the centre.

When the seat is filled the hair will need to be teased out to open up the filling and produce an evenness all over. This will take some time and can be quite tiring to the hands. Evenness and thickness of hair filling can only be judged by feel. Edges and corners should be well filled to medium firmness. As the seat is covered in calico, which is the next operation, any noticeably soft or empty areas can be topped up as the first covering progresses.

The traditional lining cloth is unbleached calico. It is used to pull down the hair filling to the required outline and shape. In this case the calico is stretched over the hair filling and used as the shaping medium, a technique that has been used for two hundred years or so. Scrims and canvasses are also used in the same way.

Calico is stretched over the hair stuffing.

Temporary tacks set the cloth in place. It is adjusted until the seat is tight and firm with smooth, well stretched edges. This first covering is finished off by completing the front corners with small, tightly folded pleats, which are inverted to form a 'V'.

The back two corners of the seat need careful cutting and some firm manipulation to get the calico to lay into the recess

Cutting into the back corners (see also FIG 2).

An incut corner of this kind can often prove difficult. While some fabrics will stretch and allow themselves to be pulled and eased in place, there are less resilient types of cover which will call for much firmer handling.

Final adjustment of the calico is usually necessary. Do this by removing some of the temporary tacks and adding more until all the edges are set tight and the outer line of the cloth is smooth and evenly pulled.

Calico linings also come in a variety of widths. For this job each piece was cut to 610mm (24IN) square and 1.2 metres (4FT) was used for the set at a cost of £4.80.

The top stuffing is 71g (2½oz) cotton felt. This gives the seat a full and rounded appearance, which is in keeping with the origi-

nal intended design of the chairs.

A traditional drop-in (rather than drop-on) seat which sits inside a rebated chair has a slimmer and less rounded appearance.

The dining chairs I was working on required 3 metres of cotton felt, which cost £4.80.

The top covering is a fine ribbed silk and cotton blend fabric with a roll width of 1350mm (just over 53IN). Six pieces were cut 650mm square, which meant a length of 2 metres (a little more than 2YD) was needed for the job.

The seat is covered with the silk/cotton fabric in the same way as it was with the calico. Temporary tacks set the cover along the underside of the back rail. It is pulled over to the front by stretching and tacking again. The sides are set by smoothing, stretching and holding with temporary tacking.

The silk/cotton fabric is put on in the same way as the calico was.

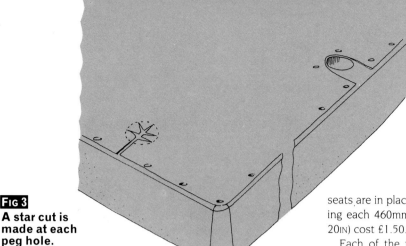

FIG 3
A star cut is made at each peg hole.

Take care to keep the grain, or thread of the fabric straight and square to the front rail. The front corners are pulled down and tacked in place before the back corners are cut and eased into the leg recess.

Excess cover is cut away and a single fold or pleat is tightly placed at each of the points of the two back corners.

Before any tacks are driven home, each of the four sides of the seat is given a final horizontal stretch to adjust the cover and ease it taut.

As the cover I used is a finely woven ribbed silk with a surface sheen it, like most covers of this sort, is vulnerable to tack bites. These show up along the edges of the work as lines, or pulls where each tack is placed. A good horizontal, end to end stretch along all sides helps to smooth the cover and stop the bites being obvious.

Bottom linings, or dust covers, were not always used on this type of dining chair upholstery. However, in this case I used a lightweight hessian, turned in and tacked to the undersides, as it had been on the originals.

Black cotton lining underneath gives a neat finish.

To finish, use a black cotton lining underneath neatly turned in and tacked. The outer edges of the lining covers all the previous work, but is kept just back from the edge so it cannot be seen when the

seats are in place. Six pieces of lining each 460mm x 510mm (18IN x 20IN) cost £1.50.

Each of the three peg holes is trimmed with a star cut and turned in (FIG 3). An extra tack or two ensures a clean, acceptable finish to the undersides.

From stripping to finish the complete restoration of the upholstery of the set took about 14 hours. It was a pleasing and worthwhile project since the total material costs were low – the total cost for fabric was £30 and sundry items such as tacks and twine cost only £2. Wood and fillings added about £35.

The number stamped on to each of the seat frames was chalked on to the under lining so that each seat found its matching chair ●

Trim round the dowel holes.

INDEX

Woodturning

Adventures in Woodturning	*David Springett*	Practical Tips for Turners & Carvers	*GMC Publications*
Bert Marsh: Woodturner	*Bert Marsh*	Practical Tips for Woodturners	*GMC Publications*
Bill Jones' Notes from the Turning Shop	*Bill Jones*	Spindle Turning	*GMC Publications*
Bill Jones' Further Notes from the Turning Shop	*Bill Jones*	Turning Miniatures in Wood	*John Sainsbury*
Carving on Turning	*Chris Pye*	Turning Wooden Toys	*Terry Lawrence*
Colouring Techniques for Woodturners	*Jan Sanders*	Understanding Woodturning	*Ann & Bob Phillips*
Decorative Techniques for Woodturners	*Hilary Bowen*	Useful Woodturning Projects	*GMC Publications*
Faceplate Turning: Features, Projects, Practice	*GMC Publications*	Woodturning: A Foundation Course	*Keith Rowley*
Green Woodwork	*Mike Abbott*	Woodturning Jewellery	*Hilary Bowen*
Illustrated Woodturning Techniques	*John Hunnex*	Woodturning Masterclass	*Tony Boase*
Keith Rowley's Woodturning Projects	*Keith Rowley*	Woodturning: A Source Book of Shapes	*John Hunnex*
Make Money from Woodturning	*Ann & Bob Phillips*	Woodturning Techniques	*GMC Publications*
Multi-Centre Woodturning	*Ray Hopper*	Woodturning Wizardry	*David Springett*
Pleasure & Profit from Woodturning	*Reg Sherwin*		

Woodcarving

The Art of the Woodcarver	*GMC Publications*	Understanding Woodcarving	*GMC Publications*
Carving Birds & Beasts	*GMC Publications*	Wildfowl Carving Volume 1	*Jim Pearce*
Carving Realistic Birds	*David Tippey*	Wildfowl Carving Volume 2	*Jim Pearce*
Carving on Turning	*Chris Pye*	The Woodcarvers	*GMC Publications*
Decorative Woodcarving	*Jeremy Williams*	Woodcarving: A Complete Course	*Ron Butterfield*
Essential Woodcarving Techniques	*Dick Onians*	Woodcarving for Beginners: Projects, Techniques & Tools	
Lettercarving in Wood	*Chris Pye*		*GMC Publications*
Practical Tips for Turners & Carvers	*GMC Publications*	Woodcarving Tools, Materials & Equipment	*Chris Pye*

Plans, Projects, Tools & The Workshop

The Incredible Router	*Jeremy Broun*	Sharpening Pocket Reference Book	*Jim Kingshott*
Making & Modifying Woodworking Tools	*Jim Kingshott*	The Workshop	*Jim Kingshott*
Sharpening: The Complete Guide	*Jim Kingshott*		

Toys & Miniatures

Designing & Making Wooden Toys	*Terry Kelly*	Making Wooden Toys & Games	*Jeff & Jennie Loader*
Fun to Make Wooden Toys & Games	*Jeff & Jennie Loader*	Miniature Needlepoint Carpets	*Janet Granger*
Making Board, Peg & Dice Games	*Jeff & Jennie Loader*	Turning Miniatures in Wood	*John Sainsbury*
Making Little Boxes from Wood	*John Bennett*	Turning Wooden Toys	*Terry Lawrence*

Creative Crafts

Celtic Knotwork Designs	*Sheila Sturrock*	Embroidery Tips & Hints	*Harold Hayes*
Collage from Seeds, Leaves and Flowers	*Joan Carver*	Making Knitwear Fit	*Pat Ashforth & Steve Plummer*
The Complete Pyrography	*Stephen Poole*	Miniature Needlepoint Carpets	*Janet Granger*
Creating Knitwear Designs	*Pat Ashforth & Steve Plummer*	Tatting Collage	*Lindsay Rogers*
Cross Stitch on Colour	*Sheena Rogers*		

Upholstery and Furniture

Care & Repair	*GMC Publications*	Making Shaker Furniture	*Barry Jackson*
Complete Woodfinishing	*Ian Hosker*	Pine Furniture Projects	*Dave Mackenzie*
Furniture Projects	*Rod Wales*	Seat Weaving (Practical Crafts)	*Ricky Holdstock*
Furniture Restoration (Practical Crafts)	*Kevin Jan Bonner*	Upholsterer's Pocket Reference Book	*David James*
Furniture Restoration & Repair for Beginners	*Kevin Jan Bonner*	Upholstery: A Complete Course	*David James*
Green Woodwork	*Mike Abbott*	Upholstery: Techniques & Projects	*David James*
Making Fine Furniture	*Tom Darby*	Woodfinishing Handbook (Practical Crafts)	*Ian Hosker*

Dolls' houses & dolls' house furniture

Architecture for Dolls' Houses	*Joyce Percival*	Making Period Dolls' House Accessories	*Andrea Barham*
A Beginners' Guide to the Dolls' House Hobby	*Jean Nisbett*	Making Period Dolls' House Furniture	*Derek & Sheila Rowbottom*
The Complete Dolls' House Book	*Jean Nisbett*	Making Victorian Dolls' House Furniture	*Patricia King*
Easy-to-Make Dolls' House Accessories	*Andrea Barham*	Miniature Needlepoint Carpets	*Janet Granger*
Make Your Own Dolls' House Furniture	*Maurice Harper*	The Secrets of the Dolls' House Makers	*Jean Nisbett*
Making Dolls' House Furniture	*Patricia King*		

Other books

Guide to Marketing	*GMC Publications*	Woodworkers' Career & Educational Source Book	*GMC Publications*

VIDEOS

Carving a Figure: The Female Form	*Ray Gonzalez*	Woodturning: A Foundation Course	*Keith Rowley*
The Traditional Upholstery Workshop		Elliptical Turning	*David Springett*
Part 1: *Drop-in & Pinstuffed Seats*	*David James*	Woodturning Wizardry	*David Springett*
The Traditional Upholstery Workshop		Turning Between Centres: The Basics	*Dennis White*
Part 2: *Stuffover Upholstery*	*David James*	Turning Bowls	*Dennis White*
Hollow Turning	*John Jordan*	Boxes, Goblets & Screw Threads	*Dennis White*
Bowl Turning	*John Jordan*	Novelties & Projects	*Dennis White*
Sharpening Turning & Carving Tools	*Jim Kingshott*	Classic Profiles	*Dennis White*
Sharpening the Professional Way	*Jim Kingshott*	Twists & Advanced Turning	*Dennis White*

MAGAZINES

Woodturning • Woodcarving • Toymaking
Furniture & Cabinetmaking • BusinessMatters
Creative Ideas for the Home

The above represents a full list of all titles currently published or scheduled to be published. All are available direct from the Publishers or through bookshops, newsagents and specialist retailers. To place an order, or to obtain a complete catalogue, contact:

GMC Publications, 166 High Street, Lewes, East Sussex BN7 1XU United Kingdom
Tel: 01273 488005 Fax: 01273 478606
Orders by credit card are accepted